911

Community Canada

Community
Canada

J. Bradley Cruxton

Robert J. Walker

Toronto
Oxford University Press

*To our parents who instilled in us
a love of history.*

Oxford University Press
70 Wynford Drive, Don Mills, Ontario M3C 1J9

Oxford   New York
Athens   Auckland   Bangkok   Bombay
Calcutta   Cape Town   Dar es Salaam   Delhi
Florence   Hong Kong   Istanbul   Karachi
Kuala Lumpur   Madras   Madrid   Melbourne
Mexico City   Nairobi   Paris   Singapore
Taipei   Tokyo   Toronto

and associated companies in
Berlin   Ibadan

This book is printed on permanent (acid-free)
paper ∞ .

Oxford is a trademark of Oxford University Press

Canadian Cataloguing in Publication Data

Cruxton, J. Bradley
Community Canada

Full colour ed.
Includes index.

ISBN 0-19-541169-2

1. Canada – History – To 1763 (New France) –
Juvenile literature.   2. Canada – History –
1763-1867 – Juvenile literature.   3. Canada –
Social conditions – To 1763 – Juvenile literature.
4. Canada – Social conditions – 1763-1867 –
Juvenile literature.*   5. Indians of North America –
Canada – History – Juvenile literature.
6. Indians of North America – Canada – Social
conditions – Juvenile literature.   I. Walker,
Robert J. (Robert John), 1941- .   II. Title.

FC161.C78 1995   971   C95-931764-3
F1032.C78 1995

Senior editor: Geraldine Kikuta
Project editor: Monica Schwalbe
Photo researcher: Natalie Pavlenko Lomaga
Cartographer: Daniel Cartography
Illustrators: Dean Kalmantis/Tasoula Koutsourakis
Cover illustration: David Craig
Production: Joanna Gertler

Printed and bound in Canada
          5   BP   99   98

CONTENTS

ACKNOWLEDGEMENTS

We would like to thank the following reviewers for their helpful comments on parts of the manuscript: Richard Atleo, University of British Columbia Museum of Anthropology; Don Bogle, Head of History, York Region Board of Education; Robert W.C. Burgar, Project Archaeologist, Metropolitan Toronto and Region Conservation Authority; J. Peter Hill, Head of English, The Haldimand Board of Education; Harold Franklin McGee Jr., Department of Anthropology, St. Mary's University, Nova Scotia; Glenda J. Redden, Consultant for Multicultural Services, Nova Scotia Department of Education; Siksika Elders for consultation on the Blackfoot chapter; and Christopher Moore for consultation on the cover illustration.

We would also like to thank the principal, teacher, and students of Dr. S.J. Phillips Public School in Oshawa for their kind help with the classroom photographs.

UNIT ONE

Discovering History

CHAPTER 1

What Is History?

One of my ancestors was a French soldier. When he was only seventeen he was sent to Quebec. He helped defend New France against the British. Last summer I visited Quebec City. I saw the Plains of Abraham where the bloody battle was fought in 1759. Imagine! I stood on the exact spot where one of my ancestors had fought beside General Montcalm more than 200 years ago!

My grandmother would often tell me stories of times gone by. Among my favourites were stories about when her mother was a young girl. Her mother went to school in a one-room log school house. Those were the days when students used quill pens. They carried their own ink in stone bottles. The thing she remembered most about her school though was the big box stove. It stood in the middle of the room. The children would gather around the stove at recess or before school hours. On cold, frosty mornings in the winter they would place their stone ink bottles on that big box stove to thaw out the ink. Sometimes some mischievous student would leave the cork in the bottle. Then there would be an explosion and a large black spot on the ceiling of the room.

There was only one store in our town in the early days. You could buy almost anything there. There were tins of tea, sacks of flour and sugar, barrels of dried apples, and huge wheels of cheese. Bales of cloth, kerosene lamps, boxes of fish hooks, and work boots stood on the shelves. But on the counter were the huge glass jars that every girl and boy dreamed about. They were filled with lollipops, sticks of red and white peppermints, and white candies as hard as rocks, called "Gibralters."

Who or what are these stories about?
What is being described?
When did the events take place?
Who might be telling the stories?

These stories are part of **history**. History deals with people and events of the past. It explores the changes that have taken place in the way people live. Everything that has happened from the beginning of time to the most recent moment is part of history. You are about to begin an exploration of history. It is important to realize that history is the study of the people and events in the past that have helped to make us what we are today.

History can start close to home with a study of you and your family. It can help you to better understand who you are. Once you have studied your own history and that of your family, you can explore the history of other groups you belong to.

Groups you belong to can be called **communities**. A community is a group of people who share common interests and experiences. They often live or work in the same area. Your family, for example, is your closest and most personal community.

Your school is also a community. All of the students, teachers, custodians, and administrative assistants who work or study in the school are part of the school community. Your school has a history. People and events of the past and all of the changes that have taken place are part of its history.

Your town or city is a community too. It has a history. Your province and country are communities. They have a history too.

In this Unit, you will discover your own history and that of your family. Then you will be ready to move on to the history of your local community. You will learn many skills along the way. These skills will help prepare you to explore some of the early communities that were part of Canada's history.

You Are History

If history is the study of people and events of the past and changes in the way people live, then you are history. There are stories you can tell about your life in the past. There are events that you have experienced. Even in your lifetime many changes have taken place. You are a valuable source of information. Yet each one of you has had a different past. It is that past, your own personal history, that makes you a special person.

Explore your own past. Recall some of the highlights of your life. Use the questions below to get you started. Answer as many questions as you can. You may want to ask other members of your family to help you.

What was the most important event or experience of your life to this point?

What other events stand out as special?

Where and when were you born?

When did you get your first tooth or take your first step?

Are there any stories people tell about you as a baby or young child?

Did your family move during your childhood? When? Where?

Did you have any favourite pets as you were growing up? How old were you when you got your pets?

Did your pets ever do anything exciting, such as scare away a prowler? When?

Can you recall your first day at school? What was your teacher's name? Does any single grade stand out especially in your mind? Why?

Who were your early friends and playmates? How old were you when you met them?

Do you have younger sisters or brothers? When were they born?

Which family celebrations stand out in your memory? Why? How old were you? (examples: Birthdays? Halloween? New Year's Eve?)

Have you belonged to any teams or clubs? When did you join them? Have they organized any special events? What were they? When were they held?

What are your memories of family vacations? Where did you go?

What is the best time you remember on a vacation with your family?

What were the best and worst years of your life so far? Why? What happened?

By the time you have worked your way through these questions, you should have a list of many important events in your life history. So far though, these events are all mixed up. You need to put them in order. How old were you when each event took place? Go back and write your age beside each one. Now put the events in the order in which they occurred. Which events took place before your first birthday? Which happened between your first and second birthdays, and so on? This task is called putting events in **chronological order**. Once you have the events in order, you can make a **timeline**.

Skill Building: Making a Simple Timeline

A timeline is an excellent way to record the important events from your past. It allows you to show the events in chronological order. You will be able to get an overall picture of your life from the beginning to the present.

1. Find a long piece of paper or tape two pieces of paper together end to end. Draw a line from the top of the paper to the bottom in the centre.

2. Divide the line with a mark for your birth and for each year of your life. Mark your birth date at the top.

3. Record the important events of your life on the timeline. Put them in chronological order. Use the space on both sides of the line to note the events.

4. Add drawings or photos to your timeline to illustrate the events.

5. Compare your timeline with a classmate's. Are there any events you have in common? Which events are different?

6. What did you discover by making your timeline? Did it help you remember important events? What did it tell you about yourself?

Students at work on their timelines.

1
2
3
4
5
6
7
8
9
10
11
12
13

Born at the Calgary General Hospital
My first birthday
Favourite food: apple sauce!
Learned to walk

Baby sister born
Mom brought home a small white kitten
Got my first tricycle
Family moved from Calgary to Ottawa

Started grade one
First visit to the zoo (scared by a camel!)
Moved to new house on Fairfax Drive
My first two-wheel bike

Used to play with Bobby and Chantal
On Halloween, I was a Viking
Learned to swim
First ride on a horse
Went to summer camp in Huntsville
Got a big puppy for Christmas (Taffy)
Visited my grandparents in Calgary
        and saw the Calgary Stampede
Met my best friend Joseph
Teacher Ms. Muir

Flew on jet alone to Calgary
Teacher Mr. Jacobi

Exploring Your Roots

Your timeline outlines your own personal history. The ways in which your history is different from that of others makes you unique.

Yet, some of your experiences will be similar to those of others in your class. Some of your common experiences have to do with growing up such as getting your first teeth or learning to walk. Others may be experiences you have shared with your family such as vacations and special holidays. Your family is part of what you are.

We all belong to a family. That is, we all live with and depend on at least one other person. There are two ways that you become part of a family. You are born into the family or you join by adoption, marriage, or by being asked to live with the family. You share many things with your family. Your family is your closest and most personal community.

How could you find out more about your family? What about your family's history? By exploring your family roots, you can find out more about your family and yourself.

Getting Organized

Before you begin to explore your family history, you need to make some important decisions.

1. What would you like to know about your family roots that you don't already know?
2. What sources could you use to gather information?
3. What are some of the important questions that will help to guide your investigation?

Skill Building: Finding a Focus

The topic of exploring your roots or examining the history of your family is a large one. Where would you start? You might be tempted to write down all kinds of details. But these details won't be in any order. They probably won't make a lot of sense.

How should you start? First, it is important to break your large topic down into smaller packages. These smaller packages are called **sub-topics**. Sub-topics will help you organize your investigation. They will help you find a focus.

For example:
The topic is Family History.
Sub-topics might be:
1. Family Origins
2. Family Treasures and Stories
3. Important Events
4. Family Customs and Traditions
5. Occupations of Family Members

6. Changes the Family Experienced
Suggest other sub-topics that are of special interest to you.

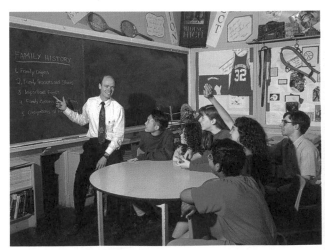

Students brainstorming sub-topics for their family history.

Now you have your topic divided into sub-topics. What do you want to find out about each of the sub-topics? What questions can you develop to guide your study? Remember the "Five W's"–Who? What? Where? When? Why? These are key questions to ask when gathering information.

For each sub-topic, list questions you want to answer. The first two sub-topics have been done for you. Note the kinds of questions that have been set out to help you.

Family Origins

How far back can I trace my family?

Did my family come to Canada from another country?

When? Why did they come?

Where did the early members of my family live?

Family Treasures and Stories

What special family treasures or possessions have been passed down from one generation to another?

Where are they now? Who in the family has them?

Are there any stories about important events in the lives of my relatives?

Arc there any unusual characters in my family?

What special story stands out in my mind about my family members?

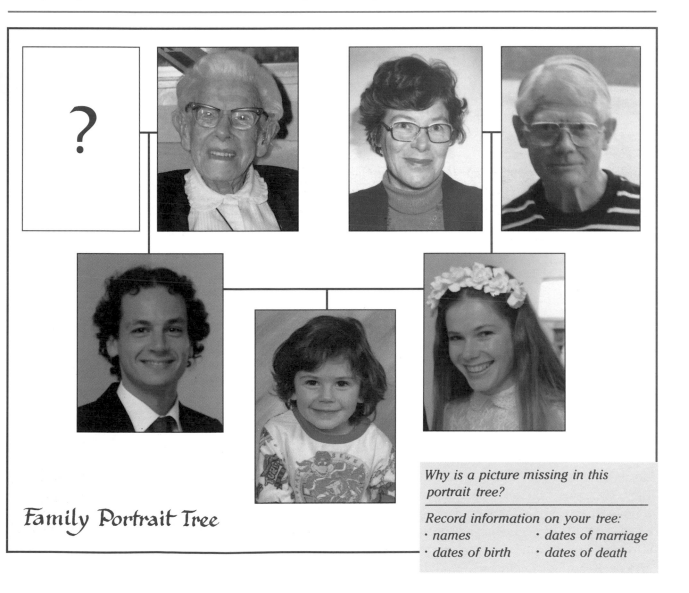

Family Portrait Tree

Why is a picture missing in this portrait tree?

Record information on your tree:
- *names*
- *dates of birth*
- *dates of marriage*
- *dates of death*

The picture on page 7 shows a family portrait tree. A family portrait tree is one way of recording information about your ancestors.

The study of your family line through your ancestors is called **genealogy**. Your ancestors are all of the people from whom you are descended. Your parents, grandparents, great-grandparents, and all of your relatives before them are your ancestors.

Genealogy can be like eating peanuts. Once you get started, it's hard to stop. Tracing your roots is not a day- or a week-long project. In fact, some people have spent their whole lives doing it. Ancient peoples kept track of their family history by reciting poems and songs about their families. The Native peoples of Canada, the Incas of Peru, and the Hebrews are just some of the peoples who could repeat their genealogies from memory.

Someday you might enjoy reading *Roots* by Alex Haley. He asked, "Who am I?" To find an answer he traced his ancestors back through slavery to their beginnings in Africa. The book was later made into a popular television mini-series. His story created a lot of interest in genealogy. Haley believes that when people develop an interest in their own roots they will have more respect for the beginnings of other people. That way the world will move closer to peace.

Locating Information

How would you put together a family portrait tree? Your family may have kept old photographs of family members. They might even go back to the days of your great, great-grandparents. Pictures could be hiding in unmarked boxes in attics and basements. They might be tucked into old books or be lying at the bottom of drawers. You could find them in old albums or old school year-books. Our ancestors were fascinated by cameras and excited about having their pictures taken. They would often put on their best clothes and pose with serious expressions. The photos captured important events in the life of the family.

Don't ignore the possibility that old photographs might also tell you more than you first imagined. Information written on the back could help to answer the important questions: Who? What? Where? When? Why?

Photographs are **artifacts**. Artifacts are objects made by people in the past. You might have many other artifacts from your family's history in your home. Antique furniture and clocks, and old dishes and toys are artifacts too. Can you think of others? These artifacts can tell you a great deal about how your family lived in the past.

Artifacts though are not the only sources of information about your family. **Books and documents** are other valuable sources. **Documents** are original printed materials from the past. They may be government papers such as birth and death certificates, population records, or passenger arrival lists. They could also be diaries or journals, or personal letters written by people about their experiences. They could also be maps, drawings, or paintings. Look at the collage on pages 9 and 10. Can you identify each document? Where might you find them?

Books that might help you learn more about your roots are histories of common family names, how-to books on tracing your family line, or old atlases.

Look at the following chart. It lists some key sources of information and where you might locate them. The first

place to look is at home in your family records. Ask your family members for help. Then try your school and community library. You can also write to government offices for help.

But there is another very important source of information about your family history. It is found in the memory of living relatives. Your parents and grandparents are a storehouse of facts and events. They can share with you their earliest memories. They can describe what life was like when they were growing up. They will be able to tell you about the changes in your family over time. They can show you some of the family treasures. They have many of the answers to the focus questions you developed. One way to get information from your parents or grandparents is through an **interview**.

Family Records	Libraries	Government Records
letters	printed family histories	passenger arrival lists
birth certificates	old atlases	citizenship records
death certificates	"how-to" books on	census records
marriage licences	tracing your roots	birth certificates
diaries	histories of common	marriage licences
passports	family names	death certificates
deeds to property	old telephone books	land registrations
recipes	old newspapers	
family treasures		

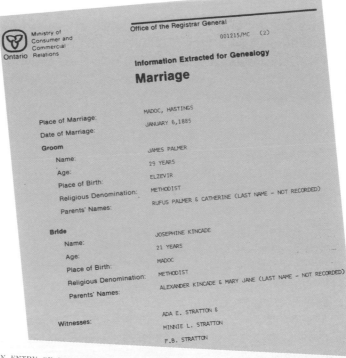

Learning More About Your Roots
Can you identify these documents? Which is not a document, but an artifact?

Skill Building: Collecting Data Through an Interview

What is an interview? It is a meeting during which you collect information from a person. The best way to get information is by asking questions.

Journalists make a living by asking questions. Journalists work for magazines, newspapers, and radio and television stations. They often interview people such as politicians, athletes, and movie stars. They want to find out more about the experiences, interests, and opinions of these people. But not all interviews have to be with someone famous. For example, you could interview a relative to find out more about your family's history. Remember, everyone has a story to tell if only someone will ask and listen.

One of the best ways to collect "people history" is to use a portable cassette tape recorder. It is much easier to record an interview than to write down the answers to questions.

Audio tapes will last a very long time. Your children and your grandchildren will be able to listen to the family history you capture on tape. They will hear the actual voice of the special person you interview. Exciting stories of your family history will be preserved for future generations.

The tape recorder should be looked on as the interviewer's friend. So before you begin interviewing, try it out. Practise with it until you feel comfortable using it.

Here is an outline of the steps to follow for a successful interview.

Getting Started

1. Write down the key questions that you wish to ask in the interview. Ask questions that focus on Who? What? When? Where? and Why?

2. Keep a balance between fact and opinion questions. Fact questions ask for information about actual events. Opinion questions ask about thoughts and feelings.

Fact question: When did you come to Canada?

Opinion question: How did you feel when you first arrived?

3. Make certain that you ask open-ended questions. Open-ended questions require more than one-word answers. In other words, you want to know more than "Yes" or "No." For example, "What did you like most about school?" will lead to more information than "Did you like school?"

4. Listening is very important. If you hear something that is interesting, encourage the person to talk about it. Be ready to leave your set questions for a few minutes. Let the person wander a little in the answer. This approach will often get you more exciting information. The best interviews occur when people have a chance to really talk about their own experiences.

5. Arrange the time and place for the interview. The interviewer and the person being interviewed should both have a little time to prepare and think about the interview.

6. If you plan to use a tape recorder, be certain that the person being interviewed does not object to being taped. Then, be sure the equipment is in working order.

Practice Makes Perfect

Work in groups of three in your class to practise interviewing. Interview each other about your life histories. Prepare your questions first. Then take turns asking your questions, being the person interviewed, and observing the interview. This will help the interviewer to improve his or her techniques.

The observer should watch for such things as:

1. Are the physical arrangements comfortable for an interview? A good arrangement is to sit facing each other with the tape recorder on a table or sofa between you.

2. Does the interviewer start with friendly questions and try to put the person being interviewed at ease?

3. Is it an interesting interview? Are the questions balanced and open-ended?

4. Does the interviewer talk too much and not listen enough?

5. Does the interviewer listen carefully? Does he or she encourage the person to talk more about interesting experiences and events?

6. Does the interviewer keep the conversation moving along? Is the pace too fast? Is it too slow?

Doing It

1. Be on time for the interview. Introduce yourself if you do not know the person.

2. Try to conduct the interview in a quiet place. This should help both of you concentrate on the questions and answers.

3. If you are using a tape recorder, start the tape by stating your name, the name of the person being interviewed, and the date. For example: "This is Joe Sawchuk speaking. This is an interview with my grandmother, Mary Ellen Tomins. It is being recorded on October 30, 1995."

4. Be flexible. If you are collecting interesting information, don't be afraid to get into a topic you had not planned.

5. Don't allow the interview to go on too long. A half-hour or forty minutes is a reasonable time for an interview.

6. Remember to thank the person at the end of the interview. He or she has helped you to gather valuable information.

7. Review your tapes (or notes) as soon as possible after the interview. Write a summary of what you discovered from the interview.

A student interviewing her grandmother. What questions might she be asking?

Exploring Your School Community

You have discovered how you and your family are part of history. Your school is also part of history. Your school may be 100 years old or it may be new. It does not matter. There is information that needs to be collected, organized, and preserved for future generations. You have learned some skills in examining your personal and family histories. Now you can put those skills to work in exploring your school community.

How could you tell people about your school's history? Sometimes we think the only way to communicate history is to write about it. But historians have many ways to tell about the past. For example, a museum could set up an exhibit to explain pioneer life. This is done by the **curator**. A curator is an historian who works in a museum. The curator collects photographs, costumes, documents, and even household items. He or she carefully records and identifies all of the objects.

Then the curator displays them so that they tell the story of the past for the visitors.

Another interesting way to communicate history is to use a **time capsule**. A time capsule is a collection of objects that help to describe what everyday life is like. Time capsules are often placed in the cornerstones of public buildings such as banks and town halls. Usually, the capsule is a steel box or container. It can hold almost anything as long as the objects describe everyday life. It could contain such things as a soft drink can, a green garbage bag, a newspaper headline, a poem or book, ticket stubs for a rock concert, or glossy photographs of the latest car models. The idea is that people from some future generation will open the time capsule. They will discover what life was like for the people who put the time capsule together.

Here is a class at work making a time capsule for their school. Look at the ideas they have developed. They should help you to get started on your time capsule.

People
· *pictures of students, teachers, principals, and school helpers*
· *interviews with famous graduates*
· *information on cultural groups represented in the school*

School Achievements
· *photos of champions past and present*
· *photos of honour students*
· *samples of yearbooks or school newspapers*
· *drama presentations*
· *class trips*
· *music nights and concerts*
· *multicultural festivals*

A Day in the Life of the School
· *student life-clothes, timetables, homework assignments*
· *interviews with graduates about a typical day thirty years ago*

School Location and Design
· *collection of photos*
showing how the
building has changed
· *map showing the*
location of the school
in the community
· *floor plan of the building*

Skill Building: Communicating History Using a Time Capsule

Plan a time capsule for your school to be opened in thirty years at an assembly. What would you want the students of the future to know about the school community today? What might you include in the time capsule?

1. As a class, make a list of sub-topics that will help you describe everyday life at your school.

2. Divide the class into groups. Each group chooses one or two sub-topics and makes a list of what to collect for their part of the capsule.

3. Decide where you might find the materials for your part of the time capsule. Then collect the information and materials you need.

4. Sort through the material you have collected. Make a final decision on what to include in the time capsule. Keep it interesting for future generations.

5. Decide how to present the information in an exciting way. Remember a future generation will open your capsule. They must be able to understand it easily. You could include written descriptions, drawings, photos or photo collages, models, posters, or audio tapes.

6. Share your part of the time capsule with the class. Explain what you have included and what it will mean to future generations.

7. Place the time capsule in a safe place. Leave a record of its location and when it should be opened.

Activities

Looking Back

1. Start a personal dictionary of key words. You can add to your dictionary as you meet new words and concepts in this book.
   a) Divide a page in your notebook into three columns. Make the middle column the widest.
   b) In the left column, write the key word. In the middle column, write the meaning of the word. Try to write the definition in your own words.
   c) In the third column, give an example. You could use the word in a sentence or draw a sketch.

   Start your dictionary with the following:

history	genealogy	curator
community	artifact	time capsule
chronological order	document	
timeline	interview	

Using Your Knowledge

2. Make a timeline to record what you have done today. Start with when you woke up at 8:00 a.m., for example. Does this example tell you how to divide your timeline?

3. Look at the following topics. Choose one topic and break it down into sub-topics. Then develop focus questions for each sub-topic.
   a) My Ancestors
   b) Leisure Time Activities and Recreation in My Family
   c) All About My Grandmother

4. Make your own family portrait tree. Use photocopies of your family pictures. There may be a machine at your school or public library that you could use. Stick small rolled pieces of masking tape on the back of the pictures. Then arrange them on a blank white sheet for copying. The tape will not damage the pictures and will hold them in place. If you cannot find pictures for some of your ancestors, leave a blank circle. Try to make your portrait tree for three or four generations.

5. Make a collection of favourite family recipes. Try to determine how old the recipe might be and which ancestor or family member introduced it to the family. Put the collection together in a family recipe book or make a family recipe calendar.

6. Remember the three key sources you can use to find historical information? They are artifacts, books and documents, and people and memories. Write these headings in your notebook. Place the items in the list below under the correct headings.

   birth certificate
   telephone book
   your grandfather's diary
   the antique rocking chair in your family room
   the old set of dishes your grandmother gave to your mother
   your great-uncle's story about his experiences in the war
   your great-aunt's old passport
   plans of your old family home
   Alex Haley's *Roots*

Extending Your Thinking

7. Interview an older relative about your family history. Remember the skills you learned for an effective interview. Make a list of the questions you want to ask first. Read your questions to a partner. Ask your partner to evaluate your questions. Are they friendly questions? Do they ask for both facts and opinions? Are they clear and open-ended? Make improvements to your questions. Then arrange the interview.

8. "To forget one's ancestors is to be a brook without a source, a tree without a root."–Proverb
   Discuss the meaning of this proverb? Do you agree? Why?

9. Plan a time capsule that will describe the everyday life of teenagers today. Remember to start by outlining your sub-topics. Then make a list of the materials you want to include and collect them. Present your finished time capsule to the class.

CHAPTER 2

Exploring Your Local Community – People

Colonel Sam McLaughlin

Stefan was in the attic. He was poking through a box of photographs. It was then he spotted it. Something shiny was lying at the bottom of the box. Stefan fished it out and held it up. It was some kind of medal. On it was the face of an elderly man and the words, "Colonel R. S. McLaughlin: 1871-1971."

At dinner Stefan asked his mother about the medal. She recalled that every elementary school student in Oshawa had received one of these medals in 1971. They were part of a celebration to mark the 100th birthday of Colonel Sam McLaughlin. Colonel McLaughlin was one of Oshawa's most illustrious citizens.

The next day, Stefan took his discovery to history class. As he passed the medal around, he was bombarded with questions. Who was Colonel McLaughlin anyway? Why was he so important that they would make a medal to honour his birthday? How much did Stefan think the medal was worth? When did Colonel Sam die? And what were the accomplishments of his life?

Most students in Stefan's class knew that Samuel McLaughlin had been Chairman of the Board at General Motors, Canada. After all, there were lots of reminders of his name in Oshawa. Two schools, a library, streets, and an art gallery were named after him or members of his family. His home, Parkwood, was open to the public. The McLaughlin Planetarium in nearby Toronto was also named after him. He had provided funds to help build it. But the class wanted to know more about the man whose face was on the medal.

It was at that moment that their history teacher suggested a local history project. Why not find out more about this remarkable citizen? The whole class could get involved. The first car made in Oshawa appeared in 1907. What was it like, that car with the McLaughlin body and the Buick engine? Were there any 1907 models still around that the class could see? What happened in 1915 when Louis Chevrolet, a daring racing car driver, offered McLaughlin the chance to make the Chevrolet automobile in Oshawa? Why did McLaughlin sell his company to General Motors in 1918? How did the manufacturing of cars and parts grow into one of Canada's most important industries? Were there still people around who remembered Colonel Sam?

During the following weeks the class collected a remarkable amount of information. They did some of their research in school, but they also looked for information in the community. They read several books and articles about McLaughlin. They searched through community newspapers from the early 1900s. They were determined to find every bit of information about the McLaughlin Carriage Works and General Motors. Some students located and interviewed people who had worked for Colonel Sam. The class visited the McLaughlin home to try to imagine his lifestyle. The public relations office at General Motors provided information, photographs, and the names of people class members could talk to. Dozens of photographs were sifted through and studied.

When the project was finished the students were proud of their research. Experts who read it encouraged them to publish it. So the class published its first booklet. It was a ninety-two page booklet entitled Colonel Sam and the Horseless Carriage.

Stefan, whose discovery of the medal started it all, summed up the project this way: "It was a really good place for us to start our study of local history. After all, Colonel Sam lived right here in our own community. We got to know him well. He became a person who lived and breathed. It made history come alive for us. I'm glad I found the medal."

Why did Stefan's class decide to explore the community's history?

What sources of information did they use?

What did the class accomplish?

Stefan's class learned a great deal about the local community. They studied written sources that helped them put events in chronological order. They examined artifacts such as photographs, the medal, old buildings, and early automobiles. These artifacts helped them to actually *see* what the past was like. The class talked to people to learn about their memories. Memories gave the students a feel for the past. Interviews helped to turn fragile memories into a permanent record.

Your **local community** is the city, town, or village in which you live. Everyone who lives and works in your area is part of your local community. People and events of the past and all the changes that have taken place in your local community are part of its history.

You can locate information about the history of your own community. These next three chapters present a variety of activities for planning a local community study. This chapter explores people. The next two chapters cover the environment and the economy. Select sub-topics that interest you from each chapter. Remember the skills you learned as you explored your family's and your school's history.

Skill Building: Planning a Local Community Study

When you explored the history of your family and your school, you learned how to focus your topic, locate and record information, and communicate what you found. You made timelines and time capsules. You talked to people and learned about their memories and feelings. Now you can apply your skills to explore the history of your local community. Here are the general steps you will follow.

FIND A FOCUS
The first step is to narrow down your broad topic. Break it down into sub-topics and develop focus questions to guide your study.

LOCATE INFORMATION
Identify your main sources of information. In history, some main sources are artifacts, books and documents, and people and memories. Explore these sources for information to answer your focus questions.

ORGANIZE AND RECORD INFORMATION
In this step, you use an organizer such as a chart or timeline to organize and record your information.

EVALUATE THE INFORMATION
Review your information. Make sure it answers your focus questions. Be sure it is accurate.

DRAW CONCLUSIONS
What does the information tell you? What important facts have you discovered?

COMMUNICATE YOUR CONCLUSIONS
Choose the best way to tell about what you have discovered. You could prepare a talk, write a paragraph, design a poster or a mural, or put together a scrapbook.

Now let's go through each step. These steps will help you plan your local community study.

FIND A FOCUS

Your topic is "The History of Your Local Community." The sub-topics have been set out for you. They are People, the Environment, and the Economy. These sub-topics have been broken down into even smaller topics for your study.

People
Origins and Early Settlement
Multiculturalism
Recreation and Leisure
Community Leaders

The Environment
The Natural Environment
Main Street
Architecture

The Economy
Industry
Transportation and Communication

Your teacher will help you choose activities from several of these sub-topics. As you explore these sub-topics, you will develop focus questions for each one.

LOCATE INFORMATION

You will explore artifacts, books and documents, and people and their memories to find answers to your questions.

ORGANIZE AND RECORD INFORMATION

Chart organizers, lists, timelines, and interviews are just some of the ways you will use to record and organize your information.

EVALUATE THE INFORMATION

Review your information. Does it answer your questions? Do you need to look further? Is the information accurate? Check it again.

DRAW CONCLUSIONS

You will discover interesting facts about your community's past. There are mysteries to be solved. Think about what the information tells you.

COMMUNICATE YOUR CONCLUSIONS

You will find many ways of telling about your discoveries. Posters, murals, scrapbooks, talks, and newspaper reports are some ways you will use.

Origins and Early Settlement

Do you know what community names such as Ottawa, Winnipeg, and Niagara mean? Do you know why some communities have names such as Victoria, Charlottetown, or Cornwall? Community names are important clues. They can tell you about the origins and early settlers of your community.

Many communities still have the names given to them by the Native peoples. The Native peoples were the first settlers. They named many of their communities after the natural features of the area. Niagara, for example, means "thunder of waters." Winnipeg means "murky waters," and Toronto means "meeting place." Some names we use today are translations of original Native names such as Yellowknife, Medicine Hat, Moose Jaw, and Thunder Bay.

Other names are clues to the first European settlers who came to an area. These settlers often named communities after kings and queens, government or military leaders, religious leaders, or community founders. Victoria, Regina, Georgetown, Prince Albert, Halifax, Brockville, and Wesleyville are examples. Then there are names that describe the location of a community. Peekaboo Corner, New Brunswick; Hairy Hill, Alberta; and Horsefly, British Columbia are real places.

Find out what the name of your community means. The following activities will help you to learn more about the origins and early settlers of your community.

Making a rubbing of a gravestone.

A Cemetery Study

Did you ever think that a visit to your local cemetery could tell you about the history of your community?

Visit a local cemetery and examine various gravestones. Find one gravestone that is at least fifty years old. Find another gravestone that is more recent (less than ten years old).

Examine the gravestones carefully. Use an organizer like the one on page 23 to record information from the gravestones. Fill in as many facts as you can.

You may be able to make rubbings of the gravestones. Check with the cemetery officials for permission. Old gravestones can be damaged by constant rubbing. This is because they were often made of soft stone. If you cannot make rubbings, sketch the gravestones on the back of your organizer.

To make a rubbing you will need large sheets of newsprint, tape, and a thick wax crayon or stick of artist's charcoal. Tape the large sheets of newsprint over the gravestone. Then lightly rub over the paper with the wax crayon or charcoal.

The letters and images on the gravestone will appear on the paper.

Display your rubbings in the classroom when you return. Examine the information you recorded on your organizers.

1. As a class, list the ages at death of all the people on the recent gravestones. Make another list of the ages at death of all the people on the old gravestones.

    a) Who was the oldest person recorded?

    b) Who was the youngest?

    c) Calculate the *average* age at death of the people on the recent gravestones. Do the same for the people on the old gravestones. Do

people live longer today than in the past? Why?

2. Is there any evidence that disease or disasters struck the citizens of your community?
3. What occupations or skills are identified?
4. What religions are identified?
5. What countries or other Canadian communities did the people in your community come from? How many were born in the community?

While you are visiting the cemetery, gather information for your family history if your ancestors are buried there. Check for dates you need and the original family names of women in your family's past.

Things to Consider	Recent Gravestone	Old Gravestone
Name on gravestone		
Birth date		
Place of birth		
Death date		
Age at death		
Cause of death		
Religion		
Occupation		
Decorations on gravestone		
Size of gravestone		
Condition of gravestone		
Additional names on gravestone and relationship to deceased person		
Additional information		

Researching the Past

Most libraries keep collections about the history of the local community. These collections often include books on local history and early citizens, photographs, newspaper files, old diaries, and early maps. The librarian can help you find these resources. If the information you want is not in the library, the librarian will often be able to tell you where you can find it.

Locate information in your school or community library on the origins and early settlement of your community. Use the resources to answer the following questions:

1. **a)** What does your community's name mean?

    b) Did your community have a different name when it was founded? If so, what was it? When was the name changed? Why was it changed?
2. Who were the first people in your community?
3. When was your community first settled?
4. Why was your community first settled?
5. What part of the present community was settled first?
6. Who were some early community leaders? For example, who was the first mayor?

Use a chart organizer like the one below to record your findings.

Memories and Recollections

Senior citizens are a valuable source of community history. They can be asked to recall memories of their origins within the community. They can tell how the community has developed in their lifetime. You have an opportunity to practise the skills of an effective interviewer. Ask a senior citizen living in your neighbourhood or an older relative for an interview. You might also ask a resident of a local senior citizens' home.

Review the steps in conducting a successful interview. Develop your key questions. Below are some examples of focus questions. Add others. Think of what you would like to know about life in your community's past. Think about what interesting information a senior citizen could give you.

1. Were you born in the community or did you move here?
2. Where have you lived in the community?
3. How big was the community when you were young or when you first arrived?
4. What impressed you about this community?
5. How has the landscape changed over the years?
6. What other major changes have you observed in the community?
7. What do you think this community will be like in the future?

Conduct the interview and share the results with your class.

Community Name	When Settled	Why Settled	First Area Settled	First People	Early Leaders

Multiculturalism

The Native peoples were the first inhabitants of Canada. More than three hundred years ago the French joined the Native peoples. Soon after the British and Americans settled in the area. Later people from many different parts of the world came to Canada. Each group of people brought its own language, religion, customs, art, and music. These distinguishing features make up the group's **heritage**. All of these groups have contributed to the mixture of people and traditions that make up Canada's multicultural society.

What evidence is there of multiculturalism in your community? Examine street signs and store fronts. Look at the different kinds of restaurants. Check the special events and celebrations that are planned. What cultural groups are represented in your community?

A traditional dance performed at the Japanese pavilion during Caravan in Toronto.

A Heritage Festival

Canadians celebrate their various heritages in different ways. Many communities, for example, have annual multicultural festivals. Every summer Toronto has a festival called Caravan. In Regina, the multicultural festival is called Mosaic. Winnipeg's festival is called Folklorama.

During Caravan in Toronto, each cultural group has its own building called a pavilion. Inside the pavilions, the groups showcase their food, native costumes, crafts, music, dance, and other arts. People in the community buy "passports" as tickets to the different pavilions. They "travel" from country to country each evening to learn more about the cultural groups in the community.

Plan a multicultural festival for your class or school. Start by giving your festival a name. Then make a list of all of

the cultural groups in your class. Are there other cultural groups in your community that are not on the list? Add those as well.

Divide your class into groups. Each group can choose one culture to investigate. Find out about that culture's traditional costumes, food, arts, crafts, music, dance, or other customs. Talk to your families and friends for help. Check your library.

Set up a display to showcase the culture's heritage. You could include food or recipes, taped music, costumes, crafts, pictures, drawings, or demonstrations of dancing.

As a class, design passports that could be stamped at each display as visitors come by.

Discuss how the cultural groups in your festival have helped to give your community its character. What contributions have the various groups brought to the community?

Discovering the Cultural Mosaic

People of different cultural groups live in every Canadian community. Select a group from your school or neighbourhood. Interview individuals from that group. Find out about their special customs and experiences. Here are some focus questions to get you started:

1. What nationality were your ancestors?

2. What language did they originally speak? Do any family members still speak that language?

3. What occupations and skills did they bring?

4. Why did you or your ancestors settle in this community?

5. Did you or your ancestors have any problems getting used to living in this community? If so, what were they?

6. What are some of your culture's special customs?

Share your results with the class. Compare what you learned about the various cultural groups in your community.

A celebration of Native culture at Folklorama in Winnipeg.

Swedish dancers performing for a cultural festival.

Customs and Traditions

Each cultural group in the community has its own customs and traditions. For example, groups celebrate special holidays in different ways. Christmas, Hanukka, Ramadan, and New Year's Day are examples of special holidays.

Choose a cultural group and a holiday it celebrates. Research answers to these questions:

1. When is the holiday celebrated?
2. Why is it celebrated?
3. What preparations are made for the holiday?
4. What foods are prepared?
5. What decorations are used?
6. What special music is played or sung?
7. What other customs and traditions are followed to celebrate the holiday?

Ask the librarian to help you locate books about the cultural group. Check the library for any clipping files on special events or holidays. These files often contain interesting articles from newspapers and magazines. Look at cookbooks for special recipes.

Use an organizer like the one below to record your information.

Recreation and Leisure

Sports arenas, playing fields, local churches, and schools were all important parts of early life in your community. Social events were often held in church basements or school rooms. People gathered at the local sports arena or playing field to cheer local teams or join in a game. In the winter, the fields might be flooded to make skating rinks. The steepest hillside in the community would be the favourite tobogganing place for families.

These sports and social events are all examples of leisure activities in the early days of the community. Each generation had its favourite activities. Do you know what kind of music your parents listened to when they were teenagers? Who were their sports heroes? What were their clothes like?

Cultural Holiday:
When celebrated
Why celebrated
Preparations
Food
Decorations
Music
Other customs

Skill Building: Understanding Timelines

Remember your personal timeline. Each section of the timeline represented a year in your life. A year is one way we record and measure time. But there are other ways too. We can also divide time into hours, minutes, and seconds. If you wanted to make a timeline of your activities for a day, how might you divide your timeline? You would probably use hours.

If you wanted to record events over a long period of time, you might divide your timeline into ten-year periods or even one-hundred year periods. Ten-year periods are **decades**. One-hundred year periods are **centuries**.

Copy the list below into your notebook. Identify the time period. Write your answer beside each example.

January

1990-1999

Tuesday

2001

1800-1899

Now suppose you wanted to make a timeline to record important events for each time period. How would you divide your timeline? Copy the chart below into your notebook. Give an example of each time period listed. Then explain how you would divide your timeline. The first time period is done for you as an example.

Look at the timeline on pages 30-31. This timeline is divided into decades starting at 1900. It gives an overview of the important facts about recreation and leisure in the 1900s.

Notice how there is more than one important fact under each decade. Ten years is a long time. Many important events happened during the decade. There were many noteworthy people. To help organize the facts, the information is divided into sub-topics. The same sub-topics are used to record information for each decade.

Examine the information on the timeline. Does the timeline give you a good overview of recreation and leisure from 1900-1939?

Time Period	Example	Timeline Organization
Day	Monday	Divided into hours
Week		
Month		
Year		
Decade		
Century		

Life as a Teenager in Your Community

In groups, choose a decade from the incomplete section of the timeline shown below. Use the same sub-topics. Find out as much as you can about teenage life in your community during that decade. Books, magazines, newspapers, and personal interviews can all be used as sources of information.

Plan a sight and sound show to present your decade to an audience.

1900-1909

What they wore:
Girls–high button boots, skirts to the ankles, sashes and lace, huge hats
Boys–knickerbockers with suspenders, shirts with bow ties, caps

What they listened to:
Ragtime piano music

What was new:
The horseless carriage (automobile), the Marconi wireless

Famous athletes:
Tom Longboat (long distance running), Tommy Burns (boxing)

Favourite entertainers:
Sarah Bernhardt

Leisure activities:
Singsongs around the piano, local church concerts, listening to the gramophone

1910-1919

What they wore:
Girls–simple blouses and long flared tunics
Boys–knickerbockers with suspenders

What they listened to:
Jazz, music hall songs

What was new:
Airplanes, silent movies, women working in offices

Famous athletes:
George Hodgson (swimming), Joe Malone (hockey), The Winnipeg Falcons

Favourite entertainers:
Theda Bara, Lillian Gish, Charlie Chaplin, Eva Tanguay, The Dumbells

Leisure activities:
Listening to the gramophone, cycling

1920-1929

What they wore:
Girls–short dresses with no waistline, short hair, silk stockings rolled down to the knees
Boys–bell bottom trousers, baggy sweaters

What they listened to:
Charleston, the Black Bottom, Ballin' the Jack, Fox Trot

What was new:
Model T Ford, talkies, women getting the vote

Famous athletes:
"Bobbie" Rosenfeld (track), Ethel Calderwood (track), Lionel Conacher (football), The Edmonton Grads (basketball), Babe Ruth (baseball), Howie Morenz (hockey), Jack Dempsey (boxing)

Favourite entertainers:
Mary Pickford, Marie Dressler, Rudolph Valentino

Leisure activities:
Going to the movies, listening to the Victrola, dancing

1930-1939

What they wore:
Girls–fitted fashions with waists, ruffles, butterfly sleeves, high spiked heels, nail polish, nylon stockings
Boys–argyle sweaters and socks, slacks and shirts

What they listened to:
Swing, boogie-woogie, rumba

What was new:
Penicillin, commercial airline flights

Famous athletes:
Fritz Hanson (football), Francis Amyot (canoeing), Sandy Somerville (golf), "Torchy" Peden (cycling)

Favourite entertainers:
Ginger Rogers and Fred Astaire, Marx Brothers, Clark Gable, Norma Shearer, Raymond Massey, Beatrice Lillie, Fay Wray, Jeanette MacDonald

Leisure activities:
Horror and adventure movies, listening to the radio, dancing

1940-1949

What they wore:

What they listened to:

What was new:

Famous athletes:

Favourite entertainers:

Leisure activities:

Television in living rooms

RECREATION AND LEISURE

1950-1959	1960-1969	1970-1979	1980-1989

1950-1959

A 1950s juke box

What they wore:

What they listened to:

What was new:

Famous athletes:

Favourite entertainers:

Leisure activities:

1960-1969

What they wore:

What they listened to:

Leisure activities:

Famous athletes:

Favourite entertainers:

What was new:

The first astronaut on the moon

1970-1979

What they wore:

What they listened to:

Famous athletes:

Secretariat wins the Triple Crown

What was new:

Favourite entertainers:

Leisure activities:

1980-1989

The technological revolution

What they wore:

What they listened to:

What was new:

Famous athletes:

Favourite entertainers:

Leisure activities:

The Sports Arena

HISTORIC TERRACE SOLD
By Frances Kelly *The Toronto Star*

For thousands of Metro roller skaters, it will be the end of an era.

Employees of the Terrace roller rink, where skaters have been spinning their wheels for half a century, have been told the Toronto landmark has been sold and is expected to close in May.

Built in 1912 as the "Dominion's largest auditorium," it takes up most of a downtown block formed by Mutual, Dalhousie, Dundas and Shuter Streets.

It was the first home to the Toronto Maple Leafs, who started out as the Toronto Arenas hockey team and became the St. Pats before becoming the Leafs. They played there until 1932.

In 1925, the United Church of Canada held its inaugural service there, bringing together the Congregational, Methodist and Presbyterian churches.

During the Big Band Era, it echoed with the sounds of Glenn Miller, Duke Ellington, Count Basie, and Woody Herman. And in 1949, Frank Sinatra held his first Toronto concert there.

William Dickson, who owned Ontario News Co., bought it from the city in 1938, renamed it Mutual St. Arena and brought in roller skating.

It became The Terrace in 1962 after a $3-million renovation that converted it to the three levels and added 18 curling sheets.

Just about now you are thinking that there can't be any more hiding places for local history. Are you sure you have found them all? What about the local sports arena? Almost every community has an arena that has played an important role in its history.

Visit a local arena in your community. Look carefully at the trophies displayed in the showcases. Check the photographs mounted on the walls. Were there championship teams in your community's past?

Were there local athletes who made the community proud? Who were they? What names of families who still live in your community do you recognize?

Select a local team from the past. Imagine you are a sports writer for the local paper. Write a column for the newspaper that captures the excitement of an important game or championship. A reporter's column should answer the questions: Who? What? Where? When? Why? and How?

Women's hockey team, early 1900s.

A friendly game of hockey in Saskatchewan, 1899. Hockey was then already a half-century old.

Community Facilities

Arenas, gyms, clubs, and parks are all examples of recreation facilities. Investigate the recreation facilities in your community. In groups, list all the facilities you can think of. Consider all age groups from pre-schoolers to senior citizens. Check other sources to add to your list. Go through the blue or yellow pages of your local telephone book. Talk to people in your community to gather information.

Review your list. Do you know which facilities are the newest? Which do you think are the oldest? Do they date back to the earliest days of your community?

Ask an official from your local Parks and Recreation Department or your local Community Centre to come to your class. Have the official talk about the earliest facilities in the community. Ask about the changes that have taken place. Have some questions ready. Find out if you were right about the oldest and newest facilities in the community.

Community Leaders

HENRY'S GIFT   By Sam Pazzano *The Toronto Sun*

Young Henry Orbe received the most precious gift of all–a chance for a healthy life.

The nine-year-old Peruvian boy arrived at Pearson International Airport yesterday and was greeted by Ron Fox, who is raising $200 000 so that Henry can have life-saving kidney surgery at the Hospital For Sick Children.

Henry also suffers from osteomielitis, a painful bone-rotting condition that has crippled him.

The child was taken into surgery at the Hospital For Sick Children at 8:30 p.m. last night so surgeons could put pins in his right leg to help support it.

Fox said doctors found Henry's leg had been broken a couple of weeks ago "and nobody was aware of it because of the weakness in his leg."

Fox said even while Henry's leg is being repaired and is in traction, they can still treat the infection that is eating away his bones and try to correct his kidney problem.

"I'm very happy, I never thought I would come to Canada," said Henry's father, Segundo Guerra, 37, through an interpreter, Fox's wife Clara.

Fox found Henry's weeping father, carrying his crippled son from a hospital in the Peruvian city of Iquitos at Christmas time. Fox was visiting his wife's family.

Guerra, who earns the equivalent of about $1 a day as a courier, couldn't afford medical treatment.

Fox, 49, and father of seven, has raised $100 000 for Henry's treatment so far. And the aircraft leasing company owner pledged a $50 000 lien on his North York house to ensure medical costs are covered.

Generous donations and pledges have flooded in: A St. Catharines group called Hands Across The City has offered to collect $30 000. Fund-raising events, including a gourmet dinner, chili-making competition and art auction are scheduled for this summer.

The Good Citizen's Award

How would you describe Ron Fox? He is not a famous person you would hear about often in the news. He is an ordinary citizen who has made a special effort to help someone else. Many people like Ron Fox are never recognized and honoured. Every community has ordinary people who have helped others or made a special contribution. Do some detective work to find the good citizens in your community. They may be people from the past or the present.

First, think about your criteria for a good citizen. The criteria are qualities you feel a good citizen should have. Some criteria are listed in the chart on the next page. Add others and give examples.

Now start your search for your good citizen. Listen to the local news and watch the newspaper stories for clues. Search through the newspaper files in the library. Ask people in your school or community for suggestions.

Once you have made your decision, design a scroll to honour the good citizen. Write a **citation** to go on the scroll. A citation describes the special qualities of the person receiving an award. Present your award before the class.

Criteria	Example
This person is: brave	person rescues a child or animal in danger
generous with his or her own time	person volunteers many hours for the local food drive
a leader of young people	person spends a lot of time and effort coaching teenagers in the community
fair-minded and unprejudiced	person encourages multiculturalism and good relations in the community

Why might you choose this volunteer for a Good Citizen's Award?

Local Heroes and Heroines

Every community in Canada has produced heroes and heroines. Choose a famous citizen, of the past or present, from your community. He or she may be a political or business leader. Consider also famous inventors, entertainers, or athletes. Do not overlook men and women who are leaders in the social or religious life of the community.

Research the person you select. Check books and newspaper files. Use these questions as a guide:

1. Who is your local hero or heroine?
2. When did that person live in your community?
3. What leadership characteristics did that person have?
4. How did that person contribute to the life of the community or Canada?
5. In what ways is that person remembered in the community today? (Are there streets, schools, buildings, or parks named after that person?)
6. Why did you choose this hero or heroine?

Put together a scrapbook that tells about your famous citizen.

Acting as Decision-Makers

What problems do you think the early settlers of your community faced? When did they get their first school? How did they decide where to build roads? Where did they get the water they needed? How did they protect the community from fire?

Imagine you are the early leaders of your community. You have called a town meeting to decide on what the community needs. As a class, make a list of the first things you think the community will need.

Divide the class into groups. Each group can choose one item from the list. Discuss how you would provide the building or service to the community. Consider the following questions:

1. What materials will you need?

2. Where will you get the materials?

3. How will you transport them to the community?

4. Where will you locate your building or service? Explain why.

5. What problems have you come across? How might you solve them?

Select a spokesperson for your group to present your plan to the class. Make certain you present the problems you discovered and the possible solutions.

Discuss each group's presentation. Are there any other problems that haven't been solved?

CHAPTER 3

Exploring Your Local Community–The Environment

The Natural Environment

Where is your community located? Is it on a lake or river, in a valley, or on a plain? These features are all part of the **natural environment**. The natural environment has always been important in deciding the location of communities. Native peoples chose the locations of their communities with care. They were aware of the need for fresh water, good hunting and fishing grounds, and nearby rivers for travel.

The first fur traders and settlers also used waterways as their highways. Towns often sprang up around natural harbours. Ships carrying passengers and products could anchor there. Soon streets were laid out around the harbour. Lots were marked out for homes, schools, and churches. Other desired locations for towns were along rivers, or near good soil, stands of timber, and minerals.

Historical Maps

What are the features of the natural environment around your community? How has the natural environment changed through history? Maps of your community can tell you about the development of your area.

First let's look at the sample map on page 38. Check the **legend** beside the map. The legend shows the symbols used on the map. A **symbol** is something that stands for or represents an object. The legend tells you what the symbols on the map mean. It helps you to read the map.

Answer these questions:

1. What features of the natural environment may have helped to decide the location of Comstock?
2. What other factors might explain why Comstock developed where it did?
3. What two major highways run through the community?
4. Locate the mills on the map. Explain their location.
5. Explain the location of the industrial area.
6. How would you describe the pattern of the streets in the main residential area?
7. Why did the main residential area develop where it did?
8. Where would you expect the Main Street in Comstock to be? Explain why.

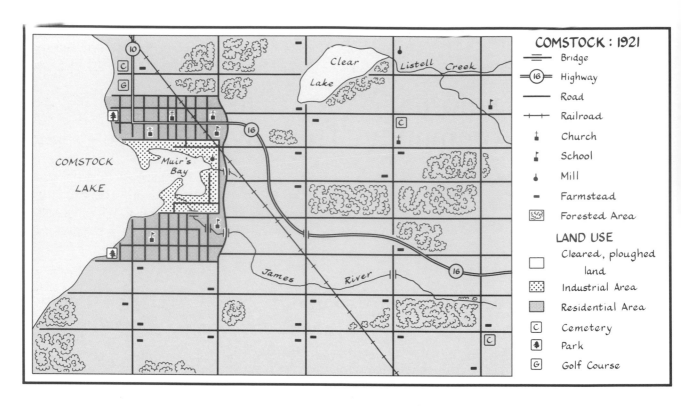

COMSTOCK : 1921

═══	Bridge
═⑯═	Highway
───	Road
┼┼┼	Railroad
♰	Church
♪	School
♦	Mill
─	Farmstead
▨	Forested Area

LAND USE

☐	Cleared, ploughed land
▦	Industrial Area
▨	Residential Area
C	Cemetery
♠	Park
G	Golf Course

Students examining a map of their community in an historical atlas.

Now you are ready to examine historical maps of your own community. Locate one old map and one recent map. One place to look for an old map is in an historical atlas of your area. You will find these atlases in libraries and local museums. Many museums and historical societies also have copies of old maps. You can find recent maps in your library. You probably also have one at home. By comparing old and new maps of your community, you can find out how the community has changed.

Examine the two maps carefully. Check the legends and find the symbols on the maps. Use an organizer like the one below to record information from the maps.

Study the information in your organizer. Can you explain why your community developed where it did? What major changes did you discover from your map study?

Local Environmental Concerns

What concerns do people in your community have about the natural environment?

Check local newspapers and magazines. Collect articles on local environmental concerns. Make a list of all the concerns your class identifies.

Divide the class into groups. Each group can investigate one area of local environmental concern. In your group, read the articles on your topic. Summarize the concern outlined in the articles in one or two sentences. Discuss why people are concerned. When did they become concerned? What solutions can you see?

Find or draw pictures to illustrate the concern. Design a poster to make the community more aware of this environmental problem. Display the posters in the school hall or public library. Use this display to raise community awareness about your local environment.

The Community Speaks

In every community there are groups who work to protect the environment. They voice concerns about environmental problems. Do you know of any groups in your community? These are some common environmental groups:

	Old Map	Recent Map
Title and date		
Source (where did you find the map?)		
Main features of the natural environment		
Main roads		
Railways		
Location of main residential areas		
Location of farms		
Location of industries		

Environment Canada
  (Federal Government)
Ministry of Natural Resources
  (Provincial Government)
Parks and Recreation
  (Municipal Government)
Local Conservation Authority
Local Field Naturalist Club
Pollution Probe
  (or other concerned citizen's group)

Invite a guest speaker from one of these groups to your class. Ask the speaker to talk about his or her organization. When was it founded? Why was it founded? What are its major concerns? What changes in the community's environment has the speaker seen? Which have been good changes? Which have caused damage to the environment?

Main Street

Does your town or city have a Main Street, a Centre Street, a town square, or a First Avenue? It probably does and this is likely the oldest and most important area of your community. In the early days, farmers brought their produce to sell at the market on Main Street. The post office and community shops were concentrated there. The first doctor's or dentist's office was probably located above a store. The first churches were often built right along Main Street.

Main Street was also the social and entertainment centre of town. Parades, concerts, and theatre presentations all took place there. People met on Main Street and exchanged community news in the days before the telephone. Main Street, like all other parts of the local community, has changed over the years.

A Stroll Down Main Street

Take a walking tour along your "Main Street" (it may have a different name). If possible, arrange to have a long-time resident of your community go with you. This person can offer important information about changes that have occurred along the street. A walking tour is one of the best ways to find out about your present community and its past.

Work with a partner. You and your partner will have a map organizer of your Main Street. As you stroll along the street, use your observational skills. Mark the names of stores, churches, and other buildings on your organizer. As you identify each building, look for clues about the past. Try to find evidence of changes on the street.

Here are some clues to watch for:

• old or painted-over signs on buildings
• dates engraved on cornerstones, around the doors of buildings, or on metal plaques
• dates printed on sidewalks, maintenance hole covers, and on gates
• storefronts that look old (did the building once have some other use?)
• the kinds of materials used in the buildings
• evidence of old railway tracks and stations

Note any clues you find on your organizer.

When you return to the classroom, compare your organizers with those of your classmates. Examine all the clues the class found about the past. Try to reconstruct what your Main Street looked like in the past from the clues. Discuss some of the changes that have taken place along your Main Street. This could be over the last 25, 50, or 100 years. Suggest reasons for these changes. What is the most important change? How do you think Main Street will change in the future?

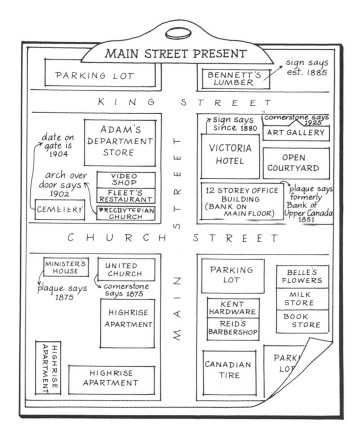

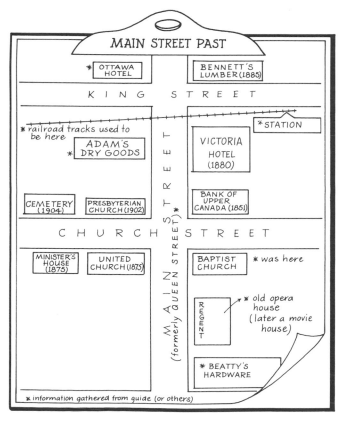

Testing Your Conclusions

Test the conclusions you reached after your walking tour. Interview long-time owners of businesses on Main Street. Ask them how Main Street has changed during the time they have worked there. Prepare your questions ahead of time. Here are some focus questions to get you started:

1. Do you have any old photographs of your business or Main Street?
2. What kinds of businesses have opened and closed on the street?
3. Have customers changed in any ways? For example, do they spend more or less than they used to? How do prices compare?
4. Is there more theft or crime on Main Street now?
5. Have attempts been made to restore the historic buildings? Which buildings have been restored?
6. What changes do you expect on Main Street in the next twenty-five years?

After the interview, report to the class on any new information you discovered. What changes did the business owner describe that you didn't notice on your walking tour?

TOP: Main Street Present. Use a map organizer like this one to identify the buildings on the street and the clues to the past.
BOTTOM: Main Street Past. Use the clues the class has gathered to reconstruct what your Main Street looked like in the past.

Skill Building: Developing Observational Skills Using Photographs

Photographs are excellent sources of historical information. By comparing an old photograph of a Main Street with a recent photograph, you can see some of the ways the street has changed. Examine the photographs like a detective searching for clues. Ask questions.

Look at these photos of a Main Street. Discover the important changes on the street by answering the following questions.

1. Where was each photograph taken?

2. When was each photograph taken?

3. What features are the same in the two photographs? For example, which buildings are the same?

4. What features are different? For example, which buildings have been altered? Which buildings have disappeared? Which buildings have been added?

5. What headings or categories can you use to organize the similarities and differences in the two photographs?

Here are some examples:

    vehicles

    buildings

Add other headings based on the similarities and differences you noticed.

Lincoln Street in Lunenburg, Nova Scotia, around 1900.

Lincoln Street in Lunenburg, Nova Scotia, 1990.

Windows Into Time

Collect historical photographs of your Main Street. Search for them in the local library, museum, or newspaper offices. You might find them in your own family albums or in the attic. Ask the business owners along Main Street if they have old pictures you could see. Ask the owner of the photograph to help you date it and identify the buildings. Rephotograph or photocopy the picture for permanent record. Indicate important information on the back. Identify the source and date. Bring the photocopies to class.

In groups compare one historical photo of your Main Street with a recent photo. Remember the questions you used to examine the photographs in the skill-building exercise. List your observations under the headings "Similarities" and "Differences" in your notebooks. Discuss the changes that have taken place on your Main Street.

Make a scrapbook of the photos the class collected. Indicate dates, sources, and important changes. Your scrapbook will be a valuable permanent record for your school library.

A painting of King Street, Toronto in the 1840s. Paintings and drawings are other important sources of information about the early streets in your community.

Architecture

Architecture is the planning and building of houses, churches, schools, stores, and other buildings.

One of the best ways to begin to understand and enjoy architecture is to look closely at the buildings in your community. Look up to see what kind of roof a building has. Look down to find an unusual fence in the yard. Look around for ornaments that decorate the building. Look inside at the arrangement of the rooms. Look closely to see what kinds of materials were used in the building. How old do you think the building is? Find out about its special features. What can these features tell you about the people who lived or worked there?

Most communities have old buildings that are considered town treasures. They are reminders of the early history of the community. They may be homes, railway stations, banks, or even old stables. Often they have been restored to look as they did when they were built. Some have become tourist attractions and are open for the public to visit.

Trained people are often present to guide you around these historic buildings. They can answer your questions. Sometimes a printed brochure is also available. The brochure can give you valuable information about the site. Don't overlook buildings that may not be so obvious though. Old stores, banks, and railway stations won't have guides, but by looking closely you can uncover many interesting details about the past.

Campbell House in Toronto is an example of a restored home from the early 1800s. Read the information that follows about the house.

CAMPBELL HOUSE

The residence of Sir William Campbell,
Chief Justice of Upper Canada
1825-1829

Sir William Campbell was 64 years of age when he built his "fine mansion of brick, at the head of Frederick Street with a view of the bay." It was constructed to his specifications and was suited to an important man in 1822 York (Toronto).

William Campbell was born in Scotland in 1758. Young William enlisted as a private in a Highland regiment and was sent to America where he fought in the Revolutionary War and was taken prisoner.

After his release he decided to stay in the New World. He settled in the Maritimes, studied law, and in 1804 was appointed Attorney-General of Cape Breton and elected to the Provincial Assembly. In 1811 he became a judge in Upper Canada. At the age of 66 he was named Chief Justice of Upper Canada.

In 1829 Sir William retired to his mansion. A later resident of the house, Mr. John Fensom, kept a pet alligator there (it lived in the garden).

In 1969 the Sir William Campbell Foundation was established to re-locate and restore the stately Campbell home.

Starting at daybreak, March 31, 1972, it took only six and a half hours to

Moving Campbell House through the streets of Toronto.

move the 150-year-old Campbell House from its original location on Adelaide Street East to its new site at Queen Street and University Avenue.

The house measuring 11 m wide, 16 m long, and 13 m high was carefully jacked up to a height of 3 m off the ground. About 1 km of trolley wire, 82 street lights, several electricity poles, traffic lights, and signs had to be moved to make way for the house. Some 65 maintenance holes in the streets had to be shored up to support the weight.

The move itself became a major spectator sport and crowds lined the downtown streets to witness "the Campbell's stately journey."

According to the experts, the house weathered the move very well.

The Campbell House has been restored to its original elegance. It is believed to be the third oldest structure remaining in Toronto, and is preserved as an example of our heritage dating back to the "early brick period of York" from 1807 to about 1825.

The fireplace in the Campbell House kitchen.

The Kitchen

During this period, kitchens were generally located in the basement. Other rooms in the basement would include the wine cellar, wood chute, and food storage rooms.

The large kitchen has the original colonial brick bake oven. The oven is next to the open-hearth fireplace, where all the cooking was done. It was one of the warmest places in the house in the winter, and must have been a good place to sew. Many needles were found buried in the hearth. The floor also has been reconstructed from the original bricks, which have been cleaned and sealed to protect them.

The kitchen has been furnished with a 3-m long ash table, a sink with a rack above for drying plates, a pine linen press, a settee on which the cook could have rested, an armchair, and ladder-back chairs with elm seats. Other historic details include the copper cauldron over the water heater and a number of antique kitchen utensils.

Complete the following organizer on the special features of Campbell House.

Historic Building: Campbell House
Location
When built (approximate date)
Size (number of floors)
Main features of the outside (materials used, number of windows, design of doorway, for example) **1.** **2.** **3.**
Main features of the inside (Describe the kitchen. Where is it located? What are the main pieces of furniture? etc.) **1.** **2.** **3.**

What does the information in your organizer tell you about how the people in the house lived?

Planning a Class Trip

An individual or group can plan a class trip to a restored historic building in your community. The local Historical Society or museum can make suggestions about places to visit. The class can learn a great deal about how people lived in the past from visiting an historic site.

If you are involved in the planning, visit the site well in advance of the class trip. As you tour the house, keep notes on what you see, hear, and feel. Your task is to develop a worksheet for your classmates. It could be a list of focus questions that can be answered by careful observation. It could be an organizer to guide your classmates' observation of special features.

For example, you might notice that the doorways are low. A tall person would have to duck to pass through. The beds are short. Most of us would find our feet dangling out the end. On your worksheet, direct your class's attention to these features. Ask: What clues can you find that show people were shorter in the past?

Visit the rooms of the house. In the kitchen, notice the storage crocks, the spices hanging from the rafters, the fireplace, and the kitchen utensils. These might lead to questions about types of food eaten, food preparation, fuel and energy, and sources of light.

Make arrangements for the class visit. Consult your teacher about the plans. Prepare your worksheet. Every student in the class should have a copy.

After the class trip, lead a discussion with your classmates about what they observed.

Heritage Sites

Contact the municipal office. Ask if there is a Local Architectural Conservation Advisory Committee (LACAC) in your area. You could also contact the local Historical Society or museum. Invite a speaker from one of these organizations to your class. Ask the speaker to tell you about the Heritage Act of your province. What buildings or sites in your community have been placed under the Heritage Act? Find out why these sites were chosen. Make a picture collection of historic buildings in your community. Include a short description of each building. Try to note the dates the buildings were constructed and some key features.

Province House in Charlottetown, Prince Edward Island. The first meeting of the Fathers of Confederation was held here in September, 1864. Today it is the seat of the provincial government and a National Historic Site.

An Historic Landmark

Explore the history of an old building in your community. The building could be a railway station, a church, temple, or synagogue, a mill, or the town hall. It could be an historic home like Campbell House in Toronto. Work alone or in groups.

Research to find out:

1. Who built it?

2. When was it built?

3. What are the important features of the building?

4. Who has lived in it or used it?

5. What changes have been made inside or outside?

6. What important events or activities have taken place there over the years?

7. Are there stories or legends connected with the building? (For example, is it "haunted"?)

Sources of information may include the local history section of libraries, people who have lived or worked in the building, tourist brochures, and file clippings at the library or newspaper office.

Summarize your research in a chart organizer. Include pictures or sketches of the building.

Bellevue House in Kingston, Ontario. Sir John A. Macdonald, who became Canada's first prime minister, lived in the house in 1848-49.

CHAPTER 4

Exploring Your Local Community –The Economy

Industry in the Community

How do people in your community earn their living? Some might work in industries that harvest natural resources. For example, they might work in mining, farming, fishing, or lumbering. Others might work in industries that use natural resources to make other products. Almost every community has factories. They might produce automobiles, televisions, parts for jet planes, or compact discs. Or, people might earn their living in service industries. These industries provide a service rather than make an actual product. For example, people might operate a tourist resort, work in a hospital, sell real estate, or work in a bank. Find out about the industries in your community.

Labour: Past and Present

Choose an industry in your community that has been there for a long time. Imagine that you are a worker in that industry sixty or seventy years ago. What would your typical working day be like?

For example, if you were a logger, you would start work very early in the morning. You would be staying in a logging camp in the woods. To cut down trees, you would work in groups and use large hand saws and axes.

If you were a bake shop owner, you would also start work very early. You would bake your bread first thing to make sure it was fresh for your customers. You would bake your goods in a large oven at the back of your shop.

You may have to do some research to find out what the job you select involves. Interview people who have worked in the industry. Make a timeline to record the important tasks in a typical day, or write a journal entry to describe your day.

How was a working day seventy years ago different from what it is today?

Profile of an Industry

Research an important industry in your community. Work alone or in groups. Investigate the products or services the industry provides. Find out about the people who work there. Discover how the industry has changed over the years.

Below are some focus questions to get you started. Add other questions to the

TOP: A tailoring workshop in the early 1900s. What changes have taken place in the way clothes are made?
BOTTOM: A general store around 1920. Notice the wide variety of goods on the store shelves.

list. Develop a chart organizer to record your information. Each focus question in the list should suggest a heading for your organizer.

Locate resources that will help you find the answers. Search through your library for books and newspaper clippings. Even advertisements can give you interesting information. You might also contact the industry's public relations office for help.

1. Why is this an important industry in your community?
2. What goods or services does it provide?
3. How long has the industry been in your community?
4. Why did the industry develop here?
5. How many people work in the industry?
6. What changes have occurred in the industry over the years? For example, has it grown? How have the products or services changed?

Review your information. How does the industry help your community? Are there any negative effects on the community?

Tour of a Local Industry

Visit an industry in your community. Practise your observational and listening skills. You could tour a local factory, a nearby farm, or a service industry such as a bank or tourist resort. Whatever industry you

visit, you will see how people work together. You will find out about the resources used in that industry. You will learn *how* those resources are used. Try to identify the special skills of the workers.

Prepare a worksheet like the one below for your tour. The sample worksheet is for a tour of a factory. If you visit a farm or service industry, you will want to change some questions. Give a copy of your worksheet to the guide at the industry well in advance of your tour. It will tell the guide what you would like to know. Everyone in the class should have a copy of the worksheet for the tour. When the tour is over, compare your worksheet with those of your classmates. Discuss your findings.

Worksheet Sample

Name of industry:

How long has this factory
been in the community?

Who started it?

Why was it located here?

How many people are employed?

What is produced?

What materials are needed to
make the product?

Where do these raw materials come
from?

Where do the finished products go?

How are they transported?

Choose one job within the factory.
What skills does the employee need
to do that job?

How did the employee learn to do
the job?

Does the employee like the job? Why?

Transportation and Communication

Transportation

Transportation is all the means of moving people and goods from one place to another. Transportation has always been important to Canada because the country is so large. Distances between communities can be vast.

Earliest settlers had only the lakes and rivers for transport. Later they built canals to link waterways and make transportation easier. After the steam engine was invented, railways were built. Settlements then grew up along the railway lines. With the invention of cars and trucks, roads and highways became more important. Today we have air transport. Now even remote parts of Canada can be reached.

Transportation Past and Present

Develop a list of all the forms of transportation that have been used in your community. Include vehicles from the past as well as the present. To help you identify forms of transportation from the past, ask your parents and grandparents. Talk to people in your community. Check books on the history of your community and pioneer transportation.

On your list underline the forms of transportation still used in the community. Circle the forms of transportation no longer used. Prepare a timeline mural on the development of transportation in your community. Use pictures, drawings, and artifacts in your mural.

An early airplane. Why were airplanes one of the most important inventions in transportation history?

Skill Building: Developing a Timeline Mural

By now you are almost an expert on timelines. You have developed your own personal timeline. You may have looked at a timeline of recreational activities in the 1900s on pages 30-31. Now you are ready to create a timeline mural of historical events.

Historians sometimes talk about **historical periods**. You have probably heard that you live in the "Technological Age." The Technological Age is an historical period. We give it that name because of the many advances in technology we have experienced. For example, in the Technological Age computers, calculators, and specialized space craft were invented.

Other examples of historical periods are the Age of the Automobile and the Industrial Age. It is not always easy to say exactly when these historical periods began or when they ended. Historical periods often overlap. But they help us to describe important events in history.

How could you make a timeline mural using historical periods?

1. Decide what you want your mural to show. For example, it could show the development of transportation or communication through history.

2. Decide on the historical periods you will include in your mural. You will need to choose these carefully. They should show the major stages in the development of your topic. For example, historical periods you might use to show the development of transportation could be The Early Days, The Railway Era, and The Age of the Automobile. What others would there be?

3. On a large sheet of heavy paper, draw columns for each historical period you have identified. Label each column. Remember to make the columns large enough for several pictures and drawings.

4. Locate information and pictures to illustrate the developments in each historical period.

5. Enter the information and pictures in the appropriate columns of your mural. Label each picture and illustration. You can use artifacts or illustrations of artifacts as well. For example, if you are showing the development of transportation you can include an old driver's licence, a bus schedule, or drawings of a hub cap, a licence plate, or a railway spike. Write a short caption to explain each artifact.

6. Present your mural to the class. Explain how the pictures show the development of your topic through history.

Communication

Communication is all the means of exchanging information and ideas. Today we have satellite television, fax machines, and computerized mail. But what forms of communication were important in the early days of your community? Are they still used today?

Newspapers were very important in early communities. The earliest newspapers were usually published weekly. As communities grew, more daily newspapers began to appear. In 1873 there were only 47 daily newspapers in Canada. By 1900 there were 112 daily newspapers. Find out how your community newspaper has changed.

The Local Newspaper: Then and Now

Obtain reproductions of old newspapers published in your community. The copies should be as old as possible. Look in the newspaper office, the library (possibly on microfilm), or in a local museum. If you can't find a complete copy, a reproduction of a front page will give you enough information. Your teacher will help you. Bring a recent edition of your community newspaper to class as well.

Divide the class into groups of four. Have two people in each group examine an old newspaper. Have the other two people examine a recent edition. Complete an organizer like the one below for the newspaper you are studying.

When your organizer is complete, share your information with the other two people in your group. Explain your findings. Discuss the changes you discovered in your community newspaper.

Newspaper

Date

Circulation of the paper

Number of pages or
sections

Names of sections and
special features

Published (daily, weekly,
monthly, bimonthly,
quarterly)

Scope of the news
(local, regional, national,
international)

List a headline as an
example of each type of news story.

Other local stories
featured

Types of advertisements
and examples

Changing With the Times

Communication systems have changed to suit the needs of the community. Today we depend on forms of communication that are easy and fast. But imagine what your community would be like without the telephone. Consider the following questions:

1. How many times do you use the telephone in a day? a week?
2. List the reasons why you use the telephone.
3. Ask your parents and members of the business community why they use the telephone.
4. Select one of the community members from the following list: doctor, grocer, farmer, taxi driver, politician, homemaker. Write a description of how that person's job would be different without the telephone.

The telephone was invented in 1876. The phone these men are using is from 1907. How is it different from our telephones today?

Looking Back at Your Local Community Study

In the study of your local community, you explored many different topics. You used a variety of resources and completed many different activities.

Some activities in your study asked you to make **comparisons**. When you compare two things, you examine how they are similar and different. You may have compared an old gravestone in your local cemetery with a recent one. You may have compared old and new maps of your community or old and new photos of your Main Street. You may have discussed how old and modern newspapers are similar and different. All of these activities helped you to see the changes that have taken place in your community.

Now that you have completed your study, you can look back at some of these changes. A **comparison organizer** can help you to discover the important changes in your local community.

Skill Building: The Comparison Organizer

A comparison organizer is a chart that summarizes information about two or more things. It can help you compare people, events, objects, or topics. Here is how to construct a comparison organizer.

1. Select two items for comparison. To see the changes in your community, you could compare two different time periods in its history. For example, you could compare "Pioneer Times" and "The Modern Day."

2. Choose the **criteria** for your comparison. Criteria are the characteristics you will compare. For example, if you are comparing two cars, the criteria you might use are appearance, comfort, and price. To compare two periods in your community's history, choose sub-topics from your local community study. These sub-topics will be your criteria.

For example: The Natural Environment Industry
                Transportation Architecture

3. Construct a chart like the one below in your notebook. The items to be compared are listed across the top of the organizer. The criteria are listed down the left side.

4. Review the activities you completed for each sub-topic you have listed. What important discoveries did you make about the natural environment in pioneer times, for example. What important discoveries did you make about the natural environment today? Decide on the important facts. Enter them on your organizer in point form.

5. Review the facts you have recorded. How do the two periods in the history of your community compare? In what ways are the two periods alike? In what ways are they different? Discuss your conclusions with the class.

Criteria	Pioneer Times	The Modern Day
The Natural Environment		
Transportation		
Industry		

UNIT TWO

Native Communities

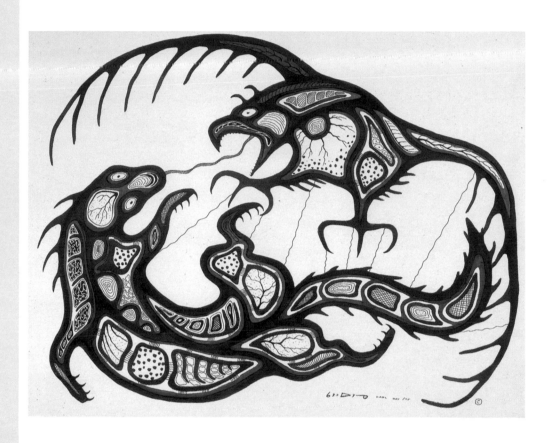

*"Conflict between
Good and Evil" by
Carl Ray.*

CHAPTER 5

The Mystery of History

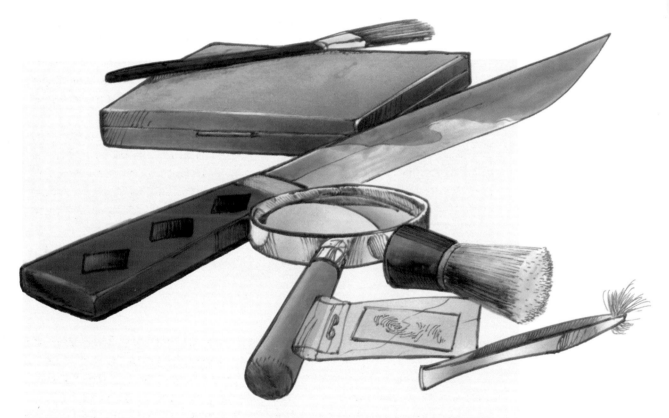

Detective Robinson was at the scene of the break-in minutes after the crime was discovered. A set of rare stamps had been stolen from an oak display cabinet in the museum gallery. The body of a museum guard had already been removed to the morgue.

Detective Robinson examined the scene of the crime. She was looking for clues. Any clues or **evidence** *might help solve the mystery at the gallery. Detective Robinson made careful notes about the evidence scattered around* *the gallery. There was a blood-stained letter opener, lint from a dark blue fabric, a brass button, a claim check from a numbered security box, and a smeared thumb print on the glass door of the oak display cabinet.*

There was also another piece of evidence. There was an eyewitness. A custodian reported that he had seen a man in a dark brown suit about one hour after the museum had closed. The man had hurried down a back staircase and gone out through a fire exit. The custodian was questioned for details. The detective prepared a report on the testimony of the eyewitness. Now the difficult task for Detective Robinson was about to begin.

Detective Robinson was haunted by the basic question. Who killed the guard and stole the rare stamps? Back in her office she began the slow process of reviewing the data she had collected. She sifted through the evidence. She re-examined each clue carefully.

Then Detective Robinson sat back and thought about what she had found. She tried to reconstruct the crime in her imagination. The real meaning of all of the clues had to be determined. Which clues were most important? Were there important pieces of the puzzle still missing? Could false clues have been planted at the scene to confuse the police? The clues had to be arranged and re-arranged until they began to form a clear picture. Detective Robinson began to develop theories about what happened at the gallery.

One theory was that it was an inside job. The eyewitness could actually be involved. This theory would have to be tested. Was the custodian telling the truth? Would he have any reason to lie? Was there any way to check his story? Each theory in turn would have to be carefully tested and weighed against the evidence. Can you suggest other theories that Detective Robinson should test?

When Detective Robinson can prove one of the theories, the mystery of the break-in at the gallery will be solved.

Exploring history is like solving a mystery. The mystery though is not a crime. The mystery is our past. Historians try to uncover the truth about what happened in our past. Sometimes their only clues are things like bits of old pottery, or legends that have been passed down from generation to generation, or the remains of old diaries. Historians try to piece together the past from these bits of evidence. Like detectives, they ask questions. They look for missing clues and explore all possible sources. They develop and test theories. Then they form conclusions based on the evidence they have uncovered. If their theory can be proven, the mystery is solved.

There are still many unsolved mysteries about the past. Historians are still trying to answer many questions. For example, where did the Native peoples of Canada come from? How did they live? We will be looking at these mysteries of history. Like detectives and historians, we will be searching for the clues.

Skill Building: Recognizing Facts and Opinions

"The eyewitness saw a man in a dark brown suit run down the staircase after the robbery. Detective Robinson, however, believes a gallery guard committed the crime." What is fact and what is opinion?

When you investigate a mystery or research any topic, you collect information from many different sources. Some of it is fact; some of it is opinion. What is the difference?

A **fact** is something that is true. It can be proven. For example, "Maple trees lose their leaves in the fall." This is a fact. We know it is true because we see it happen every year. It can be proven.

"The Huron once lived near Midland, Ontario." This is also a fact. Historians have found the remains of a Huron village near Midland. They have evidence to prove the statement.

"The coloured leaves in fall are very beautiful." This statement is an opinion. An **opinion** may or may not be true. It is based on a person's thoughts or feelings. Often it tells us how people feel about events or evidence.

"The Huron respected Father Brebeuf more than any other missionary among them." This statement is also an opinion. It cannot be proven. It is the writer's interpretation of the facts.

How can you separate statements of fact from statements of opinion?

1. Study the statement closely.

2. Ask yourself if the statement can be proven. If you investigate, can you show that the statement is true? If you can, the statement is a fact.

3. Ask yourself if the statement expresses a thought or feeling. Is it an interpretation of the facts? Can it be proven? If it cannot be proven, it is an opinion.

Test Yourself

In your notebook, create two columns. Label one column "facts." Label the other column "opinions." Study the following statements. Decide which are facts and which are opinions. Write each statement in the correct column.

1. Teenagers spend too much time watching television.
2. Canada has two official languages, French and English.
3. Smoking is dangerous to your health.
4. The Montreal Canadiens are a better hockey team than the Toronto Maple Leafs.
5. Canada is a multicultural nation.
6. British Columbia is Canada's most westerly province.
7. The Toronto Blue Jays are the best team in the American League.
8. Ontario is the largest province in Canada.
9. China has the largest population of any country in the world.
10. The Native peoples of Canada came to North America from Asia by way of a land bridge.

Where to Look for Clues

In Unit One you investigated the mystery of your own past. You examined information from many sources. You studied artifacts. You searched through books. You tapped the memories of people living in your community. You were able to compare the sources and check the evidence to find the facts.

Most information you needed was fairly easy to locate. The sources were readily available in your community. This is because the people and events you explored were part of recent history. There were written records to tell you about the past. You were exploring the sources of **recorded history**.

Imagine trying to locate information about people who lived thousands of years ago or who did not keep written records. Native peoples have lived in Canada for a very long time and have passed on their history orally. We have written records of some of the Native peoples' history since the arrival of the Europeans. These represent only a partial history and were usually written from the Europeans' point of view. For the full story we must dig deeper.

Where do we look for clues? How can we learn about the lives of the first peoples in Canada? Today historians study the customs, legends, and oral history of Native peoples to learn more about their ancestors. They examine legends that have been passed down from generation to generation. They interview Native elders. They study artifacts such as totem poles and objects from archaeological sites. They compare this evidence with the journals of the early explorers and missionaries who first met the Native peoples for a more complete story.

Finding out about life in earlier times calls for true detective work. Historians gather their evidence. They search for clues and compare the facts from as many sources as possible to form conclusions about what life was like in the early Native communities.

Finding Clues in Archaeology

THE DRAPER ARCHAEOLOGICAL SITE

For years people had been picking up Native artifacts on the Draper farm in Pickering, Ontario, near Toronto. Arrowheads, clay pipes, and bits of pottery were frequently found. Museum experts said that the farm had been the location of a large Huron village. The village dated back to 1500. It covered about five hectares (the size of about ten Canadian football fields)! Most of the land had never been disturbed by ploughing.

Archaeologists digging for Huron artifacts on the Draper farm in Pickering, Ontario.

In 1976 a new airport was to be built near the Draper site. Suddenly the site was threatened with destruction. Archaeologists had to explore the area before it was totally destroyed. A crew of about sixty students from the University of Western Ontario worked at the site for six months in 1975. Their goal was to discover the size of the village and its population. They wanted to know how many houses there had been. They wanted to locate the palisade or fence built to protect the village. They also wanted to learn what they could about the diet of the people who had lived there.

Time was short. Power equipment such as bulldozers and road graders was used to unearth the artifacts. In six months, the crew found over 200 000 pieces of clay pottery vessels. They uncovered several thousand clay fragments and thousands of bone and stone artifacts. They also unearthed a few rare items such as a small stone mask, a clay bear, and detailed clay pipes. Items made in Europe were found as well. Archaeologists located the remains of thirty-four Huron houses and twenty-four Huron **middens** or garbage dumps. Clues about plant and animal life were also found.

The archaeologists were able to piece together a great deal about this early Huron village. It had grown from a small village of ten houses to a village of forty-five to fifty houses before it was abandoned. The houses had been arranged to make them easy to defend against attack. The remains of plant life indicated that the people had a diet of corn, beans, and squash. Bones of animals suggested that deer, bear, woodchuck, and racoon may have been part of the diet as well. The early village of about 600 people had grown to about 2500 people.

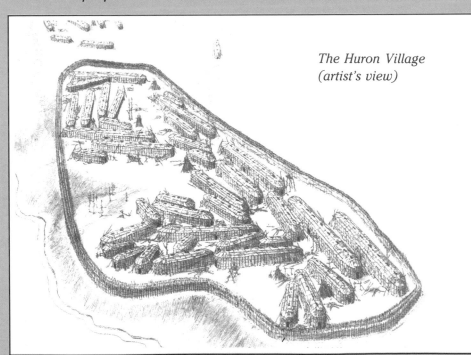

*The Huron Village
(artist's view)*

Artifacts found on the Draper site, including a pottery vessel, bone implements, and pipes.

Archaeology provides many important clues about earlier times. **Archaeology** is the study of remains from the past. Archaeologists search for artifacts and other clues at historic sites. They try to determine where houses and shelters were located. They examine cooking and storage pits and the bones of animals to find out about a people's diet. They even analyze the microscopic pollen from the soil. The pollen can tell them about the vegetation and climate at the time.

At some archaeological sites the remains are found on the surface of the ground. Paintings by Native peoples on rock surfaces such as cliffs and cave walls are an example. These rock paintings are called **pictographs**. Native carvings on rock surfaces are another example. These rock carvings are called **petroglyphs**. You might find some examples of pictographs and petroglyphs in your area.

At most archaeological sites though, the remains are buried and have to be carefully dug out. Archaeological digs are called **excavations**. The Draper site is an example of an archaeological excavation.

Two of Canada's largest sites are the Rainy River Burial Mounds in Ontario and the Head-Smashed-In Buffalo Jump in Alberta.

Archaeological sites hold a key to the history of Canada's Native peoples. The remains found at a site help to explain how the people lived. They give clues about how people changed over time and why changes took place in the community.

Today many people are concerned that these historic sites could be destroyed. Archaeologists and Native groups are working together to identify and protect these valuable sources of information.

But archaeology gives us only part of the picture. It cannot tell us everything about life at a historic site. Many clues are still missing. Stone tools and chips of pottery, for example, don't tell us things like the kind of government the people had. They don't tell us about the ideas and beliefs of the people. To find clues about this part of a community, we need to turn to other sources.

BELOW RIGHT:
Petroglyphs found at a site near Peterborough, Ontario.

BELOW LEFT:
Pictographs from the Agawa site, north of Lake Superior. These pictographs illustrate an Ojibwa legend. The horned figure is Misshipeshu, Great King of the fishes.

CARBON 14 DATING

How old are the remains found at an archaeological site? Since 1949 scientists have been able to answer this question. They can calculate the approximate age of organic (plant and animal) matter such as wood, bone, shell, seed, or charcoal discovered at an archaeological site. The method they use is called **radiocarbon (carbon 14) dating.** *The early history of Canada is dated almost entirely by this method.*

How is it done? Scientists know that all living things contain radiocarbon or carbon 14. When living things die, radiocarbon is given off at a steady rate. Scientists can measure the amount of radiocarbon in an artifact at any time. They can compare the amount of radiocarbon in the artifact with the rate of decay. Then they can calculate how long the organic artifact has been dead.

In recent years the method has been improved. The new technique is called **accelerator dating.** *It is even more accurate. Scientists can now analyze even a small sliver of bone. The latest results are astonishing. Artifacts originally thought to be many thousands of years old are proving to be more recent. As a result, many archaeological sites in Canada are being redated. Technology is helping to rewrite the pages of history.*

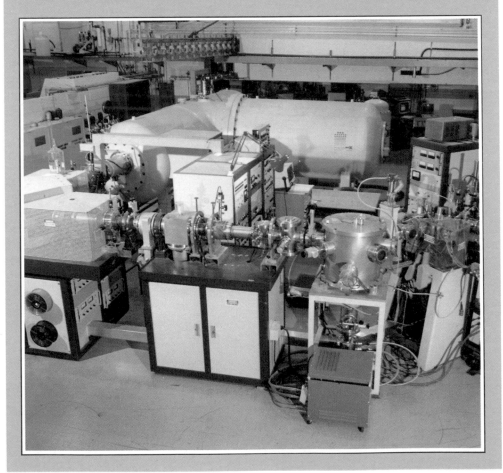

A laboratory specializing in accelerator dating. This method of radiocarbon dating can work with very small samples and produce results faster than Carbon 14 dating.

Finding Clues in Oral History

A LEGEND OF THE MICMAC

Glooscap is the central figure in the Micmac legends. He is called the Great Chief. It is a mystery where he came from. According to legend, Glooscap looked and lived like all other Micmac, but he was twice as tall and twice as strong. He was never sick, never married, never grew old, and never died. He had a belt which gave him great power, and he used this power only for good.

Glooscap took up his great bow and shot arrows into the trunks of ash trees. Out of the trees stepped men and women. They were a strong and graceful people with light brown skins and shining black hair. Glooscap called them the Wabanaki, which means "those who live where the day breaks." In Canada, the Micmac belonged to these people of Glooscap.

Glooscap told the people he was their Great Chief and would rule them with love and fairness. He taught them how to build birchbark wigwams and canoes. He showed them ways to catch fish, and even which plants were useful for healing. He taught them the names of all the stars, who were his brothers.

He showed the men how to make bows and arrows and stone-tipped spears. He taught them how to use them. He also showed the women how to scrape hides and turn them into clothing.

"Now you have power over even the largest wild creatures," he said. "Yet you must use this power gently. If you take more game for food and clothing, or kill for the pleasure of killing, then you will be visited by a terrible giant called Famine. When he comes among people they suffer and die."

–Adapted from *Glooscap and His Magic: Legends of the Wabanaki* by Kay Hill

Such stories were common in early Native communities and are still common today. They are called **legends**. Legends have been passed on by word of mouth from one generation to the next. They were told to entertain the members of the community around the fire. They explained the values and customs of the Native group and were a way of teaching the young people. All the Native communities have a rich tradition of stories and legends.

Legends answered questions the people had. How was the world created? Why is the environment the way it is? Why are the animals as they are? Who are the great heroes and heroines of our people?

These legends are a valuable source of information about life in early Native communities. They tell us a great deal about the beliefs, feelings, and ideas of Native peoples. This is something archaeology cannot do.

Examine the Micmac legend more closely.

1. What questions does this legend answer? List them.

2. What values or customs of the people does the legend show?

Finding Clues in Records and Journals

Their [Native peoples] principal food and usual sustenance is Indian corn and red beans, which they prepare in several ways. They pound them in wooden mortars [bowls] and reduce them to flour, from which they take the hull [outer covering] by means of certain fans made of tree-bark, and of this flour they make a bread. . . . Sometimes they put in blueberries or dried raspberries.

(Vol. III, p. 125)

As to their clothing, they have several kinds and styles and varieties of wild beasts' skins. . . . They dress and prepare the skins very well, making their breeches of deer-skin, and of another their leggings which reach as high as the waist, with many folds. . . . Further they have a robe of the same fur, shaped like a cloak, and sleeves which are tied behind by a cord. This is how they dressed during the winter. . . .

(Vol. III, p. 131)

Their life is wretched by comparison with ours, but happy for them since they have not tasted a better and believe that none more excellent can be found. . . . Their lodges are fashioned like bowers and arbours, covered with tree bark and inside on both sides there is a sort of platform, four feet (1.2 m) in height, on which they sleep in summer. . . .

(Vol. III, p. 122)

–From *The Works of Samuel de Champlain*

These words were recorded by the French explorer Samuel de Champlain. Champlain was one of the first Europeans to visit the Huron. In the winter of 1615-1616 he explored southern Ontario and spent about four months among the Huron. His journal is a source of facts and opinions about Huron life.

1. What is Champlain reporting on in each paragraph above?

2. What facts are helpful in trying to solve the mystery of what life was like among the Huron?

3. What is really not fact, but Champlain's opinion?

Many explorers and visitors to Native communities recorded what they saw and heard. Often their reports included information about the beliefs and ideas of the people. These early journals or diaries are an important source of information. Some, like those of Champlain, even include drawings or paintings of community life.

Often the journal entries are based on very brief encounters with the Native peoples. The writers did not stay in the Native communities for a long time. Therefore, we have to ask how well they really knew the people they were writing about.

Other explorers stayed for longer periods in Native communities. Even then we cannot always accept their journal entries without examining them carefully. Often they wrote only about things that interested them. They had strong opinions about what they saw. They saw things from their own point of view. The journals contain valuable information, but we must always examine carefully what is reported.

Skill Building: Recognizing Bias

All of us have our own point of view. It is our way of seeing things. Our point of view is shaped by our life experiences. Our family, friends, values, and interests all help to shape our point of view.

Sometimes our point of view can make it difficult to judge things fairly. A one-sided point of view is called a **bias**. Consider this example:

Maria has recently moved to a new city. She has lived there for only two months. She does not like the new city. It is not like her hometown. When she describes her new city, she tells you only about what she doesn't like.

Maria is giving you a one-sided point of view. She is describing only the negative aspects of her new city. She has not lived in the new city long enough to judge it fairly. Maria is biased in favour of her hometown.

Here is how Maria describes her new city to you:

The people here are unfriendly. No one speaks to me. Everyone is in such a hurry. I hate how rushed everything is. Getting to school is a real nightmare. I have to take a bus and a street car. Most days people are packed in like sardines. I never get a seat. I miss being able to stroll to school with my friends.

Which words or phrases show Maria's bias? Consider "real nightmare," for example. What if Maria had said,

"Getting to school takes more time." How are these two statements different?

How can we check for bias in what we read?

1. Read the source material carefully.
   Try to determine the point of view of the writer.
   For example: What is the writer's nationality?
   When did the writer live?
   What is the writer's occupation?

2. Select words and phrases that might show a bias. Explain your choices.

Use these steps to judge the bias in the following excerpt. It is taken from the journal of the French explorer Jacques Cartier when he first met the Native peoples in 1534.

We gave them knives, combs, beads of glass, and other trifles of small value, for which they made many signs of gladness.... They appeared to be a miserable people, in the lowest stage of savagery ... owning nothing of any value except their bark boats and fishing nets....

3. How do you think this journal might have affected Europeans' perceptions of Native peoples? What effect might these perceptions have on Europeans' actions when dealing with Native peoples? Re-write this excerpt using bias-free language.

Summing Up

In this chapter we have explored how historians investigate a problem or mystery. Can you outline the steps in an historical investigation? Let's review them.

1. Ask Questions
Historians ask questions about mysteries of the past. For example, how did the first peoples come to North America?

2. Search for Clues
Historians look for evidence to help

answer their questions. They look at many different sources. They examine archaeological artifacts, legends, and written records to gather as much evidence as possible.

3. Record the Information
Historians carefully organize and record the information they have gathered.

4. Evaluate the Information
Then historians evaluate the information. What is fact and what is opinion? Is there

any bias in the information? They compare evidence from all available sources. Do the clues from archaeology and legend tell the same story or a different one?

By comparing the evidence, historians are testing the information. Each fact needs to be carefully checked. Historians cannot always find absolute proof, but they test the information until they feel confident they are close to the truth.

5. Form a Theory

When historians have gathered enough evidence and tested it, they can form a **theory**. A theory is a possible explanation. It is the conclusion historians draw from their investigation.

Historians don't stop there though. They are always testing their theories. New evidence might be uncovered. Theories might be proven or disproven. They might have to be changed.

6. Communicate the Theory

Historians are not finished their task until they have told others about their study. They might write a book or an article. They might give a talk. It is important to communicate what they have learned. They share their knowledge so that others can help to take the study further.

Activities

Looking Back

1. Add new words in this Unit to the personal dictionary you started in Unit One. Begin with the following:

evidence	legend	theory
fact	midden	carbon 14 dating
opinion	pictograph	
recorded history	petroglyph	
archaeology	bias	

2. Based on evidence found at the Draper site, what conclusions were archaeologists able to draw?

3. What sorts of clues about early peoples can archaeology provide?

4. How does the radiocarbon method of dating help the historian?

5. What purposes do legends have for the Native peoples? Why are they a valuable source of information for the historian?

6. In what ways are journals a good source of information about early peoples? In what ways may they be unreliable?

Using Your Knowledge

7. You are an historian preparing a book on a Native group of Central America. The information available to you is:
   a) an archaeological discovery of arrowheads and clay bowls
   b) animal bones that can be tested by radiocarbon dating
   c) a legend about what causes thunderstorms
   d) a diary of an early explorer who visited the Native community
   e) a pictograph of a hunter on a temple wall.
   Which would be most useful if you wanted to know about:
   i) the kind of government the people had
   ii) the age of the community
   iii) the ideas and beliefs of the people
   iv) how the people obtained their food
   v) the diet of the people?
   Explain the reasons for your choices.

Extending Your Thinking

8. Investigate another Canadian archaeological site. Choose one in your own area if possible. Identify:
   a) the location of the site
   b) how the site was discovered
   c) the size of the site
   d) some artifacts found at the site
   e) the age of the artifacts
   f) the conclusions archaeologists made.
   Present your findings to the class.

9. Read another legend of a Native group. Note the questions the legend answers. Explain what it tells you about the values and beliefs of the people.

CHAPTER 6

Who Are the Native Peoples?

The Native peoples were the first inhabitants of Canada. When the Europeans arrived, about 300 000 Natives already lived in what is today called Canada. They were spread across the country. There were many different groups. All Native peoples were not the same. A variety of lifestyles was practised. Some, like the Huron, lived in settled villages. They farmed the land and grew much of their food. Some, like the Blackfoot, were hunters who moved from place to place following their game.

Look at the first map on page 71. This map identifies many Native groups.

Native Cultural Areas

One way to organize a study of Native communities is to examine different groups from different **cultural areas**. The second map on page 71 shows seven Native cultural areas in Canada before the arrival of the Europeans. Each cultural area includes Native groups that shared common experiences or ways of life.

Culture is the total way of life of a group of people. When we examine the culture of any group, we look at everything about the way they lived. We examine their homes, their clothing, and any artifacts they made. We examine their daily routines and seasonal activities. We explore their ideas and beliefs.

The culture or way of life of Canada's Native peoples was closely related to their environment. Each group adapted to its own environment. The people learned to use the resources around them without harming their environment.

In this chapter, we will look at each cultural area. As you read through the sections, try to answer these questions:

Where is the cultural area located?
What is the landscape like?
What kinds of vegetation are found there?
What is the climate like?
What animal life is found in the area?
How did the Native peoples of the area adapt to their environment?

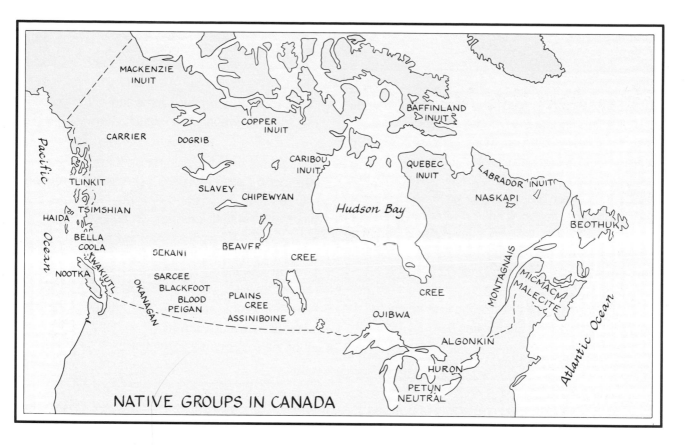

NATIVE GROUPS IN CANADA

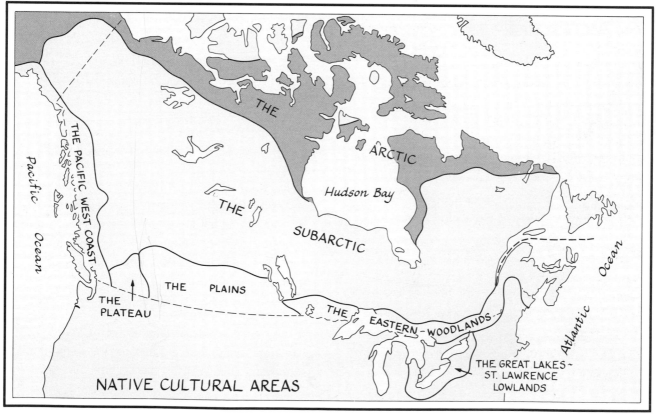

NATIVE CULTURAL AREAS

Skill Building: Keeping Good Notes

Keeping a notebook helps you to organize information. It is an important way to keep track of what you have read, seen, or heard. Many early explorers kept notebooks to record their experiences and discoveries. Historians also keep careful notes of their research. You can learn to keep good notes on what you read in your textbook and on what you learn from other sources. Let's go through an example of how to make notes for the section on the Great Lakes-St. Lawrence Lowlands cultural area on page 79.

1. Construct an organizer like the one below to help you record your information.

TOPIC:

SUB-TOPIC:

MAIN IDEA

SUPPORTING STATEMENTS
a.
b.
c.

---

2. Identify the topic of this chapter. It is Native Cultural Areas.

3. Identify the sub-topic you are working on–The Great Lakes-St. Lawrence Lowlands.

4. Read the first paragraph of the sub-topic. Look for the main idea. The **main idea** is often found in the first few sentences of the section. Sometimes it is found later in the section. Write the main idea on your organizer.

For example, the main idea in the Great Lakes-St. Lawrence Lowlands section is: The Native environment was suited to developing permanent communities.

You can make the main idea stand out in your notebook by writing it in capital letters.

5. Read the section again. Look for any **supporting statements**. The supporting statements help to prove the main idea. Write the supporting statements on your organizer in point form.

For example: –flat or gently rolling land good for farming

Here is a sample of a completed note for the Great Lakes-St. Lawrence Lowlands section. Did you find all of the supporting statements?

TOPIC: Native Cultural Areas

SUB-TOPIC: The Great Lakes–St. Lawrence Lowlands

MAIN IDEA

THE NATIVE ENVIRONMENT WAS SUITED TO DEVELOPING PERMANENT COMMUNITIES

SUPPORTING STATEMENTS

a. flat or gently rolling land good for farming
b. fertile soil
c. long hot summer for growing crops of corn, beans, squash
d. enough rainfall for crops
e. wild plants add other food
f. animals available for hunting
g. lakes well stocked with fish

---

6. Use what you have learned to make notes on the Arctic cultural area. Look for the main idea and supporting statements in the section.

The Pacific West Coast

The cultural area of the Pacific West Coast stretched north along the west coast from California to the panhandle of Alaska. The area was hemmed in by snowcapped mountains on the east and the indented coastline of the Pacific Ocean on the west.

The climate was moderated by the Pacific Ocean. Mild temperatures and heavy rainfall were common. In this type of climate, forests of huge trees thrived. These forests characterized the landscape. Giant cedars were abundant and thick underbrush covered the forest floors.

The Native peoples of the Pacific West Coast adapted well to their environment. The forests provided wood for their large dugout canoes, plank houses, and huge totem poles. Fish and shellfish were plentiful along the west coast and were an important source of food. Salmon was the main catch. Cod and halibut from the ocean and deer and bear from the dense forests added to the people's diet.

The abundance of fish meant that there was no need to travel over great distances in search of food. The people could live year round in the same location.

Giant trees and thick underbrush were common features of the Pacific West Coast environment.

The Plateau

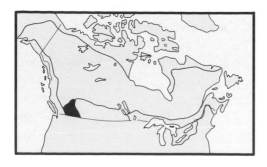

The Plateau was a high, flat stretch of land between the Coast Mountains and the Rocky Mountains in southern British Columbia. It was a rugged environment. Several rivers drained through the area. Many cut deep valleys called **canyons** or **gorges** into the surface of the Plateau.

In some parts of the Plateau the soil was desert-like. Vegetation was mainly sagebrush, rough grasses, and cacti. Other areas had better soil with stands of Ponderosa pine and coarse grasses. In the far north of the Plateau, mixed evergreen trees and richer grasses replaced the pines.

Summers on the Plateau were generally hot and dry while the winters were cold. There were differences in climate from north to south. The north with its high mountains and dense forests received more rainfall than the south. The country to the south became drier and drier toward the British Columbia Dry Belt. In the south, summers were very hot and winters were severely cold.

The Plateau was home to animals such as the white-tailed deer, caribou, black bear, grizzly bear, elk, and mountain sheep. Coyote, fox, lynx, and beaver were found in the area as well. Salmon came upstream to spawn every autumn. Trout, whitefish, suckers, and pike were also important sources of food.

The Native peoples of the Plateau travelled in small family groups to hunt and fish in the spring, summer, and fall. In the winter, larger groups gathered together in settled villages. Some Plateau people lived in lodges covered with bark or mats of grass. Others lived in circular pit houses dug into the ground. These were protected by a cone-shaped roof of poles covered with brush and earth. Hide-covered tipis were also used by the peoples of the Plateau.

The landscape of the Plateau was rugged and varied. The southern region, shown in this photograph, was generally dry with few trees.

The Plains

The cultural area of the Plains stretched from central Alberta and Saskatchewan in Canada, into the south central United States. The land was flat or gently rolling. Only a few rivers flowed through the area. They provided almost all of the available water.

The main vegetation on the Plains was grass. Trees were found only along the banks of rivers and in the foothills of the mountains. The foothills ran along the western edge of the area.

The seasons presented great variations

Grass was the main vegetation on the dry landscape of the Plains.

in climate. Summers were hot and dry. The Native peoples could live and hunt on the open plains in summer. But the winters with their severe winds were bitterly cold. The Native groups left the open plains at the end of the summer. They sought the protection of the foothills or the river valleys to escape the severe conditions of the winter. The Plains peoples therefore did not have permanent, year-round villages. They were **nomadic**. That is, they travelled from place to place.

Antelope, elk, and deer lived in the region, but the most important animal on the Plains was the buffalo. Large herds of buffalo roamed over the land and fed on the grasses. The buffalo was central to the life of the Plains peoples. The Native bands gathered on the Plains each summer to hunt the buffalo. The meat was important for food. The hide was used for tipi coverings, shields, and moccasins. The sinew was used for thread and the buffalo bones were fashioned into tools. The buffalo provided for many of the peoples' daily needs.

The Subarctic

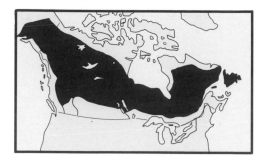

The cultural area of the Subarctic stretched across North America from Labrador in the east to Alaska in the west. It was an area dotted with many lakes and crossed by innumerable rivers. **Coniferous** (evergreen) forest was the main vegetation.

Winters were long and harsh in the Subarctic. Temperatures often dipped as low as −50° C in winter. The dense forest and the deep snow provided cover for the peoples and the animals of the region. The summers were short and mild. The harsh environment of the Subarctic made life more difficult than in many of the other cultural areas, but the Native peoples adapted.

The Native groups of the Subarctic travelled through the year to secure their food. They were nomadic. Since they were always on the move, they did not need permanent villages. Their homes were made of hides that could be quickly packed up and carried from one location to another. The peoples lived mainly by fishing in the summer months and hunting in the fall and winter.

The most important big game animals for the Subarctic hunters were moose, caribou, and black bear. They also hunted smaller animals such as beaver, rabbit, and groundhog. The streams and lakes of the Subarctic provided trout, whitefish, and pike. Waterfowl, which passed through the Subarctic in huge numbers on their annual migration, were hunted as well. Berries were gathered and dried in the fall or stored in pits in the ground. Often the berries were mixed with dried meat and grease to make pemmican.

Evergreen forests, mountains, and rivers were characteristic of the vast Subarctic region.

The Arctic

The Arctic is the region north of the tree line. Only plants such as low shrubs, mosses, and lichens could survive there. There were no trees. The landscape varied over the vast area of the Arctic. Some regions were lowlands studded with lakes. Other parts had ice-covered mountains.

Summer in the Arctic was a very short season, but the daylight hours were long. In fact, the sun did not set for several weeks. The temperature was moderate enough for colourful flowers to blossom and dot the barren landscape. In summer much of the land was covered with bogs and ponds. Then blackflies and mosquitoes plagued humans and animals.

Winters in the Arctic were long and cold. Severe storms were common. In the far north, winter might last for ten months. The sun was absent in mid-winter. There was little precipitation and the land was a cold desert.

The peoples of the Arctic adapted to their environment. They built domed snowhouses or igloos to live in. Cone-shaped tents were also made from caribou skins. These served as summer homes or were used when there wasn't enough snow to build snowhouses.

Hunting sea mammals such as the seal was basic to Native life in the Arctic. The peoples ate the meat, used the oil for fuel, and fashioned the skins into clothing. They fished and gathered birds' eggs, shellfish, and several types of edible berries.

Vast stretches of snow and ice covered the Arctic landscape for most of the year.

The Eastern Woodlands

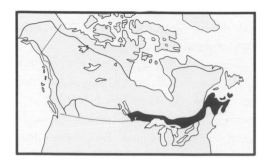

The Eastern Woodlands stretched from the Plains in the west to the shores of the Atlantic Ocean in the east. The land was mainly flat or gently rolling. It was dotted with many lakes, rivers, and streams. Hardwood forests of oak, beech, maple, and elm were characteristic of the area. Large stands of pine, hemlock, and spruce were also common, particularly in the north. A variety of wild plants, seeds, and nuts could be found as well.

The winters of the Eastern Woodlands were quite cold. Snow covered the ground. The lakes and rivers froze. Fortunately though the winter was usually short. Summers were long and usually hot. Rainfall in the area was abundant.

The people of the Eastern Woodlands lived in semi-permanent homes. Many lived in cone- or dome-shaped wigwams. The wigwams were made of a wooden frame covered with birchbark or animal skins. The coverings could be easily packed up and moved.

The forests of the Eastern Woodlands were home to deer, elk, bear, beaver, porcupine, and a variety of other small, furbearing animals. Game birds such as geese, ducks, turkeys, and grouse could be found. The lakes and rivers supplied pike, bass, perch, and trout. The Natives of the Eastern Woodlands took advantage of the abundant wildlife. They hunted and fished according to the seasons.

Hardwood forests provided the peoples of the Eastern Woodlands with a wide variety of food and materials for their everyday lives.

The Great Lakes–St. Lawrence Lowlands

The Great Lakes–St. Lawrence Lowlands stretched along the shores of the Upper St. Lawrence River. The area included the territory north and south of Lake Ontario and Lake Erie. For the Native peoples, the environment was well suited to developing permanent communities.

The land was generally flat or gently rolling and good for farming. The soil was fertile. Summers were long and hot and there was enough rain to grow crops such as corn, beans, and squash. Winters were short and cold.

The environment provided other sources of food as well. A variety of berries, shrubs, and other plants grew in the wild. Many were gathered for medicines as well as food. The peoples also hunted and fished. The **deciduous** forests (trees that shed their leaves) were home to deer, beaver, otter, fox, and other small animals. The lakes and rivers were well stocked with pike, pickerel, sturgeon, trout, whitefish, bass, perch, and other fish.

The Natives of these lowlands took advantage of the good farming conditions. They developed permanent villages and lived off the land. They built large longhouses made of wood and bark.

Little of the original forest that was home to the peoples of the Great Lakes–St. Lawrence Lowlands remains today. This photo, taken in Rondeau Provincial Park, is one of the few areas where the forest remains.

Our study of Native communities in the next few chapters will take us into four different cultural areas. We will examine the culture of one group from each area.

Before you begin your study of the Native groups, there is one other question to explore. Where did the Native peoples of Canada come from? What are their origins?

Group	Cultural Area
The Huron	The Great Lakes–St. Lawrence Lowlands
The Micmac	The Eastern Woodlands
The Blackfoot	The Plains
The Haida	The Pacific West Coast

Skill Building: The Comparison Wheel

You have examined the environments of the various Native cultural areas in Canada. Did you notice how they are alike and how they are different?

One way to help you see the similarities and differences is to make a comparison wheel. A comparison wheel is a type of comparison organizer. It will help you organize information about the environments.

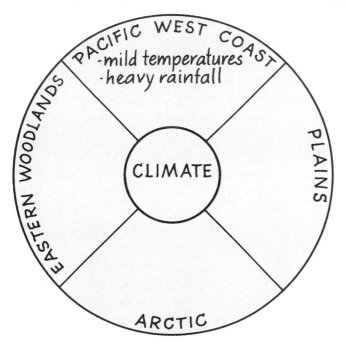

1. Draw a large circle with a diameter of about 20 cm on heavy white paper or cardboard. In the centre of your large circle, draw a smaller circle with a diameter of about 4 cm.

2. Divide the large circle into sections like the spokes of a wheel. Create at least four sections.

3. Choose the environments you want to compare. Write them at the top of each section on your wheel.

Examples: Pacific West Coast, Eastern Woodlands

4. Choose the criteria for your comparison. Remember the criteria are the characteristics you will compare. Choose one characteristic from the following list and write it in the centre of your wheel.

Criteria: Location, Landscape, Vegetation, Climate, Animal Life

5. Select the information you need. If you have decided to compare climates, pick out the facts about the climate from each environment. Print them in the correct section of your wheel. Use point form. Don't copy word-for-word from the text. Include pictures or drawings as well.

6. Examine your wheel when it is complete. What differences can you see among the environments? List them. How might these differences affect the way the people of the regions lived?

The Origins of Canada's Native Peoples

Without written records from the distant past, historians have developed different theories to explain the origins of Canada's Native population. Remember that a **theory** is a possible explanation. It is not always supported by hard facts or written evidence. Even written evidence is sometimes biased. However, all theories should be considered carefully.

Where did the Native peoples of Canada come from? Scientists suggest that the Native peoples are the descendants of people who travelled by way of a **land bridge** from Asia. This land bridge connected Asia to North America thousands of years ago. The Native peoples also have their own explanations of their origins. They tell of their origins in **creation stories**.

A Creation Story

Each Native cultural group has its own creation stories to explain its origins. In all the stories, a Great Spirit plays a leading role. The Great Spirit has various names such as Gitchie Manitou, Napi, Nanabush, or Glooscap. To the Native peoples, the Great Spirit is a mighty creative power. This mighty power, however, can take on human and animal forms. The Great Spirit can become one of the people.

Read the following Blackfoot creation story.

Napi looked down upon his world. It was still covered with water. Napi wanted land upon which he could walk. He decided to do something about it. Diving to the bottom of the sea, he came up with a handful of mud. As the mud dried it was allowed to blow in all directions. Land masses formed where it fell on the water. Soon there was firm countryside stretching to the horizons. Napi took pleasure in walking on the new land.

But the Great Spirit wanted living creatures to share the joy of the earth. From mud he shaped an object with two arms and two legs. He left it in the sun to dry. He breathed life into it. The sun-baked figure came to life in the form of the first man. Napi repeated the miracle and created the first woman.

At first the two humans showed no interest in each other. They lived apart. The man chose country to the east and the woman chose country to the west. Napi was not satisfied with the arrangement. He wanted man and woman to live together.

After many moons Napi went westward to discuss the issue with the woman. When he arrived he was very surprised. The woman had multiplied and was the chieftain of a whole village of women. The woman listened to Napi. She was interested in his ideas of men and women marrying and living together. She instructed Napi to bring the men to the west. If the women liked them, they would marry.

Napi was satisfied. He secretly hoped the beautiful lady chief would choose him. When the men arrived, the female leader was in disguise. She looked ragged, old, and unattractive. She asked Napi to be her husband, but he refused.

The clever head-woman continued with her test. She instructed the women to ignore Napi completely when choosing a husband. Napi was left alone and felt unwanted. Then the clever chieftain reappeared without disguise. Napi asked her to become his wife. At first she rejected his proposal. Napi suffered the world's first disappointment in love. Finally the woman relented and agreed to become his wife. This was the beginning of the family arrangement.

Napi then took more mud and moulded it into other shapes. Mud was the source of essential things. He created remarkable birds and animals. He produced the muskrat, bear, fox, coyote, buffalo, eagle, and many other creatures. He watched them bound or fly away to find food and freedom.

–Adapted from
"The Great Spirit"
by Grant MacEwan

How does the story explain the creation of the continents?

How does it explain the creation of men, women, and animals?

How did families begin?

How would you describe the Great Spirit?

How did the Great Spirit become part of the people's lives?

The Land Bridge Theory

Thousands of years ago, the earth was in the final stage of the last ice age. Much of the earth's water was locked up in huge sheets of ice called **glaciers**. Sea levels dropped and the floor of the ocean was revealed in many areas. One place where this happened was the shallow Bering Strait. This waterway separates Asia from North America. It is only 90 km wide.

Some scientists believe that a land bridge formed across the Bering Strait between Asia and North America. This land bridge is called **Beringia**. It was more than 1000 km wide. It is believed that the first people in North America came across Beringia from Asia. Herds of animals such as caribou, bison, and wool-ly mammoth began to feed on the grasses of the land bridge and moved into North America. Hunters came from Asia to North America following the animals which were their source of food. They did not know that they were populating a new continent as they followed the herds. It is difficult to say exactly when this **migration** or movement of people took place. Scientists do not agree. It is estimated at somewhere between 30 000 and 100 000 years ago.

What evidence suggests that this migration happened? Some similar types of animals exist in both Asia and North America. There are physical similarities between North American Natives and Asian peoples. Human remains found on other continents date back many thousands of years. Yet, human remains found in North America are not as old. Therefore, scientists believe the ancestors of the Native peoples must have come from another continent.

About 17 000 years ago the climate in North America began to warm up. The ice, which had been 3 km thick over the Rocky Mountains and the area around

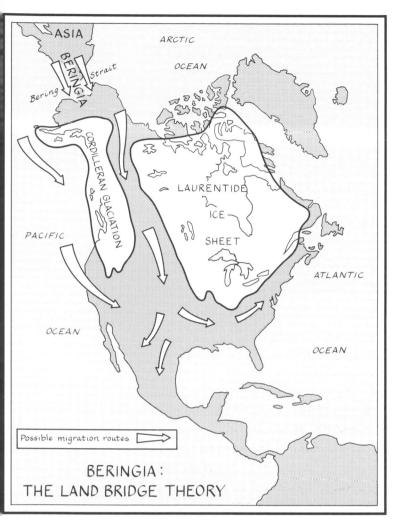

ASIA

BERINGIA

Bering Strait

ARCTIC

OCEAN

CORDILLERAN GLACIATION

LAURENTIDE

ICE

SHEET

PACIFIC

ATLANTIC

OCEAN

OCEAN

Possible migration routes

BERINGIA:
THE LAND BRIDGE THEORY

Hudson Bay, slowly began to melt. The sea levels began to rise. The land bridge of Beringia slowly disappeared about 10 000 years ago. The hunters could not return to Asia.

Migration

The hunters who crossed Beringia first came into what is now Alaska and the Yukon. The route they followed in moving south is not certain. One theory is that as the climate changed, the animals began to move south through corridors in the ice. The hunters followed. The route was along the eastern slope of the Rocky Mountains. The conditions for travel and the climate would have been difficult.

Another recent theory suggests that the Natives travelled along the coast of British Columbia by watercraft. At this time there were ice-free areas along the coast where people could have lived. They might have collected shellfish and hunted sea mammals. This theory is difficult to prove because these areas are now under water.

The climate of North America changed drastically over the next few thousand years. It gradually became much warmer. The people spread farther south and east through North America. We do not know much about these ancient peoples except that they survived mainly by hunting. In each new area they settled, they developed their own way of life. They met the challenge of surviving in the area that became their new home. These first peoples are the ancestors of the Native groups we know today.

The woolly mammoth was one of the animals that came across Beringia into North America.

Activities

Looking Back

1. Define each of the following words and add them to your dictionary.

cultural area	deciduous
culture	creation story
plateau	land bridge
canyon	glacier
nomadic	Beringia
coniferous	migration

2. How do the Native peoples explain their origins?

3. **a)** Why do some scientists believe that a land bridge formed between North America and Asia?
   b) According to the theory, why did early peoples cross the land bridge?

Using Your Knowledge

4. Read another creation story of a Native group. How does this story explain the origin of the Native group? Why would this story be passed on from generation to generation?

5. Role play a meeting of early Native peoples from two very different cultural areas of Canada. Have each group explain its own environment and lifestyle to the other.

Extending Your Thinking

6. Find out more about one of the Native cultural areas. Use an atlas to learn more about landforms and climate. Check other sources for information about resources and wildlife. Consider how the Native peoples of the area adapted to the environment. Create a mural to present your findings.

7. Create a legend, as the Native peoples might tell it, to describe the perils of the journey across Beringia and to the south.

8. Do research on glaciers. Consider these questions:
   a) When did glaciers cover large parts of North America?
   b) What areas did they cover?
   c) What were the effects of glaciers on animals, people, and the environment?

CHAPTER 7

The Huron of the Great Lakes –St. Lawrence Lowlands

Skill Building: Writing a Comparison Report

Over the next four chapters you will be exploring different Native communities of Canada. You will discover what life was like in a Native community before the Europeans arrived. You can add to your study of a particular Native community by locating other sources in your resource centre or library.

Your main task will be to observe how life in the Native communities you study is similar and how it is different. To present your findings, you can prepare a comparison report.

There are three main steps in preparing a comparison report:

Step 1: Getting Ready

Your first main step is to choose your topic, do your research, and record your information. This step gives you an opportunity to practise skills you have already learned.

Step 2: Writing the Report

In this step, you develop some conclusions about the information you found. Then you present your conclusions in a clear and organized way.

Step 3: The Final Touches

The last step is to reread your report, check it for spelling or grammatical errors, and add your title page and list of sources. Your report won't be your best work if you overlook this step.

Let's go through each step.

Step 1: Getting Ready

1. Choose one aspect of Native culture. This will be the topic of your comparison report.
For example: Native Homes
2. Choose the Native groups you would like to compare.
For example: Blackfoot Homes
                      Huron Homes

3. Select the criteria for your comparison. What characteristics of Native homes could you compare?
For example: Materials
                      Size
                      Method of construction
                      Outside appearance
                      Inside appearance
4. Draw a comparison organizer to record your information.

Criteria	Blackfoot Homes	Huron Homes
Materials		
Size		
Method of construction		
Outside appearance		
Inside appearance		

5. Locate your information. Reread the sections in this textbook on your topic. Check your library for other sources of information. Ask your librarian for help.

6. Read your source material carefully. Remember to look for the main idea (topic) and supporting information (the most important details). Be sure to stay on topic. You want to pick out the information that fits your criteria.

7. Record the information in the correct location on your organizer. Use point form.

8. Review your information. Look for similarities and differences. Come to a conclusion about your comparison of Native homes. Are Native homes alike or different? Write a sentence that states your conclusion.

Step 2: Writing the Report

You have gathered and organized your information. You have also come to a conclusion based on what you found. Now you are ready to start thinking about your report.

A report has three main parts: an **Introduction**, a **Body**, and a **Conclusion**. The introduction tells what your report is about. It states your topic. The body is the meat of your report. It gives all of the supporting information you found. The conclusion is a summary. It tells what you learned from your research.

Study the sample report on page 87. Examine each section carefully. Look at what each section should do.

Step 3: The Final Touches

When you have finished your report, reread it. Check that it is clearly written. Check for spelling mistakes.

Finally, give your report a title page. A title page should list the title of the report, your name, the date, and the name of your teacher. Also add a list of the sources you used to gather your information. Put this list at the back of your report. Ask your teacher for help. A list of sources is called a **bibliography**.

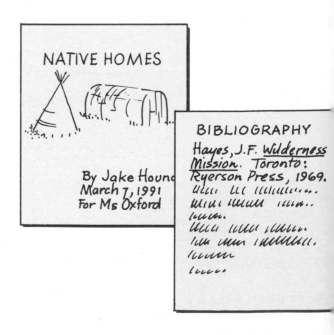

Now it's your turn. Choose a different aspect of Native life to compare, such as Native villages or winter activities. Follow the steps in writing a comparison report.

INTRODUCTION
1. States your topic.
2. States the items you are comparing.
3. Identifies the characteristics you are comparing.

BODY OF THE REPORT
1. Includes one paragraph for each characteristic you are comparing.
2. Describes the information you discovered about each characteristic.
3. Explains what you observed from the information.
4. Can include pictures or drawings to illustrate your information.

CONCLUSION
1. Sums up the most important information about the characteristics you compared.
2. States the most important observation you made from your comparison.

Native Homes

Native Homes are very different. We can see the differences if we compare Huron and Blackfoot homes. We can compare the materials used, the size of the homes, the way they were built, and their outside and inside appearance.

First we will look at the materials used in Huron and Blackfoot homes. The Huron made their longhouses mainly from cedar. They used cedar poles for their framework and crosspieces. They used slabs of cedar bark to cover the frame. The Blackfoot built their tipis of buffalo hides. They used 15 or more hides sewn together. They covered a framework of 10 to 20 poles. Both the Huron and the Blackfoot chose materials easy to obtain from their environment.

Paragraph to compare size
Paragraph to compare the way the homes were built
Paragraph to compare outside appearance
Paragraph to compare inside appearance

The Huron built large, permanent homes meant for many families. The Blackfoot built smaller homes of buffalo skins that could quickly be put up and taken down. Their homes are different because each group used materials from its own environment. The two groups built homes suited to their special way of life.

The chief was seated near the fire. Young people of the village had gathered to hear the stories of Huron creation long ago. The chief held that special knowledge about the past. He would pass it along to the younger generation. The smoky longhouse grew silent as the chief began his story.

In the beginning, there was nothing but water–nothing but a wide, wide sea. The only people in the world were the animals that live in and on water.

Then down from the sky world a woman fell, a divine person. Two loons flying over the water happened to look up and see her falling. Quickly they placed themselves under her to make a cushion for her to rest upon. They saved her from drowning.

While they held her, they cried with a loud voice to the other animals, asking their help. Now the cry of the loon can be heard at a great distance over water, and so the other creatures gathered quickly.

As soon as Great Turtle learned the reason for the call, he stepped forth.

"Give her to me," he said to the loons. "Put her on my back. My back is broad."

And so the loons were relieved of their burden. Then the animals, discussing what they should do to save the life of the woman, decided that she must have earth to live on. Great Turtle sent the creatures, one by one, to dive to the bottom of the sea and bring up some earth. Beaver, Muskrat, Diver, and others made the attempt. Some remained below so long that when they rose they were dead. Great Turtle looked in the mouth of each one, but could find no trace of earth. At last Toad dived. After a long time he arose, almost dead from weariness. Searching Toad's mouth, Great Turtle found some earth. This he gave to the woman.

She took the earth and placed it carefully around the edge of Great Turtle's shell. There it became the beginning of dry land. On all sides, the land grew larger and larger, until at last it formed a great country. It was a country where trees and other plants could live and grow. All this country was borne on the back of Great Turtle, and it is yet today. Great Turtle still bears the earth on his back.

–Adapted from
Indian Legends of Canada
by Ella Elizabeth Clark

"Deliverance of Sky-Woman" by Arnold Jacobs, Six Nations Iroquois.

Who Were the Huron?

The Huron were a nation of Native people living in the region of the Great Lakes. These Native people called themselves Wendat, which might mean "Islander". Wendat might also mean "Dwellers on a Peninsula," describing where these people lived. However, the French called them Huron. This is still the more commonly used name for the Wendat Nation.

The Huron lands stretched across the peninsula between Georgian Bay and Lake Simcoe. Their total territory covered about 56 km from east to west and 32 km from north to south. It was an area that the Huron could travel easily in three or four days.

THE GREAT LAKES - ST. LAWRENCE LOWLANDS

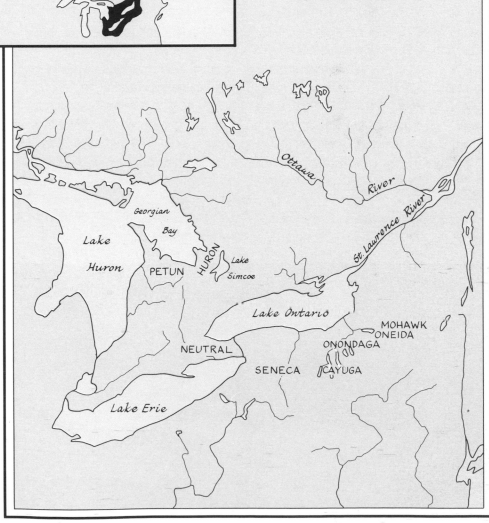

HURON COUNTRY

The Huron Village

The Huron lived in permanent villages. Most of their villages were located near streams that flowed to Lake Huron. In times of war the streams were excellent routes for escape to Lake Huron. A network of trails linked the Huron villages together.

The site for a village was chosen with great care. The Huron looked for a location close to a source of spring water. They chose areas near sandy, well-drained soil that was good for farming. Villages were not built on the shores of Lake Huron because of the strong northwesterly winds.

Every ten to twenty years it was necessary to move the villages. Farming over several years exhausted the soil. New fields had to be cleared. New villages were built only a few kilometres from the old ones.

Huron villages varied in size. Large villages had a population of 1500 to 2000 people and contained forty or more longhouses. These large villages were the centres for feasts and important council meetings.

The large villages were also protected against attack. They were surrounded by strong fences called **palisades**. A palisade was made from wooden poles. Poles 4 m or more in length were pointed and twisted into the ground a few centimetres apart. There were often several rows of poles. These fence posts were then woven together with small branches. Large pieces of bark were placed over this frame to give it strength. The Huron then fastened tree trunks lengthwise at the base of the palisade or piled earth against it for extra strength.

Other measures were taken to protect the village as well. Watchtowers or galleries were built on the inside of the palisade. They were used to keep an eye out for intruders. Often only one entrance was built through the palisade into the village. The way in was protected by wooden bars.

Small Huron villages were not fortified with palisades. In times of danger the people fled to the large villages for protection. Smaller villages did have some advantages. The smaller population wasn't as hard on the land. The soil was not exhausted as quickly, and people were able to stay in one location longer. Sometimes large villages divided to form two or more smaller villages.

Types of palisades.

A model of a Huron village.

The Huron Longhouse

TOP: Building a longhouse. What are the Huron on the top of the longhouse doing?

BOTTOM: The interior of a longhouse. What tools, utensils, and other objects of everyday Huron life can you identify in this picture?

The Huron homes were called **long-houses**. If you look at the picture you will see why they were given this name. The longhouses varied in size. The length depended on the number of families that occupied it. Most longhouses were probably 30 m long and 7 m wide.

The house was usually built with the ends facing the prevailing winds so that the narrowest part would receive the force of the gale. Longhouses were set back from the palisade for defence. To save space only three or four paces separated the longhouses. The spread of fire was always a danger in a Huron village because the houses were so close together.

The frame of the longhouse was made of flexible wooden poles. They were driven into the ground to support the walls. The tops were bent and tied together to form the roof. The main poles were fastened with wooden cross pieces to make them sturdier. Slabs of cedar bark were tied onto the frame and over-lapped like roofing tiles. Holes were left in the ceiling to let smoke out and light in. The ends of the longhouse were usually rounded. An enclosed porch was often built at each end for storing corn and firewood. The outside of the longhouse was sometimes decorated with red paint-ings. These were symbols of the families living in the longhouse.

Several families lived in the same longhouse. A mother and her daughters might live there with their husbands and children. Or it might be a woman, her sisters, and their husbands and children. All the women in the longhouse would be related. Historians are not certain why this pattern was followed. It might be because the women worked together as a team to produce food. It might have been for protection since the men were away so much of the year.

On the inside a row of fireplaces ran down the centre of each longhouse. The fireplaces were about 4 m apart. They helped to heat the entire longhouse. There were other smaller fireplaces as well that were used for cooking. All of the smoke from these fires did not escape through the holes in the roof and the longhouse was often quite smoky. Rolled torches of birchbark were used for light. Since fire was such a danger, valuable possessions were buried in shallow pits to keep them safe.

One family lived on each side of a fireplace. A bark or reed mat covered their ground space. A bark platform was built against the wall about 2 m above the ground. In the summer the family would sleep on the platform or outside in the open air. In winter the family slept on the ground to be closer to the fire.

Huron Society

A Huron chief in 1825.

A Huron Native belonged to many different groups. One group was the family. The family was made up of parents and their children. The size of the average Huron family was five to eight people.

The Huron also belonged to larger family groups. These included relatives such as aunts, uncles, grandparents, and cousins. These larger family groups were called **clans**.* The members of a clan were all descendants of the same female relative. A Huron belonged to the same clan as his or her mother. There were eight different clans. They were identified by animal names: Wolf, Deer, Bear, Turtle, Beaver, Hawk, Porcupine, Snake. Each clan protected its members from harm. People of several different clans often lived in the same Huron village. Each clan had its own section in the village.

Each clan had two chiefs, a civil chief who looked after everyday problems and a war chief. They held their positions for life. When a chief died, the title was passed to another member of the clan. A Huron chief tried to win the support of the people and seldom used force.

All of the civil chiefs of the clans belonged to the village council. The council met frequently in the house of the village chief. The village chief might be chosen from an important clan in the village.

The council talked about the concerns of the villagers. The chiefs made certain that no family in the village was without food or shelter. They organized community projects such as feasts, dances, and building palisades. They settled arguments between people of different clans. At the council meeting the village chief sat on the floor in front of the fire. The other members of the council formed a circle.

Before any battle, a council of war chiefs would meet. They would decide if the village would send out a raiding party. The oldest chief was the war chief for the entire village.

Several villages grouped together to form a **tribe**.* There were four different Huron tribes. Each tribe had its own tribal council. The clan chiefs of each village took part in the tribal council. One chief was named the chief of the tribe. He would call the meetings of the tribal council and send messengers out to the villages to announce it. The tribal council would settle disputes between villages. Problems were discussed until agreements were reached by the members.

The four Huron tribes grouped together in a larger organization called a **confederacy**.* In the spring of each year a meeting of the confederacy council was held. It would last for several weeks. The chiefs of all the tribes attended. Feasts were held and gifts were exchanged. The confederacy council discussed problems that were of concern to all Huron.

*See note on page 93.

NOTE: *Some Native groups prefer the terms extended family (clan), kinship (tribe) and Alliance (Confederacy).*

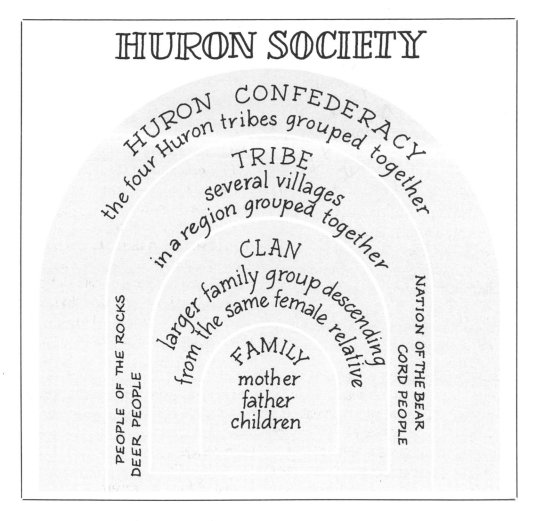

HURON SOCIETY

HURON CONFEDERACY
the four Huron tribes grouped together

TRIBE
several villages in a region grouped together

CLAN
larger family group descending from the same female relative

FAMILY
mother
father
children

PEOPLE OF THE ROCKS
DEER PEOPLE

NATION OF THE BEAR
CORD PEOPLE

HURON WOMEN IN SOCIETY

Women had an important role in Huron society. The legend you read earlier spoke of the first woman on earth. Her name was Aataentsic. She was the mother of all people. She had charge of the souls of all the Huron dead.

*The Huron traced their ancestry through their mother. This pattern of descent is called **matrilineal**. The chief woman of each clan had influence. She consulted with the other clan women to choose the chiefs. The chiefs were men. They held their positions for life but they could be removed for a serious offense or if they became ill.*

*The Huron living arrangements also show the importance of women. The people living in a house were all related through the women. The families were usually a woman and her daughters and their husbands and children or a woman and her sisters living there with their husbands and children. This pattern is called **matrilocal**.*

Everyday Life Among the Huron

In Huron country, the different seasons brought changes to the environment. Many of the day-to-day activities of the Huron followed the changing seasons.

Spring

The Huron were farmers. They grew three-quarters of their food. As farmers, they were different from many other Native groups that hunted and gathered. The Huron's environment allowed them to farm and develop a settled way of life.

Spring was the time of year when the Huron cleared the land and prepared it for planting. The men and women worked together. A couple could clear as much land as they needed. They had the right to the land as long as they used it. When they no longer used it, it became part of the common land once again. To the Huron, the land was there for everyone.

Clearing land took hard work and skill. Smaller trees were cut down with stone axes. The larger trees were killed by burning piles of branches around the base of the trunk. The stumps would remain and the crops would later be planted between them.

Spring was also the season for making repairs to the village. The palisade likely needed to be strengthened after a severe winter. New longhouses had to be built. Extensions had to be added to older houses to make room for growing families. Spring was the best season for building the longhouses. The sap was running in the trees. This made the branches more flexible. It was easier to shape the poles for building the framework of the longhouse. Spring was also the season for building light and sturdy birchbark canoes. They were important for hunting and trading.

The women of the village had the important responsibility of planting and tending the crops and gathering firewood. They worked together to help provide for the village. The men were often away from the village trading or hunting and fishing. Sometimes the men also helped with the crops.

In March and April the women often travelled great distances from their village to gather firewood. They worked together in teams to make certain that each longhouse was well supplied with dry wood for the year to come.

Late spring was the time for planting crops of corn, beans, and squash. Sunflowers were also planted for their seeds. Sunflower oil was used to garnish food.

Corn was the most important crop. The cornfields were close to the village. To prepare for planting, the women sorted kernels of corn and soaked them in water for several days. Between the stumps in the fields, they shaped the soil into little mounds about a metre apart. Nine or ten corn kernels were planted in each mound. Once the kernels began to grow,

A Huron woman working in the corn fields.

the plants were thinned out. Only the strongest plants were left in the mound.

Beans and squash were planted about two weeks after the corn. Squash seedlings were started indoors to avoid frost. The seeds were placed in bark trays filled with powdered wood. They were kept near the longhouse fire for warmth. When the seeds sprouted the women transplanted them to the fields.

Summer

Summer was the season for tending the fields and trading with friendly neighbours. The Huron women and children often moved temporarily to be closer to the fields. The women of one longhouse worked together to clear the weeds from their fields. Spare time was spent gathering wild plants and berries to add to their diet. Some of the berries were dried for winter use. Others were used to flavour corn soup or were added to small cakes before they were baked.

During the summer, most Huron men were away from their villages. Only a few remained at home to protect the village. The men set out on long journeys to trade with their neighbours the Petun, Neutral, and Algonkians. The Petun and Neutral had tobacco, black squirrel skins, and furs to trade. The Algonkians had skins and winter clothing decorated with porcupine quills. The Huron prized the skins they obtained from their neighbours. They were sometimes unable to find enough animal skins at home to make all their own clothes. In exchange, the Huron offered their neighbours cornmeal. The cornmeal helped their neighbours get through the hard winter.

The trade routes to neighbouring tribes were closely guarded. The main routes were controlled by important chiefs. This gave them wealth and importance. Anyone who wanted to use the route offered gifts to the chief. The confederacy decided how many men from the villages could go out to trade. The Huron protected the trade routes from outsiders.

Trading was conducted with much ceremony, much as modern-day diplomats and businesspersons do today when meeting trading partners. The event often lasted several days. The traders painted their faces. Gifts were exchanged and speeches were made. Feasts were held before and after trading.

Summer, quite naturally, was the usual time for battle during wartime. The Huron and the Iroquois had been enemies for a long time because the Huron had not joined the Iroquois confederacy.

Being a brave fighter in wartime, just as being a good hunter or provider in peacetime, helped young men gain respect in their village.

Autumn

The Huron women were responsible for the fall harvest. When the corn was harvested, the women tied the ripe cobs in bundles. Then they hung the bundles to dry from poles under the roof of the longhouse. After drying, the kernels were shelled from the cob, cleaned, and stored in large bark chests. The women ground the dried kernels into flour. A hollowed out tree trunk was used as a mortar. A long pole was used as the grinder. Sometimes women ground the corn between two stones and blew the husks away using a bark fan. The harvest included more than just bringing the crops in from the fields. Acorns, walnuts, and wild grapes were also gathered from the woods.

SAGAMITE
(Cornmeal soup)

The Huron usually had two meals per day, one in the morning and the other in the evening. Corn was the main item in their diet. A corn soup called sagamite was the most common dish.

> *Boil cornmeal (ground corn) in water*
> *Place whole fish in the pot*
> *Continue to boil*
> *Remove the fish and pound into a mash*
> *Return the mash to the pot*
> *Add sliced squash and continue to boil*

For the men of the village, autumn was the season for fishing and hunting. Fishing was more important than hunting as a source of food. Different kinds of fish were caught, but herring and whitefish were among the most important. Fishing for herring was a village adventure. Villagers helped to carry home the catch in large wooden bowls.

The Huron used many different methods to secure their catch. Sometimes they used a line with a wooden hook and a bone barb at the end. Sometimes they landed their catch using wooden spears with barbed heads carved from bone. Large schools of herring were caught using nets made of woven Indian hemp rope.

The Huron used the nets on the open waters of Georgian Bay and on the rivers and streams in their territory. They also built **weirs**. A weir was a row of stakes set in a stream or river at a spot where it narrowed. The idea was that the row of stakes trapped the fish. The Huron then used their nets to catch them. The most important Huron weirs were at the narrows between Lake Simcoe and Lake Couchiching.

The whitefish season was most important. Fishing groups left the villages each October for the islands of Georgian Bay. There they stayed for a month or more to catch whitefish, sturgeon, and trout. They built bark cabins on the islands to house the fishing parties. Each evening they set their nets about two kilometres from shore and drew them in at daybreak. The catch was cleaned and spread on wooden racks to dry. It might also be smoked. Then it was packed into bark containers.

The fall hunt also took Huron men away from their villages for one or two

Netting fish at a weir. Why would a weir be an effective way of catching fish?

months. Animal skins and furs were the main prize. Travel was by foot and birch-bark canoe. Along with weapons, the Huron hunter carried a supply of corn-meal and a bowl. The bowl was very

BOTTOM: A deer hunt, from an illustration by the early French explorer Samuel de Champlain.

TOP: Preparing weapons for the hunt.

handy. It could be used for bailing out the canoe if needed.

The Huron hunted a variety of game. Beaver skins were valued for clothing. The four large teeth of the beaver were useful for wood working. They made excellent tools for scraping and shaping wooden bowls. Bear, muskrat, and rabbit were also hunted for their fur. But the most important game was deer. The Huron used the skins for clothing and the fat for flavouring their food.

Large hunting parties journeyed several days from Huronia to hunt deer. The deer were taken in drives. Several hundred hunters formed a line through the forest parallel to a river. Together they moved toward the river armed with bows and arrows. They made a great deal of noise as they moved. The idea was to frighten any deer in their path and drive them toward the river. When the animals reached the riverfront, they were trapped. Some were killed with sharpened poles by men in canoes. Others were shot with arrows as they tried to break through the line.

Huron hunters had another interesting method of hunting deer. They built **enclosures**. An enclosure was triangular-shaped. One side of the triangle was open. The other two sides were fences built from brush and wooden poles. These sides were 3 m high but might be as long as half a kilometre! It was difficult work to build an enclosure. Twenty-five Huron hunters might work steadily for about ten days to complete the job.

The narrow end of the enclosure led into a pen. At dawn, hunters lined up at the open end of the enclosure and beat sticks together. The frightened deer were driven back into the enclosure. They had no place for escape. Finally they were forced into the pen where they were killed with arrows. Huron women sometimes went on the deer hunting expeditions to butcher the game and help bring back the skins.

also moulded clay pots and sewed birch-bark into bowls and chests. They wove reed mats to cover doors and sleeping platforms. They made wicker baskets for carrying grain and for storing food.

Winter

Winter was the season for tribal council meetings and festivals. The Huron travelled from village to village to take part in these events. They were times for singing, dancing, and feasting. Feasts were very important to the Huron. There were singing feasts, feasts of thanksgiving, and feasts held to cure people of illness.

Hosting a feast was a sign of generosity. It would bring great honour to your family if you hosted a feast in your village. Sometimes an entire village would organize a feast and invite people from other villages. It was a great occasion. A feast might last for fifteen days!

Huron men used the winter months to prepare their tools and weapons. They wove their fishing nets from Indian hemp rope. They made bows and arrows and suits of armour to be used for hunting and possible future wars. Chisels and axes were fashioned from hard stone. Awls, needles, and small amulets were carved from bone. An **awl** is a tool used to punch holes in skins.

The women also used the winter months to make clothing and utensils. Animal skins from the fall hunt were scraped and softened. They were sewn into clothing using bone needles and animal sinew as thread. For decoration, the women painted designs on the skins and added dyed porcupine quills. They

Growing Up Among the Huron

The birth of a child was a joyous event in the Huron family. The average family had three children.

A newborn infant was often given the name of an honoured dead relative. The baby was wrapped in fur and the down of cattails was often used as a diaper. The baby's ears were pierced with an awl or fish bone. Infants were often kept on a cradleboard. It could stand on the floor of the longhouse where the family could watch over the baby while they did their work. The cradleboard was also used to transport the baby. When the mother wanted to go out, she strapped the cradleboard to her back.

Young people learned the skills they would need for adult life. They were taught by their parents, family members, and other adults from their village. They learned how to farm and look after the longhouse. They learned how to hunt and how to fish.

When the time came for marriage, a young man's mother usually chose the bride. All arrangements for the wedding were made by the mothers of the couple. Presents were exchanged to seal the marriage. The bride might receive bundles of firewood as wedding gifts. The man went to live in the woman's house after the marriage.

HURON GAMES

Lacrosse
Lacrosse was a very popular team sport with the young people. It was played with sticks, which had webbed pouches, and a hard ball. The ball was passed down the field toward the opposing goal. The object was to score in the opponent's net.

Dish
Dish was a game played with six flat stones painted white on one side and black on the other. The stones were placed in an unbreakable dish. The dish was then hit on the ground and the stone pieces jumped. A point was scored if all of the pieces landed the same side up.

Straws
In the game of straws, a handful of straws, all the same size, was thrown down on the ground. The players had to pick up some of the straws without looking. Points were scored if the players picked up an odd number of straws.

Contact: The Huron Meet the Europeans

The first Europeans the Huron met were the French. Between 1610 and 1650 French explorers, traders, and missionaries came to Huronia. The explorer Samuel de Champlain visited the Huron in 1615-1616 and lived in several of their villages. French missionaries, particularly the Jesuits, came to spread Christianity shortly after Champlain's contact. Contact with the Europeans brought measles and smallpox. These were diseases unknown in Huron country. The Natives had little resistance. Thousands died.

The Europeans who came to Huron country were interested in furs. The beaver was most highly prized. The Huron traded furs with the French who settled along the St. Lawrence River. In exchange they received European goods.

The Iroquois, the enemy of the Huron, traded with the Dutch. The Dutch had settled along the Hudson River in present-day New York State. Competition for furs made the old feud between the Huron and Iroquois much worse. The rivalry led to a bloody war in 1648. The Iroquois destroyed whole villages and killed thousands of Huron. The Dutch helped their allies by providing them with guns.

In the spring of 1649 the Huron fled from their villages. Hundreds died from cold and famine. Some fled to the Upper Great Lakes and joined with the Ottawa and Potawatomi peoples. These survivors later came to be called the Wyandot and settled near Detroit. In the nineteenth century the Wyandot were forced west to Kansas and Oklahoma, where their descendants live today.

Another large group of Huron fled to Christian Island in Georgian Bay during the war with the Iroquois. In 1650 the

Jesuits moved the group to a location near Quebec City called Lorette. About 1000 descendants of the Huron live at Lorette today. It is the only remaining Huron community in Canada. Contact with the Europeans and war with the Iroquois almost destroyed the Huron.

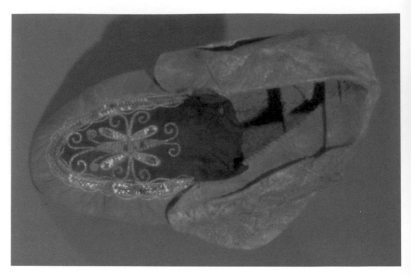

Huron chief Max Gros-Louis. Today the approximately 1000 Huron living on the reserve near Lorette are actively working to revive their language and culture and protect their rights.

Huron Arts and Crafts

A birchbark box embroidered with brown and green moose hair. These decorative boxes were greatly valued by European traders.

Huron moccasins made from tanned leather. Moccasins were often decorated with dyed moose hair and porcupine quills.

Dolls made from corn husk. The heads were carved from wood and painted.

Activities

Looking Back

1. Define the following words and enter them in your dictionary.

   palisade   matrilineal
   longhouse   weir
   clan   enclosure
   tribe   awl
   confederacy
   matrilocal

2. Where did the Huron live? Answer in two or three sentences or with a neat sketch map.

3. What foods did the Huron eat? Identify which were the most important. Include sketches to show how food was prepared.

4. In your own words, describe how the Huron built their longhouses.

5. Divide the class into four groups. Assign each group a season. List the Huron activities in that season. Create a mural to illustrate the activities.

Using Your Knowledge

6. Explain how the Huron used the resources of their natural environment to obtain food, build homes, and secure transportation.

7. The Huron were farmers. What advantages did farming give them? What problems or difficulties did the Huron face as farmers? Suggest reasons why few other groups of Native peoples in Canada were farmers.

8. In Huron society, problems were often solved through discussions. What evidence is there to support this statement? Review the section on Huron society.

Extending Your Thinking

9. Working in groups, construct models of a Huron village. Explain your model to another group. Discuss the historical accuracy of the models.

10. Imagine you are a Huron at the time of the war with the Iroquois. How would you feel? What might you be thinking? Write a journal entry to describe your experiences.

CHAPTER 8

The Micmac of the Eastern Woodlands

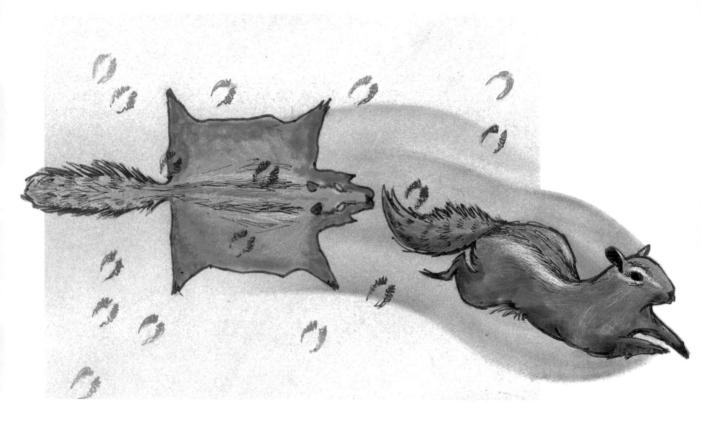

Shamans were important figures in almost all Native groups. They were thought to have special powers. They could communicate with the spirits, see into the future, and cure the sick. The people both feared and respected them. The following legend tells of Micmac shamans and their powers.

Long ago an old woman went out into the forest to get pine bark for the fire. As she was walking through the forest, she saw a long log of foxfire. She heard a noise. Something was crying. The old woman thought it must be ghosts. The noise was coming from the log of foxfire. She looked inside the foxfire log and found a child. The old woman put the baby in the hood of her robe and took him back to the wigwam.

The old woman was a shaman. She had Power. She was very strong. She could see ten days into tomorrow. She could see what was to happen. When the child was two years old, she began to make him strong too. She began to give him Power. She made him a shaman.

The old woman took a chipmunk and skinned it. She stretched the skin and pounded it. She pounded it to make it soft. All the time she pounded it, she spoke to it and sang to it. When it was ready, she gave it to her son. She said to the skin, "You must go ahead of him. You must always see ahead of him. And whatever you see, come back and report, so that he may know."

Now the people are going to war. They take the boy with them. They want him to see for them. Every morning when the sun comes up from beneath the earth, the war chief speaks to the boy, "Have you dreamed in the night? What have you seen? Have you dreamed any danger, anything ahead of us?"

Every morning the boy says no. There is no danger. But there comes a morning when he says, "Today we shall know." He takes out his chipmunk skin. He strokes it and speaks to it. "I want you to go out now, go out ahead of us, and see. I want you to see what lies ahead, what dangers are before us. Go!"

And the chipmunk skin takes on its shape and runs. It runs ahead, it sees into the tomorrows, and then it returns and crawls into the boy's robe. It crawls up on his shoulder and speaks into his ear.

"There is danger. This war chief will die."

And that same day the people come to the fighting place. The boy says, "I am going up on that mountain now. I am going to dance the War Medicine Dance. I will dance it on the top of this mountain."

The boy goes up on the mountain and dances. The whole time he is dancing the enemy are shooting at him. But they cannot kill him. When the boy comes down from the mountain, he says to the chief, "Now you must go. It is your time to dance."

The chief goes up on the mountain and it is as the chipmunk has said. The enemy kill him. The boy dreams. He tells his dream. "They are coming," he says. "They are circling around us from behind. And they are wearing caribou feet so that we may not spot their tracks. They are coming now, but they will not see us."

The enemy passed all around his people, but they could not see them. And as they passed, they lost all their caribou feet. The boy's people have the caribou feet now, and they can go wherever they want.

–Adapted from
Stories from the Six Worlds: Micmac Legends
by Ruth Holmes Whitehead

Who Were the Micmac?

The Micmac were a Native group of eastern Canada. They were a maritime group. They lived near the sea which was very important for their livelihood. It provided food and many of the things they needed for their daily lives. The Micmac lived on the peninsulas of Gaspé and Nova Scotia, on Prince Edward Island, and along the eastern coast of present-day New Brunswick.

The Micmac territory was divided into seven districts. Historians believe that most of the district names tell us about the natural features of the area. These are some of the district names and their meanings:

Sipekne'katik means "groundnut place"

Wunama'kik means "foggy land"

Piwktuk means "where explosions are made"

Epekwitk means "lying in the water"

Eskikewa'kik means "skin dressers' territory"

Kespek means "the last land."

Find these districts on the map of Micmac country. What do the names tell us about the environment of the Micmac?

The Micmac Village

Micmac villages were located on the seacoast. In the late fall, communities moved inland for a few months. The people moved to get away from the harsh winter storms that could strike the coast. But no matter where the community was located, it was never far from the sea.

The Micmac chose the sites for their villages with care. A village was usually located at the mouth of a river. The river provided fresh water and a travel route. The Micmac travelled by birchbark canoe along the coast to other villages. They would also go inland along the river to search for groundnuts and other plants. Often, the Micmac settled near good sources of food such as shellfish beds.

If a site was used for several years, firewood and possibly game around the village might be in short supply. Then the community would find a new site for the village. They might move some 75 or 80 km away from the old location, but the village would also be near the sea.

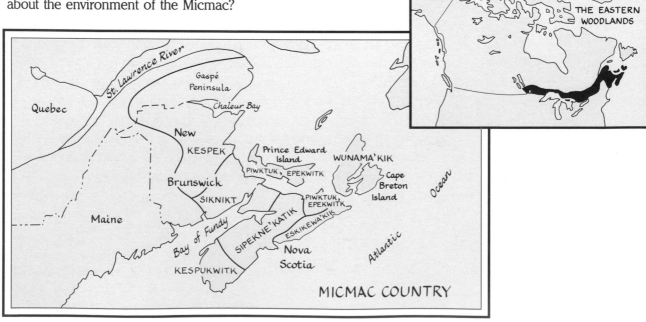

A Micmac camp. What evidence is there that these Micmac have had contact with Europeans?

A birchbark wigwam. Can you describe how this wigwam was built?

Micmac Homes

Micmac homes were designed so that they could be moved easily. The most common home was called a **wigwam**. It was a covered wooden frame shaped like a cone. The wooden frame was left standing when the people moved. The coverings were carried from location to location. Wigwams usually housed ten to twelve people.

When a new wigwam was needed, women often worked together to build it. This was an important task and one that took skill and knowledge. Some women looked for suitable poles to build the frame. They cut five to ten long spruce poles. Others found fir branches for the floor. Usually one woman oversaw everything. She told the women how to make the frame. They tied the poles together at the top with lengths of spruce root. Next they stood the poles up and spread them apart at the bottom until they formed a cone shape. Then they bent a sapling into a hoop and tied it to the inside of the frame near the top. The hoop kept the poles from slipping.

Next the women covered the framework of the wigwam with large birchbark sheets. The sheets were sewn to the frame using spruce root. Holes were punched through the bark using a bone awl. The birchbark was kept warm and wet so that it would not tear while it was being sewn. The women started at the bottom. The sheets of bark were overlapped to keep out the wind and rain. They anchored the bark by laying poles against the outside of the wigwam. A thick hide was hung over the entrance.

Often the Micmac painted the outside birchbark coverings with colourful designs. These designs had spiritual meaning to the people who lived there. The designs were animals, birds, fish, people, or abstract patterns.

Sometimes the women covered the frame of the wigwam with rush mats instead of birchbark. The mats were woven so tightly that they kept out the rain. If it was only a temporary overnight shelter the wigwam frame might be covered with fir boughs.

Fir branches were interlaced and spread on the floor of the wigwam. They acted as a comfortable springy mattress for sleeping. In winter the Micmac laid rush mats and skins on the floor over the branches. These provided extra protection against the freezing weather. The floor was dug several centimetres below the ground to help keep the inside of the wigwam warm and dry. Outside, the Micmac placed evergreen boughs against the base of the wigwam. When snow was packed against the boughs, it helped to further insulate the home.

A rock fireplace stood in the centre of the wigwam. It provided heat, light, and a place to cook. The Micmac spread sand around the edge of the fireplace to prevent the fire from spreading. The wigwam was left open at the peak for the smoke to escape. In bad weather the Micmac placed a collar of bark over the smokehole. This bark covering helped to keep the people dry, but the inside of the wigwam was very smoky.

Large families including aunts, uncles, grandparents, and cousins lived together in larger birchbark homes. These large family groups are called **extended families**. The large homes were rectangular like a cabin and could house up to twenty-five people. These homes often had two fireplaces, one at each end.

Micmac woman wearing the traditional peaked hat of the nineteenth century.

Inside a wigwam. What objects of everyday Micmac life can you identify in this wigwam?

Micmac Society

A grand chief called a **sagamore** ruled over all the Micmac people. When the French arrived at Port Royal in 1605, the grand chief lived on Cape Breton Island. His name was Membertou. He was described as a tall, majestic, bearded man. The Micmac people looked to the sagamore for leadership and advice. He led them in battle, provided dogs for hunting, canoes for transportation, and food in times of bad weather and famine.

Membertou was also a **shaman**. Both men and women could be shamans. The people believed shamans possessed power to make contact with the gods. People trusted the advice of the shamans. They believed shamans could see into the future. Shamans also had the power to cure the sick with medicines made from roots and bark.

A Micmac chief. This photo was taken sometime between 1920 and 1930.

The grand chief called Grand Council meetings. These were meetings of all other chiefs and respected Micmac. The chiefs were called together when a decision had to be made that would affect the entire Micmac nation. The Grand Council could make decisions about war and peace and trading with other Native groups.

Each Micmac district also had its own chief. The district chief called council meetings for the district when needed. He toured the district and met with local chiefs. He welcomed other visiting chiefs to his district by holding a feast. The district chief always attended the Grand Council meeting. Each year he also decided the size and location of the hunting territories for each family in the district. The size of the hunting areas changed as the size of each family changed.

A third type of Micmac chief was the local chief. A local chief headed a group of related families in the district. Some groups were as small as thirty or forty people. Most were larger. This organization by related families made certain there was always some relative to count on in time of misfortune. There would always be a family member to take care of an orphaned child. Older men within the local community helped the local chief. They were all members of a local council. The chiefs were the most respected members of the Micmac community.

Slaves were also a part of Micmac society. They were captives taken in war. Male slaves helped around the Micmac camp and did many everyday chores such as collecting firewood and water. Female and young captives were sometimes adopted into the community by families.

MICMAC SOCIETY

GRAND CHIEF

DISTRICT CHIEF

LOCAL CHIEF

EXTENDED FAMILY

Piwktuk, Epekwitk
Sipekne'katik
Eskikewa'kik

Wunama'kik
Kespukwitk
Kespek   Siknikt

Everyday Life Among the Micmac

Imagine that you could spend a year with Membertou and the Micmac. What would life be like? What could you learn from the Micmac?

The Micmac could teach you how to use the plentiful sea and land resources of their environment. They know which fish, animals, and plants are best for food. They could teach you how to build a shelter using materials close at hand. They know where to go in winter when cold winds blow into their homeland off the Atlantic Ocean. They could share their inventions–ways to travel on water and in snow. They could teach you about their legends, arts, and beliefs.

Spring

The Micmac were hunters and gatherers. In the spring, as they settled in their coastal villages, they turned to the resources of the sea, rivers, and streams for their livelihood.

In spring, the Micmac collected clams and oysters. They built traps across rivers to catch fish as they swam into fresh waters to spawn. Men and women worked together to block the fish moving upstream. They built **weirs** at a narrow place on the river. Micmac weirs were dams of rocks and wood. Large baskets were placed against the dams. As the fish tried to jump over the dams, they fell into the baskets. The Micmac caught large quantities of smelt, herring, salmon, and sturgeon.

The Micmac often went fishing for large fish and lobsters at night. They attracted the fish to their canoes with torches made of birchbark. When the fish came close enough to the canoes, they were speared with bone-tipped harpoons. Landing a very large fish such as a sturgeon took great skill. The largest fish were sometimes towed into shore.

Fish might be roasted whole on coals or they could be boiled in huge wooden kettles. Water was poured into the kettle. Then red-hot stones from the fire were dropped into the water. When the water was hot, the pieces of fish could be cooked. Kettles of stew were cooking almost constantly. All one had to do was dip a birchbark ladle into it. The Micmac preserved fish for winter by smoking them over a fire.

Spring was also a good time to collect eggs from birds' nests on off-shore islands. The Micmac also caught ducks and geese in snares or shot them with bows and arrows. Sometimes they hunted waterfowl at night. Large flocks of migrating geese would settle in the marshes at night. The Micmac would let their canoes drift in among the sleeping birds. Then, suddenly, they would light torches and create a great noise. The frightened birds would awaken and flutter around the torches. Then the Micmac would knock them down with sticks and wring their necks. This was a quick way to kill the birds the Micmac needed for

food. They did not kill more than they needed. They respected the spirits of the animals.

Summer

Summer was a time of plenty. The Micmac feasted on fish and shellfish. They caught cod fish along the coast with bone hooks and lines. On the rivers, they landed the fish in traps made of stakes. Sometimes the Micmac set out onto the ocean in birchbark canoes to hunt porpoises. Porpoise meat was considered a treat. If the Micmac were lucky enough to find a beached whale, they would take it for food. Seals were also important in their diet. Seal oil was made by melting down the fat. The oil was prized and was drunk at feasts. It was also used as an ointment and was rubbed into the skin and hair. The Micmac stored the oil in bags made from the intestines of large animals such as the moose.

Summer was also the time for harvesting wild fruits, berries, and other plants. Strawberries, raspberries, blueberries, and cranberries were enjoyed fresh. Berries were also dried and set aside for the winter. The Micmac also collected the groundnut plant. The pod, leaves, and roots could all be used for food. Roots and leaves of other plants such as the sweet-flag were also gathered for medicines. Cattails and reeds were harvested to be woven into baskets and mats.

For most of the year the Micmac travelled in small family groups. In summer they travelled mainly by birchbark canoe. Birchbark canoes were lightweight and ideal for navigating the rivers and streams. Some canoes were large enough to hold five or six people with dogs, kettles, and other heavy baggage. The Micmac used the canoes to reach their hunting and fishing grounds.

BUILDING A BIRCHBARK CANOE

The Micmac family examines the birch tree closely. It is a large tree. The bark can be cut and stripped in single sheets from the trunk. The Micmac cut around the tree in two places. Then they make a connecting cut. They loosen the bark by pounding it. Then they peel the bark from the tree.

The largest sheets are soaked in water to soften them and then they are set aside. All is ready. The young people are about to learn the age-old craft of constructing a birchbark canoe. The task will take ten days to three weeks.

The place for building the canoe has been carefully prepared. The Micmac have chosen a smooth, flat clearing. Young cedar trees have been cut down nearby. They will use the cedar for the rim and frame of the canoe.

The Micmac show the young people how to measure the ground for the size of the canoe. It will be one arm-stretch wide at the centre. It will be two double arm-stretches long. Poles are driven into the ground to outline the size. Then the Micmac lay the prized sheets of birchbark inside the frame of poles. They hold the sheets in place with rocks. The poles will help to bend the birchbark and shape the canoe.

The Micmac choose two long cedar pieces for the rim of the canoe. They tie the pieces together at the ends with spruce roots. Then they add cross pieces of cedar to shape the rim. With a sharpened bone awl, they bore holes for the lacing that will tie the crosspieces to the rim.

The completed rim is placed over the birchbark. The Micmac shape the end pieces for the front and back of the canoe. They make ribs to give the canoe strength. Then they carefully lace the end pieces and the ribs to the rim. They lay thin slats of cedar on the birchbark for the floor. The canoe is beginning to take shape.

Building a birchbark canoe. Large sheets of birchbark are laid inside the frame of poles.

The time has come to attach the bark sheets to the frame. The Micmac pierce holes through the edges of the bark for the thread. They sew the bark to the rim using spruce roots as thread. Sometimes the root is died different colours. The Micmac bind the edges with split roots of spruce. The young people watch with excitement. The canoe is almost complete.

One important step remains. The canoe has to be made waterproof. The young people help prepare a warm mixture of boiled spruce gum and fat. They paint all of the bark seams and lacing holes with this mixture. The Micmac look on with pride as the task is completed. They know this canoe will be watertight and will serve the family well.

In the late spring and summer the Micmac came together for an annual festival. They looked forward to the festival. It was a time for feasting and celebration. It was a time for dancing and storytelling. It was a time for making marriages.

Many important events in Micmac life were marked by feasts. There were feasts for marriages and funerals, for health, peace, war, and hunting. At the beginning of the hunt, for example, a feast was held as a sacred act of thanksgiving. The first animal of each species that was killed was honoured. The Micmac honoured the animals for giving up their lives so that humans could live. All the hunters gathered and shared the flesh of the first animal killed. None of the meat was wasted. The bones of these animals were treated with respect. They were hung in trees or placed in rivers to prevent dogs from gnawing on them. If the bones were shown disrespect, the Micmac believed the souls of the animals would leave the region. Then the people would go hungry.

Autumn

In late summer the Micmac began to get ready for winter. They moved inland away from the harsh storms along the coast. Some of the men went ahead to scout a good location. It was always along a river or stream. The Micmac packed what they needed from the village and followed in canoes.

September was the month for feasts of eels. Eel was a favourite food of the Micmac. In the fall eels moved into the rivers to spawn. They were caught in huge numbers in traps or by spearing. The eels were roasted over the fire or stone-boiled in wooden kettles. They were also smoked and stored for the winter.

In the late fall and winter the Micmac went beaver hunting. Micmac hunters trapped the beaver by breaking open their dams and draining the ponds. The beaver were killed with bow and arrows as they tried to escape.

Hunting beaver when the ponds were frozen was more difficult. Dogs were used to sniff out the beavers' breathing holes in the ice. Hunters then chopped their way into the beaver lodges and reached in to grab the animals by the tail. Beaver caught this way were flipped out onto the ice and killed by a quick blow from a club. Any animals that escaped from the lodge to the breathing holes found other Micmac hunters waiting for them. They too were quickly killed with harpoons or arrows.

The Micmac considered beaver meat very good to eat. They also prized the beaver's thick warm pelt. The pelts could be fashioned into robes for the winter or made into blankets. The sharp teeth of the beaver were fastened onto sticks and made into tools for cutting and gouging.

A Micmac hunter. How do you know this hunter has traded with the Europeans?

Winter

As winter came on, the Micmac hunted seals and walrus on the coast. They caught a small ocean fish called tomcod in traps or by hook and line. Micmac hunters also turned their attention to land animals. They hunted with bows and arrows and lances, or trapped animals with snares. The Micmac also had their own breed of hunting dogs. They trained the dogs to track and chase game. A pack of dogs could hold large and dangerous animals such as moose and bear at bay. The dogs would circle the animal, but keep out of its range. The animal was held until the hunters arrived.

Micmac hunters knew other ways to lure game. They fashioned "moose calls" of birchbark to attract curious moose. When the animal came close enough, it could be brought down by bow and arrow. In deep snow, the Micmac hunters had an advantage. The heavy moose were slowed down by the snowdrifts while the Micmac skimmed quickly over the surface on snowshoes.

When the animal was brought down, the hunter marked the spot with branches. The women took the responsibility of cutting up and preparing the meat. The meat was roasted on sticks over the fire or stone-boiled in large wooden kettles. These kettles were made by burning and gouging out logs. They were very heavy so the Micmac left them at hunting sites throughout their territory. The kettles were there to be used again when the people returned.

Even the bones of the moose were used. They were pounded and boiled down until they became a white grease called moose butter. Moose butter was a handy, basic food for a long journey. It was easy to carry and very nourishing and tasty. The Micmac also kept storehouses at points throughout their territory. They left food there so that they did not have to carry as many supplies when they travelled. Storehouses were filled with smoked meat, fish, and eels, as well as dried berries and boxes of animal fat.

How did the Micmac travel in winter? In the deep snow of the woodlands, the Micmac travelled by snowshoe. The Native peoples of North America invented and designed the snowshoe.

The snowshoe is a curved wooden frame with a webbing of tightly stretched raw hide. Sometimes one or two wooden bars are fitted across the shoe to give it added strength. Snowshoes are different

A Micmac birchbark moose call.

Two Native designs for snowshoes. The top snowshoe, shaped like an animal's paw, was the one most commonly used by the Micmac and other groups of the Eastern Woodlands.

shapes. The Micmac snowshoe was circular like an animal's paw. It was especially useful in the soft deep snow of the Eastern Woodlands. Other Native peoples used snowshoes that were long and narrow with a turned-up toe. These were best on the hard icy snow of open areas.

The snowshoes were tied onto the foot and ankle with leather straps. The heel and toe were left free to move. The wide frame and webbing of the snowshoe helped to spread the person's weight over a larger area. Instead of sinking into the snow, the Micmac could skim over the surface. They carried some of their goods on their backs. The packstraps were slung around their foreheads. Head, neck, shoulders, and back all helped to carry the load. Both hands were free to pull a toboggan.

Toboggans were another invention of the Native peoples. They were made of wide flat planks split from a tree trunk. The toboggans curved up at one end where the branches curved out from the trunk of a tree. Heavy loads could be placed on toboggans and pulled easily across the ice and snow.

Growing Up Among the Micmac

Large families were a source of joy and pride to the Micmac. Children were welcomed into the family. The whole community was invited to a birth feast. Feasts and dances were held to celebrate other important events in the lives of the children such as the naming, the first tooth, the first steps, the first successful hunt, and marriage.

Micmac children were amused and educated by storytelling. Stories were usually told after a meal. Grandparents might tell a dramatic tale about their ancestors or about events in the history of the family. Storytelling was very popular among the Micmac. It was a way to preserve their history and beliefs.

Children began at an early age to learn the skills they would need as adults. Older family members taught them how to care for younger children, gather firewood and water, hunt and prepare game. They learned how to make weapons and tools for hunting, fishing, and preparing food.

When the time came for marriage, a boy usually looked for a bride. If he found a girl who was willing to marry him, he would ask her father for permission. Then the young man spent a year in **bride service**. He had to prove to the girl's family that he was a good hunter and a responsible adult. During this time he would live with the girl's family.

After the year the couple were married if the father approved of the young man's behaviour and the young woman still agreed. A wedding feast with game brought in by the young man was held. Wedding speeches were made. Then the couple decided where they would live. They could move to the groom's village, they could stay with the bride's parents, or they could set up a new household of their own.

Contact: The Micmac Meet the Europeans

The first Europeans the Micmac met were probably fishing crews from France, Portugal, or England. From the early 1500s the Micmac observed strange fishing vessels off their coasts. Occasionally the crews came ashore to get fresh water or to hunt for game. When they did, they most certainly met the Micmac and traded with them.

By the time Jacques Cartier sailed into the Bay of Chaleur in 1534, the Micmac were used to seeing Europeans. Cartier reported that a party of Micmac shouted to his ship. They waved beaver skins held up on sticks like flags. The Micmac were willing to trade. Over the next two hundred years, they became partners with the French in the fur trade.

But contact with the Europeans and the fur trade changed the Micmac way of life. They no longer had time to prepare a supply of food for the winter because they were trapping. Their summer hunting and gathering pattern was disrupted. This change in lifestyle drastically affected their winter diet. They came to rely more on dried foods they could get in trade. They ate less fish and shellfish and more dried vegetables and hardtack biscuits. These new foods were not as nourishing as their traditional diet. The health of the Micmac people began to suffer.

The Europeans also brought new diseases with them. Typhoid fever, small pox, and scarlet fever were diseases the Micmac had never suffered before. The sicknesses spread quickly among them. Sometimes so many were sick that there was no one to care for them. Micmac shamans had no cures for the new diseases. The people began to lose faith in the power of the shamans.

The Micmac also became involved in conflicts with the Europeans. Both the French and the English were trying to take ownership of Micmac territory. The Micmac believed the English were the greater immediate threat. They decided to become allies of the French and so attacked English vessels which entered Micmac territory. When the English began moving into Nova Scotia, the Micmac attempted to drive them out. In response, the English tried to poison the Micmac at a "feast" and offered rewards for Micmac scalps. Rather than continuing to fight, the Micmac migrated to the deep woods.

When the English took control of the Maritimes from the French in 1763, there was peace. But there were still problems to be faced. Large numbers of English settlers were pouring into the area. Settlers cleared the forest for farms. Animals such as moose and caribou were driven from the area or killed. The Micmac could no longer continue their old way of life. They were forced to wander over much wider areas to find food. Many died of starvation.

By 1850 the Micmac people had been reduced to about 3000 persons. Sickness, starvation, and warfare had done their worst. Many old ways of life had been lost.

The Micmac adapted as best they could. They tried to keep their communities together and hold on to their language and customs. In the early 1900s, some families camped by the railroad tracks and sold baskets and porcupine quillwork. Others found work in sawmills, on the railroads, in the lobster canneries, and in fish packing plants.

A Micmac chief and his family selling baskets in 1910.

Micmac Arts and Crafts

LEFT: A Micmac chief's coat, nineteenth century. These coats were made of wool and decorated with ribbons and beads.

A splint basket. These baskets were made of shaved wood strips woven into intricate patterns.

Quilled boxes. Dyed porcupine quills were sewn through birchbark to produce the decorative patterns.

The Micmac Today

Today over 15 000 Micmac live in the three Maritime provinces and in Gaspé, Quebec. Over 600 others live in Newfoundland. Many have also settled in the city of Boston in the United States.

Some Micmac live on **reserves**. Reserves are lands set aside for the Native peoples. On the reserves, the people still practise some of their old ways. They have kept some valued beliefs and customs. They are also adapting to a new life. Some councils on the reserves have set up their own businesses. Examples are an oyster farm at Eskasoni and a sawmill at Shubenacadie. Others earn their living fishing and lobster trapping.

However, unemployment continues to be a problem on many reserves. Some Micmac have gone to cities as far away as Boston looking for work. Others are workers in the "high steel" construction industry. While some have moved permanently to the cities, others often return to the reserves for a time.

Today Canadians recognize that the ancestors of the Micmac were the first peoples of the Maritimes. Like all Native peoples, they have faced a number of challenges, but they are adapting despite problems. They have kept their distinct culture despite tremendous odds.

The late Grand Chief Donald Marshall Sr. who was the spiritual leader of the Micmac nation from 1964 to 1991.

Activities

Looking Back

1. Add each of the following words to your dictionary.

   wigwam   weir   shaman
   sagamore   bride service
   extended family   reserve

2. Where did the Micmac live? Describe their territory in two or three sentences or with a neat sketch map.

3. What foods did the Micmac eat? Describe how some of the foods were prepared. Include sketches.

4. Describe forms of transportation used by the Micmac.

5. List the materials the Micmac used to construct a wigwam.
   a) Where did the Micmac get the materials?
   b) How did the Micmac protect the wigwams against the weather?
   c) How was the wigwam especially suited to the Micmac way of life?

6. What was the role of the shaman in Micmac society? What powers did the people believe the shaman had?

Using Your Knowledge

7. How did the Micmac use the resources of their natural environment to obtain food, build homes, and secure transportation?

8. Imagine you are a Micmac boy or girl in the days before the arrival of the Europeans. Which Micmac ways would you enjoy most and why? What could the Micmac teach you?

Extending Your Thinking

9. Find out more about the Micmac today. How have they adapted to a new way of life? What problems do they face? Check newspaper files and books in your library for information. Listen to the news reports.

10. What do you know about the Native groups who live or have lived in your region of Canada? What else would you like to know about them? Where could you find answers to your questions? Divide the class into groups and do further research on the Native peoples of your region. Present a report to the class.

CHAPTER 9

The Blackfoot of the Plains

When young Native people reached adolescence, it was the custom for them to search for a spiritual helper. They found their helper through a dream or vision. But this was not an ordinary dream. Young people left camp for several days. They went out onto the prairie alone, taking no food or water. They tried to fill their minds with spiritual thoughts. They prayed and fasted and then slept. As they slept, a vision might appear. The vision was usually in the form of an animal. It would tell the young person how to use the spiritual power. The spirit-helper would protect and guard the young person throughout life.

Boys usually went out onto the prairie to search for their spiritual helper. The Blackfoot believed that girls already possessed many natural spiritual powers. But girls also sought and received special visions. Spiritual helpers gave them powers to use throughout their lives. The powers might include how to cure sickness or how to perform a ritual or song.

The boy walked by himself for several hours. Then he rested under a bush by a dried-up river bed. He was very hungry now, but he knew he must not eat. He must pray and wait for his vision. That night he slept out on the prairie alone. He slept but no vision came. For three more days he waited. He was growing weak from lack of food. The fourth night, the vision came.

The boy was tossing and turning in his sleep. In his dream he saw a coyote slinking across the prairie toward him. Its teeth were bared and its mouth was foaming. As the coyote came closer it made no attempt to bite him. Then suddenly it disappeared. A moment later, the coyote was coming toward him from another direction. Again, it was grinning at him with bared teeth. Three times the coyote appeared, but it did not hurt him. When he awoke, the boy realized that the coyote was offering him his power.

Now it was time to make a medicine bundle. The sacred medicine bundle would contain items that were reminders of the vision. The boy put bits of fur, bone, an arrowhead, eagle feathers, and some sweetgrass for incense into the bundle. These were things that he had picked up on the prairie while seeking his vision. In the future, every time he unwrapped the medicine bundle he would perform a ceremony. As each article was removed he would say the prayers or sing songs the coyote had taught him. He had received his vision. He was ready to be a hunter and a warrior.

–Adapted from Blackfoot legends

Who Were the Blackfoot?

Who were the Blackfoot people? They were the great buffalo hunters of the prairie. They called themselves "blackfoot" or "black moccasins." This name may refer to the fact that their moccasins were often covered with the black dust left from frequent prairie grass fires.

The territory of the Blackfoot stretched from the foothills of the Rockies to the present Alberta-Saskatchewan border and from the Battle River in the north to the Upper Missouri River in the south. The Blackfoot hunting area covered most of southern Alberta and northern Montana.

The Blackfoot were a nomadic people. This means they moved from place to place. The Blackfoot followed the great buffalo herds across the prairie. Buffalo were their main source of food.

The Blackfoot Village

The Blackfoot moved their villages depending on the locations of buffalo herds and the conditions of the seasons. The "moving van" of the prairie peoples was a wonderfully simple invention. It was called a **travois**. The Blackfoot made the travois by tying two poles together. Then they stretched a webbing between the poles. A family could load all the household goods onto these "moving vans."

In the early days the travois were dragged by dogs. Later North American

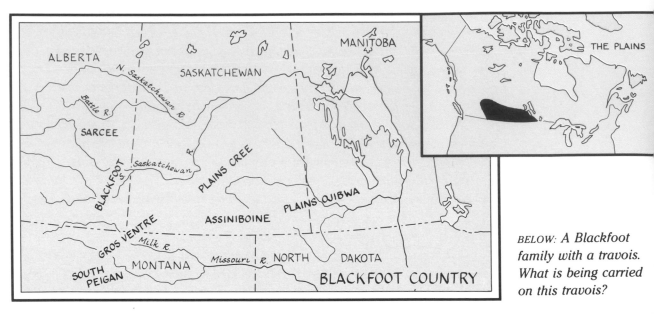

BLACKFOOT COUNTRY

THE PLAINS

BELOW: A Blackfoot family with a travois. What is being carried on this travois?

Native peoples obtained horses from trade with the Spanish in Mexico. The Blackfoot traded for horses with other Native groups or captured them in raids. Many quickly became expert riders and used horses to pull the travois. When it came time to move to a new campsite, the travois was hitched to the horse's back. Young children, the elderly, and all the family's possessions could be pulled along on the travois!

The Blackfoot Tipi

The Blackfoot home was a **tipi**. The tipi was specially suited to the Blackfoot's nomadic way of life. It was simple to put up and take down. It was also light and easy to transport.

A tipi of a young chief. Notice the symbols painted on the outside.

BELOW: A Blackfoot camp on the Plains, 1921.

The tipi was made from buffalo hides and long wooden poles. A group of women often worked together to set up the tipis. The work took special skills and knowledge. The Blackfoot made the framework with ten to twenty poles placed upright and tied together at the top. The poles were anchored with a length of rawhide that was pegged to the ground. The finished framework looked like the ribs of a huge umbrella that was partly closed.

To make the covering, the women stitched together fifteen or more buffalo hides. Then they cut the stitched hides in the form of a large half-circle. The circular covering fitted neatly around the pole framework. The women stitched the covering together at the front with wooden pins and attached a door flap. They placed pegs around the bottom of the tipi to hold it secure.

Smoke flaps were also sewn onto the hide covering. The women attached light poles to the flaps. The flaps could then be easily moved from side to side. They could be adjusted so that smoke from the fire would not be blown back into the tipi.

Winters on the plains were bitterly cold. It may be hard to imagine how the people could keep warm inside the tipis. But the tipi was carefully designed to keep out the cold. Door flaps were kept small and low. Sometimes a lining of buffalo hides was spread over the floor and stretched up the walls of the tipi. This inside lining kept out dampness and prevented drafts from blowing in under the edges of the tipi.

Inside the tipi the people sat around the central fire. They leaned against back-rests made of willow twigs laced together. At night, they slept on furs or buffalo robes.

The Blackfoot painted symbols on their tipis. In a vision or dream, the owner of the tipi was told what animal, bird, or other symbol should be painted on the buffalo hides. The paints were made from natural colours. Black paint was made from powdered charcoal. Red paint was made from a clay called red ochre. Yellow paint might also be made from clay or from buffalo gallstones. Green paint came from algae. The paint was applied thickly and rubbed into the hides with the tips of buffalo bones.

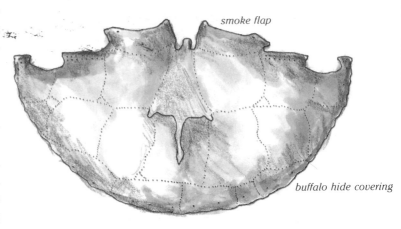

smoke flap

buffalo hide covering

Pitching a tipi. The sewn buffalo hide covering was wrapped around a framework of several poles and then sewn together at the front with wooden pins.

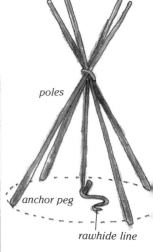

poles

anchor peg

rawhide line

A Blackfoot chief in traditional dress.

smoke flap pole

smoke flap open

smoke flap

loop pi

pegs

door flap

Blackfoot Society

The basic social group of the Blackfoot was the **clan**. The clan was a group of related families that lived and hunted together most of the year.

Several clans formed a **band**. Each band had a head chief and minor chiefs. The head chief was respected for wisdom or skill in hunting. The chief led the people by example and persuasion, not by force or by giving orders. Decisions were made by general agreement. A band also had a war chief. The war chief looked after both war matters and defence. Many bands, grouped together, formed a **tribe**.

In the summer the bands came together for a large tribal gathering. The Blackfoot people gathered for a tribal buffalo hunt. But more important, they gathered for a religious celebration. This ceremony was called the Sun Dance. You will read more about the Sun Dance later in this chapter.

Four tribes made up the Blackfoot nation or **Confederacy**. They were the Blackfoot, Blood, Peigan, and South Peigan. These four tribes spoke the same language: Siksika. They came together as allies in times of war with other peoples such as the Cree.

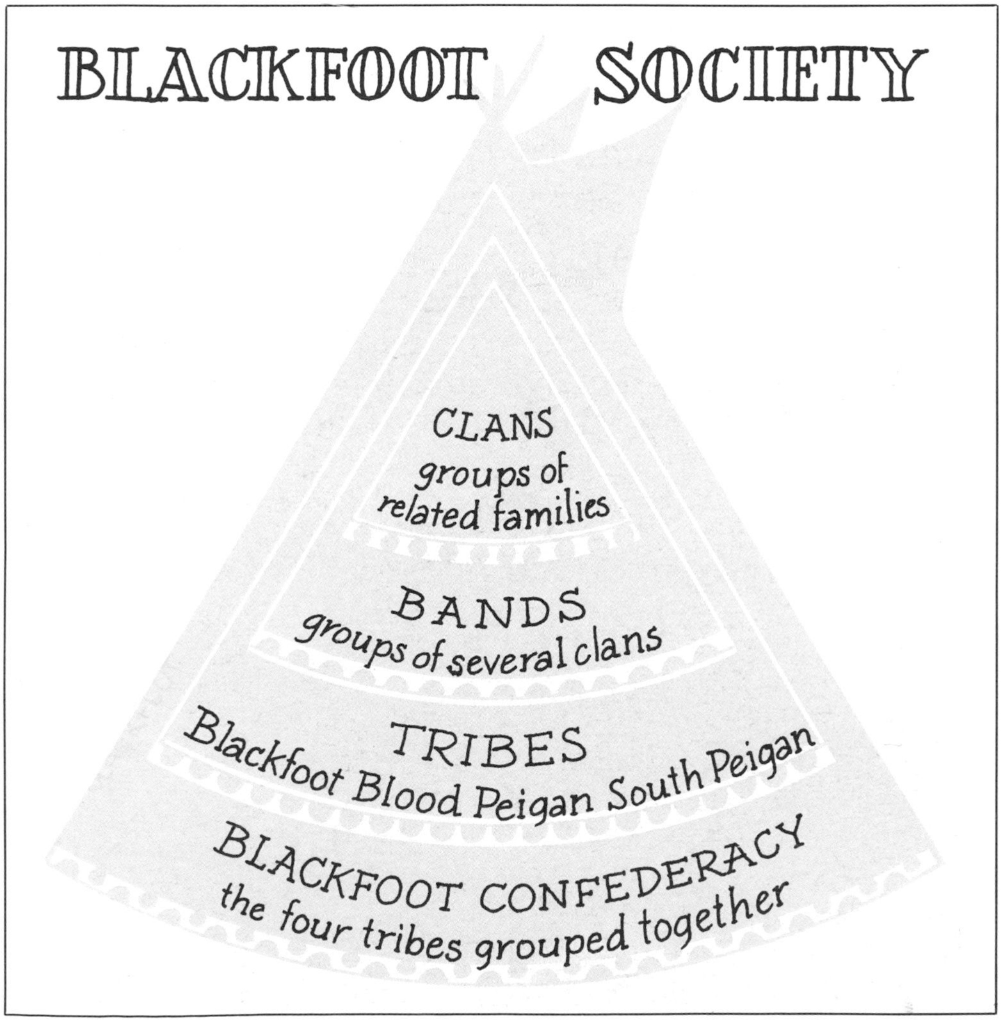

BLACKFOOT SOCIETY

CLANS
groups of related families

BANDS
groups of several clans

TRIBES
Blackfoot Blood Peigan South Peigan

BLACKFOOT CONFEDERACY
the four tribes grouped together

Everyday Life Among the Blackfoot

The Native peoples of the Plains were always on the move. They travelled across the prairie to hunt and trade. They hunted chiefly one animal, the buffalo, although they also hunted deer, antelope, and bears. Buffalo supplied them with food, clothing, shelter, and many of their daily needs.

Spring

At the first sign of spring, the hunters scouted for buffalo. If they were lucky they would sight a small herd grazing on the first green grass of the season. Then the whole camp swung into action. Everyone–men, women, and children–took part. Dogs were also used in the hunt. The idea was to surround the buffalo herd and gradually close in. Hunters tried to get as close to the animals as possible. Often they crawled forward on their hands and knees hidden under a wolf skin. Buffalo were not frightened by the wolves and allowed them to come close. At a given signal, men, women, children, and dogs would rush toward the herd from all directions. There would be a horrible noise of whooping and barking. For a moment the herd would be stunned. Then the buffalo would rush off in a panic.

The hunters had only a few seconds to aim their arrows. A well-placed arrow behind the front shoulder could pierce the buffalo's heart. The giant would fall bleeding to the ground. Wounded animals would run away across the prairie, but many would soon collapse.

After the hunt, the people would join in a great feast of fresh roasted buffalo meat.

The buffalo hunt. Hunters had to have great skill to ride after the buffalo and kill them with a well-placed arrow through the heart.

Winter was over. Soon the major herds would return from the south. There would be waterfowl and their eggs to eat. Berries and wild fruit would be plentiful. Summer was coming.

Summer

In June, the Blackfoot began to gather in huge camps. Hundreds of tipis were pitched in huge circles on the plain. Smoke from all the campfires would help to keep away those summer pests—mosquitoes.

As people from many bands came together, it was an occasion for celebration and feasting. It was a chance to hunt together. It was an opportunity for young people to meet new friends. Marriages, previously arranged by families, took place at this time. It was a time for games, singing, religious ceremonies, and dancing.

THE SUN DANCE

*The most important summer ceremony was the **Sun Dance**. In the Sun Dance, the people gave thanks to the Great Spirit. The Great Spirit caused the sun to shine and the grass to grow. The Great Spirit brought the vast herds of buffalo back to the prairies each year to feed on the grass. The Great Spirit helped the Blackfoot to hunt the buffalo so that they would have plenty to eat during the coming winter. The Great Spirit looked after the Blackfoot people. In this dance they offered their thanks.*

Sometimes a respected woman sponsored the Sun Dance. It was a way to fulfill a promise to the Great Spirit. She could give special thanks for help in a time of need, such as when sickness might have threatened her family.

The Sun Dance was held in a lodge built of cottonwood poles. Putting up the lodge was an important ceremony. Many people took part. After saying a solemn prayer the people put up a tall pole in the centre of the lodge. Near the top of the sacred pole, where it forked into a "V", they tied a bundle of branches and sage grass. This bundle represented an eagle's nest. On one wall of the lodge, the Blackfoot hung the skull of a buffalo. It was to remind them of how the Great Spirit looked after them by providing the buffalo.

At the Sun Dance some people watched while others danced. Those who danced gazed at the top of the sacred pole. They took no food and no water while the dance continued. It might last for two or more days. Often they danced until they dropped. The dance was intended as a personal sacrifice. It was a way to fulfill a promise to the spirits for their help. It was a way of seeking the guidance of the spirits through a vision.

Some dancers thought it was important to endure great physical pain to have a vision. Sometimes young men had slits cut into their chests and backs. Skewers were pushed into these slits. The skewers were fastened by cords to the top of the sacred pole. The men danced around the pole, gazing at it and blowing an eagle-bone whistle. As the men danced, the skewers pulled at their flesh and caused great pain. At the end of the dance, the dancers had to try to break free of the skewers. If they could pull them out and not faint, they had successfully completed the Sun Dance. They had proven their courage and bravery. They brought honour to themselves for the rest of their lives.

In 1885 the federal government of Canada outlawed the Sun Dance. Government officials said the dance inflicted unnecessary torture on the people who performed it. But for the Blackfoot, the Sun Dance was an important ceremony. It expressed their values and spiritual beliefs.

A modern celebration of the Sun Dance. Raising the sacred pole is one of the most important parts of the ceremony.

The most exciting buffalo hunt took place in the summer. A large number of Blackfoot people were camped together in one place. Everyone could work together in the hunt.

On the prairies there were deep valleys edged with sheer cliffs. Here the Blackfoot hunted buffalo by stampeding whole herds over the cliffs. These places were known as **buffalo jumps**. Head-Smashed-In buffalo jump is one of the most famous today.

The hunt required timing, courage, skill, and co-operation. The herd had to be lured toward the jump. This was the job of a hunter of much experience and spiritual power. Sometimes the buffalo were drawn quietly toward the cliff by a hunter dressed in buffalo robes. The hunter would use a bell to capture the animals' attention and gradually get them galloping toward the jump. Then women and children posted along the route would shout and wave buffalo robes.

An illustration of buffalo stampeding over the cliffs at Head-Smashed-In Buffalo Jump.

They kept the animals going in the right direction.

The herds would begin to stampede. Faster and faster they thundered in panic toward the jump. As they reached the cliffs they were terror-stricken and helpless. The stampeding animals plunged to their deaths. Those that were not killed in the fall were dazed and wounded. At the bottom of the cliff hunters moved in quickly with knives and spears. Soon these giants of the plains lay still on the ground.

The Blackfoot women and girls then had special work to do. They set out to butcher the buffalo. Almost every part of the animal was used. Little was wasted. They cooked the heart, kidneys, tongue, and hump. These were considered great delicacies. They stripped the hides from the bodies and cut up the meat. They needed sharp knives to cut the meat and stone choppers to shatter the bone. Bones were split so that the sweet marrow inside could be sucked out. The stomach of the buffalo was removed to be made into a cooking pot. It was suspended by short sticks over the fire and partially filled with water. Hot stones were dropped into the water to bring it to a boil. Then food could be cooked. The women and girls worked quickly, otherwise the buffalo meat would begin to spoil. In the evening, they joined in a great feast.

Autumn

All through the fall the preparation continued for winter. Berries grew on the open prairie. Raspberries, strawberries, and choke cherries were picked and dried for the winter.

The people dried buffalo meat by cutting it in strips and smoking it over the fire. They also prepared **pemmican**.

Pemmican was made of buffalo meat pounded into fine shreds between stones. The meat was mixed with melted buffalo fat and pounded choke cherries. The Blackfoot packed the pemmican into hide pouches. In these bags, it would keep indefinitely. Pemmican was ideal for long journeys. Not only was it light and easy to carry, but it was also nutritious and satisfying to eat.

Autumn was the time for curing and tanning hides for leather. Women scraped the hides again and again until no flesh was left on them. Then the hides were washed, cured, and stretched. They could be stitched together to make coverings for the tipis. Some were also used to make summer clothing and shields.

Winter

Most of the large buffalo herds left the cold northern prairies in the winter. They migrated far to the south. But a few small herds usually stayed behind in sheltered valleys or in the foothills of the Rocky Mountains. The Blackfoot also moved to take shelter for the winter. Their large camps of several hundred people broke up into smaller family groups of thirty to sixty people. The groups moved to the sheltered river valleys or to the edge of the prairies. There winter winds were not so strong and cold.

The Blackfoot had warm clothes for the winter months. They wore leggings, shirts, and moccasins of soft deer or elk hide. Some of the women wore long dresses of deerskin. They had heavy buffalo robes to wrap around their shoulders and to sleep under at night.

Strips of dried buffalo meat made up most of their meals in the winter. They also had some dried berries mixed with animal fat. By springtime, the people

might be quite thin. During very long, harsh winters food supplies could run low.

Growing Up Among the Blackfoot

Blackfoot babies were given a personal name by their mothers when they were born. Children kept these names until they became adults. Then they were given new names. An older member of the family would often declare the right to decide the adult name for the child.

Names were valued among the Blackfoot. A Blackfoot would not usually tell anyone his or her name. Someone nearby would be asked to give the information. It was believed that giving away your name was like giving away a part of yourself. When a Blackfoot died, the family

Blackfoot women and child, early 1900s.

reserved the name. Later it might be given to another family member. Sometimes special names were reserved for a long time until someone performed a great deed to earn it.

Children were usually taught by older members of the family. They learned the legends that told of their history and the ways of their people. They learned of the Great Spirit who helped them and brought the buffalo and all other animals. They were also taught the skills needed for adult life. They learned how to collect firewood and water, look after young children, use a bow and arrow, round up horses, follow game trails, and become good riders.

Young children played familiar games such as hide and seek. A particular favourite in winter was a spinning top game. The children whipped rocks across ice to make them spin. The object was to knock an opposing player's rocks out of a circle. Snow snakes made from wood were also popular. If a snake was properly hurled, it could slide for hundreds of metres across the crust of snow. Children also amused themselves with archery contests, races, and sliding down hills in the winter on sleds made from the ribs of buffalo!

The adolescent years were a time of mystery. Both boys and girls spent time alone in the wilderness fasting and seeking their spiritual visions. Marriages were arranged. They might be arranged between the father of the bride and the future groom or between the fathers of the young couple. If an agreement was reached gifts were exchanged. The young man might offer a gift of horses or furs. The young woman's family would often offer a tipi and furnishings. After marriage, the couple lived in the young man's camp.

Contact: The Blackfoot Meet the Europeans

The Blackfoot met European explorers in the mid-1700s. But even before they met Europeans, they had felt the European influence. Horses and guns had been brought to North America by the Europeans. By 1725, the Blackfoot had both. They had obtained them through trade with other Native groups.

With horses and guns the Blackfoot could hunt the buffalo more efficiently. The horses could run alongside the buffalo over the uneven ground of the prairie. Many Blackfoot became expert riders.

The fur trade with Europeans was not as important to the Blackfoot as it was to many other Native groups. There were few fur-bearing animals on the Plains. The Blackfoot traded mostly buffalo robes and dried meat.

Settlement of the west had the greatest impact on the Plains peoples. In the late 1700s settlers began moving onto the prairies. They came in increasing numbers each year. The settlers killed the buffalo by the thousands. Many killed the animals for sport. They destroyed whole herds. Sadly, by the 1870s, the buffalo were almost gone. An important part of the Blackfoot's livelihood was destroyed. The nomadic hunting life of the Blackfoot was ending.

The Native peoples also suffered from European diseases they had never experienced before. Smallpox and other illnesses swept through the villages. In 1781, a plague killed half of the Blackfoot population. Similar outbreaks killed many others later.

The Canadian government was urging all the Native groups of the Plains to sign treaties. A **treaty** is an agreement between two parties or nations. The treaties asked the Native peoples to surrender their land to the Canadian government. In exchange, the Native peoples would be paid with money or goods. They would agree to move onto **reserves**. Reserves were small pieces of land set aside for the Native peoples. Other people could not settle, hunt, or fish in these areas.

Crowfoot, a great chief, became leader of his people about this time. He believed that it was time for his people to sign a treaty with the Canadian government. Many Blackfoot were starving. In 1877 the Blackfoot signed Treaty Number 7 and took a reserve east of Calgary. Their nomadic way of life was over.

It was not easy for the Blackfoot to take up a new way of life. They were hunters. They were not experienced in farming. The food, help, and medicine that the government had promised did not always arrive. Many were discouraged and felt they had been cheated by the government. The Native people were confused and angered by the treatment they received. For many, the years that followed were full of pain, suffering, and poverty. The people had to adapt to a new way of life. At the same time, they have tried to keep their most valued ways and beliefs.

Blackfoot Arts and Crafts

LEFT: "Snake Horn" headdress, worn by a member of the Snake society. Each Blackfoot society had a particular headdress. The horn is a buffalo horn.

BELOW: A woman's saddle decorated with beadwork.

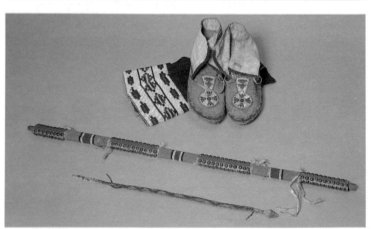

ABOVE: Moccasins, women's leggings, a pipe stem, and a beaded snake. The beaded snake was a charm used to protect the wearer against evil spirits.

LEFT: Painted symbols on a tipi. These symbols had spiritual meaning for the people who lived in the tipi and were an important form of Blackfoot art.

A modern Ghost Dance ceremony. This ceremony, which originated in the 1860s when the buffalo were disappearing from the Plains and the lives of the Blackfoot were threatened, calls on the spirits to protect the people.

The Blackfoot Today

Today many Blackfoot are cattle ranchers and farmers. On some reserves, the people have worked to develop industries and businesses. These provide jobs. For example, the Blood tribe operate a successful factory for pre-fabricated houses.

Unemployment, however, is still a problem on many reserves. Many Native people have left the reserves and moved to the cities. They are looking for new opportunities and new ways to earn a living. Regina and Winnipeg have large Native populations.

The Canadian Blackfoot today number about 12 500. They still practise many of their old ways. On the reserves, many celebrate the Sun Dance and other important ceremonies. They are forming groups to look after their own affairs and to preserve their culture.

Activities

Looking Back

1. Define the following words and enter them in your dictionary.

travois	confederacy
tipi	Sun Dance
clan	buffalo jump
band	pemmican
tribe	reserve
	treaty

2. **a)** List the materials used to build a tipi.
   b) Describe how the framework was made.
   c) How was the tipi made comfortable for the winter?
   d) Describe how the tipi was sometimes decorated.
   e) Explain how the tipi was specially suited to a nomadic lifestyle.

3. In your own words, describe the methods the Blackfoot used to hunt buffalo. What skills were needed? How did the whole community work together?

Using Your Knowledge

4. Read the following statements. In your notebook, write an "F" beside the facts and an "O" beside the opinions.
   a) The Blackfoot were a nomadic people.
   b) The Canadian government should not have outlawed the Sun Dance.
   c) One method the Blackfoot used to hunt buffalo was to herd them over cliffs.
   d) People who performed the Sun Dance endured unnecessary torture.
   e) The Blackfoot should not have signed Treaty Number 7.

5. How did the horse change the way the Blackfoot hunted the buffalo? Think of something that has changed your life as much as the horse changed the way of life of the Native peoples of the Plains.

6. Compare Blackfoot arts and crafts with those of another Native group you have studied. Look at the materials used. Ask yourself how the people used the arts and crafts. What purposes did they have? Use an organizer to record your findings.

7. How were young people in Blackfoot society educated? Who assumed the responsibility for their education? Compare the ways the Blackfoot were educated with the ways you are educated today. How are the methods different? How are they similar?

Extending Your Thinking

8. Create a mural of a Blackfoot buffalo hunt.

9. Discuss why the Sun Dance was so important to the Blackfoot. Do you think the Canadian government was justified in outlawing the Sun Dance in 1885? Why or why not?

10. The Native peoples of the Plains had lived by hunting buffalo for generations. Moving to reserves meant they would have to begin practising farming. Do further research to find out how this change would affect the peoples':

   a) diet
   b) clothing
   c) houses
   d) daily habits.

   Present your findings to the class.

CHAPTER 10

The Haida of the Pacific West Coast

Emily Carr's painting of Tanu village, Queen Charlotte Islands, 1913.

The cedar canoe glided through the water. It was paddled by two Haida. Their only passengers were the Canadian painter Emily Carr and her dog, Billie.

Emily was on a painting expedition along the wilderness coast of British Columbia. She wanted to sketch and paint as many of the magnificent Native totem poles as she could find. It was 1912. Many Native villages were already deserted. The totem poles were beginning to rot. Soon the silent forest would swallow them up.

The Haida helped Emily to set up her campsite near the deserted village of Tanu. Then they left her to paint. Around the point from the bay stood three tall totem poles. They were still standing straight and were bright in colour. Emily caught her breath at their beauty. Each pole stood in front of a cedar plank house. But the people were gone. Many had died of smallpox. Others had moved away to live in towns and cities. The forest was still. Vines, moss, and underbrush grew up around the houses and the totem poles.

Emily sat on a log and gazed for a long time at the Haida village. Finally, she picked up her brush and started to paint. The old totem poles seemed to be talking to her. They spoke of the proud people who had carved them so lovingly. They told of the families who had lived around the fires inside the cedar plank houses. Now the totems seemed sad and alone. The people had gone.

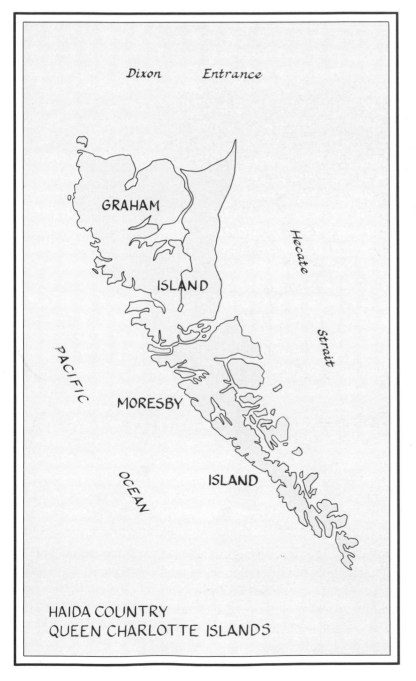

HAIDA COUNTRY
QUEEN CHARLOTTE ISLANDS

Who Were the Haida?

Who were the people who had once lived in Tanu? They were the Haida. In their language, "Haida" meant "the people." They lived on the Queen Charlotte Islands off the coast of northern British Columbia. Most Haida villages were located on the eastern side of the islands. They were built in small bays or sheltered inlets. There they were protected from the more violent winds and storms from the Pacific Ocean.

The Haida Village

The Haida stayed in one location almost year round. They did not need to travel far to find food or materials for their homes. The nearby ocean and rivers provided an abundant source of fish and other sea animals. In the forests around them, they found wood for their houses and materials for many daily needs.

The Haida preferred to build their villages right on the seashore. They travelled almost everywhere by canoe. They would draw their boats up on the sandy beach in front of their homes.

The approach to the village was always from the sea. Emily Carr could imagine the magnificent sight. Paddling in to Tanu village you would first see the huge totem poles in front of several cedar plank houses. Then you would notice the houses themselves. Each one was large enough for at least ten families.

The Haida Plank House

The Haida built sturdy homes from cedar posts and planks. Cedar trees grew abundantly in the forests. The wood is good for building because it is light and easy to work. The cedar tree also contains natu-

ral oils which help to preserve the wood from decay. Even in the damp climate of the Queen Charlotte Islands, cedar posts and planks would last for a long time.

Splitting the trees into planks took skill. Sometimes the Haida toppled the tree. They used stone axes to make a large notch in one side of the trunk. Next, they hammered wedges of bone into the opposite side until the tree fell. From the fallen cedar they made the long planks. They drove wedges into the tree along the length of the grain. The grain of the cedar is so straight that eventually the logs would split evenly into planks. Sometimes the tree was not cut down. The planks were stripped from a living tree. The Haida took planks as they needed them and the tree continued to grow.

The builders used the planks to cover the framework of their houses. Haida houses were almost square in shape and usually 15 to 18 m long. The framework was made of huge logs sunk deep into the ground. Large planks were placed upright to make the walls. The planks were fitted into slots in the supporting

framework. The roof was usually peaked with gently sloping sides. Sometimes the Haida placed large stones on the roof to hold the planks secure during a storm.

The framework of the house was meant to last for generations. But the planks of the walls and roof could be

Taking planks from a living tree. The Natives first hammered wedges into the cedar tree and then used ropes to split off planks.

LEFT: The Haida village of Skidegate in 1878. What common characteristics of Haida villages can you see in this photograph?

Interior of a plank house, from a painting by Emily Carr.

removed easily. Sometimes the people in the house decided to move temporarily to better fishing grounds. They simply removed the planks and carried them along with them.

In the roof of each house there was an opening for smoke from the fireplaces to escape. A flap over the doorway kept out the rain.

Several related families lived in each house. Woven hangings of cedar or storage boxes marked off each family's space. A raised platform ran along the inside of the walls. This platform was the sleeping area. Each family had its own sleeping area and shared a fire for cooking and warmth. People squatted around the fire or sat or lay on the platforms to keep below the level of the smoke. The inside of the house was often decorated as well. Posts were carved and painted

with animal images. The Haida also painted the sleeping platform all around the room.

The Haida once invited Emily Carr to live for a while in one of their villages. The large cedar house had an earth floor. It was full of smoke which made Emily's eyes water. Around the house dried salmon hung on racks. A baby swung in a cradle hung low from the rafters. Everyone who passed by gave the cradle a push and the happy baby gurgled and cooed. On both sides of the door stood a huge thunderbird totem with wings spread wide. To Emily, it seemed as if the great bird was protecting all the people in the house under its great wings. Emily was given a fire and a place on the sleeping bench. She lived with the Haida in their comfortable plank house for some time.

HAIDA TOTEM POLES

The Haida, like the other Native peoples of the Pacific West Coast, were famous for carving tall totem poles. These poles were fashioned from the trunks of cedar trees. They might be anywhere from 3 to 21 m tall. A tall pole rose over the entrance to each Haida home. The doorway was often the mouth of a figure at the base of the pole. Sometimes the interior poles, the outside corner posts, and even the roof beams were carved too. The peoples of the Pacific West Coast were skilled woodworkers and carved beautiful and elaborate designs.

The totem poles were carved with the figures of animals, humans, and supernatural figures. Each totem pole told the story of the family living in that house. Every figure on the pole had a face. Often the eyes and eyebrows were painted black. Nostrils and lips were red. Green, brown, yellow, and white were used as well.

Most of the old totem poles still standing or found in museums were made after 1800. Earlier poles have rotted away in the rainforests of the Pacific West Coast.

Haida Society

An individual Haida family never lived alone. A Haida **house** included parents, children, cousins, aunts, uncles, grandparents, and other relatives. The family living in a plank house could trace its roots to a common ancestor. If the family was too large, the people built another plank house or several small homes. Each village held several family houses.

Family members sometimes moved away from their villages. They might search for new fishing grounds or go to marry someone from another village. Groups larger than the family were formed. These units were called **clans**. The clans were groups of two or more houses from several villages. The Haida had two clans. They were called the Ravens and the Eagles.

Among the Haida and their neighbours the Tsimshian and the Tlinkit, there was another group even larger than the clan. This group was called a **phratry**. People of one phratry claimed descent from one common ancestor. The phratries of the Haida and the Tlinkit were called the Eagles and the Ravens. They had the same names as the clans. The Tsimshian had another phratry called the Wolf. People who belonged to the same phratry could not marry one another but they felt close. If Haida Ravens went to a Tlinkit village, they would expect a Tlinkit Raven to give them shelter and protect them. They would do the same if the Tlinkit Raven were to visit their village.

The Haida also took rank and privilege very seriously. There were three classes in Haida society–nobles, commoners, and slaves. The **nobles** were the most important. They could trace their ancestry to the founder of the house. Their wealth and privileges were inherited. They might have rights to a fish weir or a strip of hunting territory for example. The **commoners** made up the largest number of people in the villages. They had not inherited any titles or wealth. The **slaves** who lived in the villages were captives from wars. They were well treated but they had no rights.

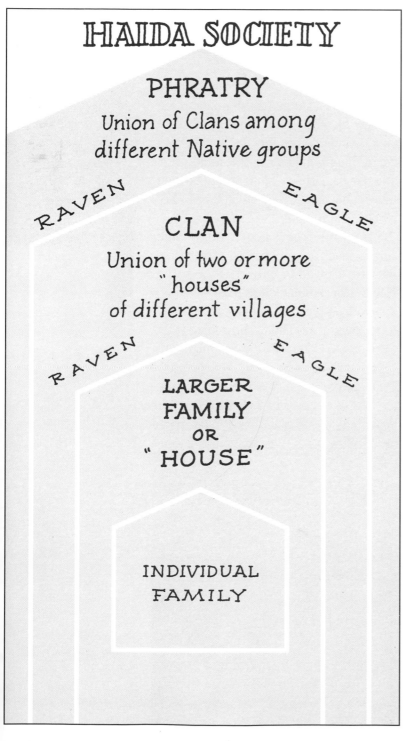

HAIDA SOCIETY

PHRATRY
Union of Clans among different Native groups

RAVEN   EAGLE

CLAN
Union of two or more "houses" of different villages

RAVEN   EAGLE

LARGER FAMILY OR "HOUSE"

INDIVIDUAL FAMILY

Everyday Life Among the Haida

Spring

Spring was a time for hunting sea lions, seals, and sea otters. The Haida were skillful canoeists. Their huge and graceful dugout canoes carried them up and down the coast. Some canoes were 18 m long. They could carry fifty or sixty passengers and two tonnes of cargo. There were also smaller vessels for hunting and short trips.

In March the Haida set off in sometimes stormy seas to hunt the sea lions. These animals often came ashore to bask in the sun on the rocks. Haida hunters would creep up on the sea lions and kill them quickly with clubs. The clubs were fashioned from very hard wood. They were elaborately carved with animal or supernatural figures such as a bear head or the eyes of a raven or whale. The Native peoples believed that the spirits provided animals as a gift. The animals allowed themselves to be caught for the benefit of human beings. Men and women were expected to treat the slain animals with respect. If they thanked the animal for giving up its life, other animals would come year after year. The head of the first sea lion killed was carried with great ceremony to the chief. A feast was held to give thanks and mark the beginning of the hunt.

A few weeks later it was time for the seal hunt. Thousands of seals passed the Queen Charlotte Islands on their annual migration north. The Haida hunted seals with clubs, bows and arrows, and light harpoons. A harpoon is a spear with an attached rope.

Sea lions and seals were sometimes eaten. More often they were boiled down for the oil in their bodies. Most food the Haida ate was dipped in some kind of oil as it was being eaten. The furs were also highly prized and were traded to other Native groups.

The Haida were famous as hunters of the sea otter. To catch the otters four hunters might set out in two light canoes. Sometimes they discovered an otter sleeping on the surface of the sea. They would harpoon it and drag it into their canoe. The sea otter would fight savagely with its razor sharp teeth and claws. Sometimes hunters were seriously wounded before the animal could be killed.

More often the sea otter would hear the hunters as the canoes approached. It would dive under the water. The two canoes would chase the otter. The hunters knew the animal had to surface for air. They tried to guess where it would appear. When it surfaced they would shoot it with their bows and arrows. Sea otter skins were highly prized. They were one of the most important trade items among the Pacific Coast peoples.

Summer

In summer, the Haida fished for salmon, their most important food. The Haida were known as "the Fish Eaters" to Native groups as far away as the prairies.

Millions of salmon ran up the coastal rivers to spawn in the summer months. The Haida then left their villages. With their families they moved closer to the best fishing grounds. They simply took some of the planks from their houses. At the fishing sites they had permanent log frameworks. The Haida could quickly put up a summer home. The planks were also handy during the trip to the fishing site. The Haida lashed the planks between two large canoes. They created a kind of freight boat to carry their supplies.

Before the fishing began, there were ceremonies to be observed. The spirits must be thanked for providing food. The Haida believed that the salmon swam up the rivers so that the people would have food. It was important to show respect for the salmon. Otherwise the fish might not return the following year. The first fish caught were eaten, but the bones were

Launching a Haida canoe, carved by artist Bill Reid, at Skidegate. The Haida used canoes like this one for their fishing expeditions.

returned to the river. The Haida took care that no bones were missing. Then the salmon could be reborn. When the ceremony was over, the fishing began.

In summer the salmon were plentiful in the rivers. It was possible to stand in the clear shallow water and spear the fish. The Haida also used wooden traps. The traps were like cages. They were cleverly designed. The Haida placed bait in the traps. Once the fish swam into the traps, they could not get out easily.

To catch large numbers of fish, the Haida built **weirs**. A Haida weir was like a fence built across a narrow river. Sometimes there was a catwalk along the top of the weir. The weir was made of twigs and poles woven through a log framework. It slowed the salmon's progress as they struggled upstream. The Haida could then direct the fish into traps using poles. They could also spear the fish or catch them in nets. The weir was a very efficient way of catching large numbers of fish. During a good salmon run, the Haida could catch enough fish to feed the village for the winter months.

The Haida spent most of the summer at these villages on the rivers. They often prepared the fish right on the shores. Fresh fish were barbecued or boiled. Fish heads were used to make soup. The fish were also cleaned and preserved for the winter. The Haida sometimes laid the fish on racks to dry in the sun. They had to keep the fish out of reach of the dogs. Most often they stretched the fish on twigs and hung them above smouldering fires. The most common sight around the summer villages was fish being smoked over fires along the river banks. Dried and smoked salmon kept for long periods. They would last through the winter.

The sea also provided plants and other foods. The people gathered octopuses, clams, and crabs. They carried them to

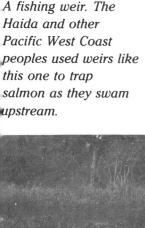

A fishing weir. The Haida and other Pacific West Coast peoples used weirs like this one to trap salmon as they swam upstream.

the village in woven baskets. They also collected seaweed from tidal pools. The seaweed was eaten raw or dried for winter use. Shells of sea creatures were used for decorations and as utensils.

Land plants were also harvested in the summer. Women dug up wild onions and fern roots with sticks. They picked plant shoots for salad greens. All kinds of wild berries were eaten fresh or dried and tightly packed for the winter.

Autumn

In late summer and fall the Haida went on great trading expeditions. They paddled hundreds of kilometres up and down the coast in their dugout canoes.

The Haida had sea otter pelts, dugout canoes, cedar boxes, and spruce root hats to trade with their neighbours. In exchange they obtained blankets made from the wool of mountain goats. They also prized the horns of the mountain goat which they could fashion into bowls, oil dishes, and ladles. From Native groups far to the north they received supplies of raw copper. Copper was highly valued and could be used for masks, family plaques, and headdresses. From the groups far to the south the Haida got abalone shells which they used for ornaments.

One of the products most sought after by the Haida was fish oil. They traded for oil with their neighbours, the Bella Coola. The best oil was made from the **oolichan** or candlefish. The oolichan is a small fish about the size of a smelt or a large minnow. It is so oily that it can be burned like a candle when dried.

The Native peoples living on the coast caught these little fish by the millions when they came in to the rivers to spawn. First they put the fish in boxes to rot for several days. Then they boiled the decay-

ing fish by dropping hot rocks into the box. The oil was skimmed off as it rose to the surface. Then it was stored in cedar boxes. At room temperature it turned into a solid block of grease. Oolichan oil was traded widely. The trails over which it was carried were called "grease" trails. These grease trails were well established trade routes through the valleys of British Columbia. The Haida carried the oolichan grease home by dugout canoe.

Trade among the peoples along the Pacific coast was extremely important. The various Native groups exchanged goods and ideas. The Haida were able to get goods they could not find in their own environment. They learned new ways of doing things. The trade benefited all the Native groups.

Winter

December, January, and February were the rainy and cold months of winter. The people did not hunt or fish as much during these months.

In winter there was time for building the dugout canoes. First the Haida would select a suitable cedar tree. Cedar is an excellent wood for canoes because it is light and waterproof. The Haida chopped down the tree and floated or towed it back to the village. Then the real work began. The log had to be hollowed out. The tools for this task were the stone axe and the adze. The Haida builders chipped away at the log until it began to take the rough shape of a canoe. Often they charred the log with fire. Then it was easier to cut away the wood. The villagers nicknamed the canoe builders "the woodpeckers" because of the constant tapping noise their tools made on the wood.

Next, the Haida had to stretch apart the sides of the canoe. There had to be space

An adze used for splitting and shaping wood. The Natives of the Pacific Coast used many different types of adzes. This one is called an elbow adze.

A Haida dugout canoe. This modern canoe was carved by artist Bill Reid. Notice the figures painted on the ends of the canoe.

for people and cargo. The hollowed out log was filled with water. Red-hot stones from the fire were dropped into the water. When the water boiled, the wood started to soften. Then the canoe builders could force posts of increasing size between the top edges. Gradually the edges could be stretched apart and the space widened.

Then the builders fashioned the long graceful curves of the canoe and perfected the shape. Each side must match the other in shape and weight. Finally the Haida took dogfish or shark skin to smooth and polish the cedar wood. Shark skin is a natural sandpaper. Then the Haida often carved or painted figures of animals on the ends of the canoe.

Winter was also the time to hold a **potlatch**. The potlatch was a gift-giving ceremony. A chief, or other person of high rank, held a potlatch to mark an important event. It could be a marriage, the death of a chief, the building of a new house, or the raising of a totem pole. Guests were invited from far away. There was dancing, feasting, and storytelling. At

a potlatch the host showered the guests with gifts. At special celebrations we often bring gifts for the host or hostess, but for the Haida giving gifts was a way to express a family's special status and wealth.

The most important people who attended the potlatch would return the favour at a future potlatch. They were expected to hold a great feast themselves. Then they would give gifts of greater value. It would be considered rude not to hold a potlatch in return.

Imagine that the chief of Tanu village has planned a great potlatch. For months the family has been making preparations. The chief will raise a mighty totem pole. Guests have been invited from far-away villages.

The potlatch begins as the guests arrive in their dugout canoes. They wait, out of sight of Tanu village, until all the canoes have gathered. Then a fleet of canoes paddles into the village. The canoes at the front are those of the most important chiefs. The others follow in order of their wealth and importance. The visitors sing as they paddle, their paddles keeping in time with their song.

The chief and the people of Tanu hurry down to the water's edge to welcome them. Some villagers wade out into the water to greet old friends and relatives. The visitors have brought their own blankets and a few personal possessions. But the host of the potlatch will provide everything else they need for the next several days.

The guests are led singing and dancing to the feast house. Here a great fire is blazing. The host family has laid out large bowls of smoked salmon, fresh steamed clams, fish oil, and berries. The next few days are full of dancing, storytelling, singing, and feasting. The dancers perform wearing elaborate masks and ceremonial costumes.

Finally the moment comes to raise the new totem pole. It is dragged or pushed on rollers to a hole in the ground that has been prepared for it. The guests are seated in order of their rank. The chief is dressed in the special ceremonial button blanket and headdress. The button blanket is made of finely woven mountain goat wool and beautifully decorated. As the drumbeat sounds, the villagers ease the base of the totem pole down a slope into the hole. Then they push with levers and pull with ropes until the pole is standing upright. Dirt is thrown back into the hole around the totem. Dancers stamp down the ground until it is firm and hard.

The chief steps forward to tell the story of all the figures carved on the totem pole. He tells of his ancestors and the history of his family. All the figures have meaning. The visitors praise the chief on the totem pole's beauty and power.

Now comes the most important part of the potlatch. It is time to distribute gifts to

the guests. The most honoured guests receive the most valuable gifts. Members of the host's family distribute blankets, tools, necklaces, bracelets, sea otter pelts, carved boxes, drums, copper plaques, and even canoes. Everyone receives a gift. The gift means they have been part of the potlatch. They have been witness to the great event that has been celebrated.

A potlatch. The host and hostess in their ceremonial dress wait to greet the guests.

Growing Up Among the Haida

The birth of a baby was a special event for the Haida. It might be celebrated with a feast or potlatch.

Children played a variety of games. They enjoyed the string game that is called cat's cradle to this day. They played guessing games. Objects were secretly hidden in one hand and the children had to guess which hand. Since the weather was mild, the children played many outdoor games such as running races and throwing javelins. They also looked to their elders to tell them stories about the traditions of their people.

As they grew older, children were taught the skills they would need for adult life. In their teenage years, both boys and girls often went on quests alone to find their own guardian spirits. Their guardian spirits would guide and protect them throughout their lives. They were also given their adult names during their early teenage years. The name-giving was also an occasion for a special celebration or potlatch. Names were very important among the Haida. They were passed on from generation to generation and were a sign of a family's honour and privileges.

Haida marriages were arranged by the parents of the bride and groom. Girls married at about age fifteen and boys at about eighteen. The engagement was celebrated by an exchange of gifts. The parents of the young man put on a series of feasts at the time of the marriage. The parents of the young woman hosted a feast on the occasion of each grandchild's birth.

Contact: The Haida Meet the Europeans

The first Europeans the Haida met were probably the Spanish. The Spanish explorer Perez recorded that he met the Haida in 1774. This was about 160 years after the French had met the Huron in eastern Canada. The Native peoples made contact with the Europeans much later in western Canada than in the east.

By 1787 the British began to trade with the Haida. The main prize the British were seeking was the soft fur of the sea otter. In exchange, the Haida drove a hard bargain for such items as knives, muskets, blankets, and kettles.

British traders sailed to China with the otter pelts. The pelts brought a high price and were made into robes for Chinese nobles. The British exchanged the furs for Chinese spices, tea, and silk. For the next fifty years the Haida were important partners in the rich, flourishing China trade.

By 1820 the supply of sea otter pelts was running out. The fur trade was declining. Fewer and fewer trading ships were calling along the coast for furs. A great source of wealth for the Haida people was disappearing.

Life had changed for the Native peoples. For furs, the Haida had obtained manufactured goods from the traders. They had become used to the manufactured goods. Items such as metal knives, kettles, and Hudson Bay blankets replaced handmade Native goods. Some old ways of making things were gradually forgotten. When the fur trade ended, the Haida suffered, much in the same way other people suffer when a major source of employment dries up.

In 1884 the Canadian government banned the potlach, mistakenly believing it was a major reason for the increasing poverty of the Haida. The real reason was the loss of a major source of revenue.

The potlatch was still practised from time to time in secret. Some Native people were thrown in jail for taking part in a potlatch. In 1921 the police seized masks and other objects used in the potlatch ceremony. Not until 1951 was the law changed. Now potlatches are being revived by the Haida.

Europeans did not settle in the Queen Charlotte Islands in large numbers until about 1900. In 1850 the Haida population was estimated at 6000 to 8000 people. By 1915 the population had dropped to 588 people. European diseases such as small-

pox, measles, and influenza had wiped
out whole families.

By 1986, the Haida population on the
Queen Charlotte Islands had grown to
about 2000 people.

A dancer performing the eagle dance at a modern potlatch. The
Haida are reviving the traditions of the potlatch.

Haida Arts and Crafts

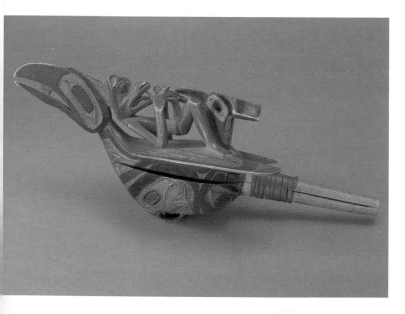

TOP: *Ceremonial masks and robes. The costumes worn during dances and ceremonies often represented various spirits.*

TOP RIGHT: *A Haida mask, carved from wood and painted.*

ABOVE: *A Haida rattle carved from wood. Rattles like this one were made in two halves and then sewn or bound together. Noisemakers, such as small pebbles, were placed inside.*

RIGHT: *A bentwood box painted with traditional Haida designs. The sides of the box were made from a single piece of wood that was soaked or steamed, scored, and then bent into shape.*

The Haida Today

Today the Native peoples of the Pacific West Coast are reviving their culture and adapting to new ways. Fishing is still important for the Haida. A fleet of fishing boats is a feature of villages such as Masset. Some groups have developed industries or formed co-operatives on their lands. But reserves, lands set aside for the Native peoples, are small and scattered. Many Natives have gone to the cities in search of new opportunities.

Today there is a re-awakening of interest in the arts of the Pacific Coast Natives. Northwest Coast art is recognized as one of the world's great artistic achievements.

Haida artists hold a prominent place in Canadian art. Bill Reid and Robert Davidson are well-known Haida artists. They are producing traditional carvings in wood. They are also using new forms to express their culture such as silkscreen prints, gold and silver jewellery, and bronze sculptures.

The Haida are also working to preserve their lands and their rights. They have led highly publicized demonstrations against logging companies. They have declared that the islands are their traditional homeland. They claim that they have the right to the resources of the forest. They want the right to govern themselves and to shape their own future.

"Elegy for an Island," a painting by Jack Shadbolt. The painting calls attention to the concerns of Native peoples over logging on their traditional homelands.

Activities

Looking Back

1. Define the following words and enter them in your dictionary.

   house   clan   phratry   noble   commoner   slave   weir   oolichan   potlatch

2. Describe the steps the Haida followed to build a cedar plank house.

3. The Native peoples made use of the animals, fish, and trees in their environment. Explain the various uses of at least two of the following:
   a) cedar trees by the Haida   c) birch trees by the Micmac
   b) buffalo by the Blackfoot   d) deer by the Huron.

4. Describe the ceremonies held at the time of salmon fishing. What were the reasons for them?

5. List the ways the arrival of the Europeans changed the Haida way of life.

Using Your Knowledge

6. Some people have the impression that all Native peoples lived in tipis or wigwams. This impression is a **stereotype**. Look up the meaning of "stereotype" in a dictionary. Explain how this impression is an example of stereotyping. How do Haida homes show this stereotype is wrong?

7. Compare a typical Haida meal with that of another Native group you have studied. What do the foods tell you about how each group used the resources of the environment?

8. Suppose you could interview a Haida man or woman about one of the following:
   a) everyday activities in the summer
   b) methods of salmon fishing
   c) making a dugout canoe.
   What questions would you ask? Stage the interview with a partner.

Extending Your Thinking

9. In an empty shoe box, make a small model to show the interior of a Haida plank house. Include as many details as possible.

10. Totem poles were an important part of Haida culture. Do further research on the symbols and designs used on totems. Draw or construct a model of a totem pole that might have been made by the Haida.

11. Hold a potlatch. Plan the event carefully. Make gifts and costumes, decorate the classroom, send out invitations, prepare food, learn some legends to tell, or write speeches for the ceremony.

CHAPTER 11

Current Issues and Concerns

The Native peoples were the first inhabitants of Canada. Their ancestors had lived in what is today Canada for thousands of years. Before European settlers came to North America, the Native peoples controlled their own lives. They hunted or grew their own food and ran their own governments. They educated their children in their traditional ways. They practised their own religion. Then one day strangers appeared on their lands.

The strangers came from distant lands in Europe. The Europeans had their own, very different ways of life. They had a different culture. To the Native peoples, they must have appeared very strange. They wore different clothes, arrived in unusual vessels, and brought new and unusual goods. The Native peoples seemed strange to the Europeans as well.

Some of the first meetings between the Native peoples and the Europeans were friendly. The Native peoples welcomed the newcomers to their land. Without help from the Native peoples, the Europeans would have had great difficulty surviving those first winters in Canada.

Jacques Cartier, for example, was one of the early European explorers to meet the Native peoples. That first winter in Canada, many of Cartier's crew fell sick and some died. They were ill with a disease called scurvy. This disease is caused by a lack of vitamin C in the diet.

The Europeans had no fresh vegetables to eat in the winter. From the Natives, Cartier learned of a cure. He discovered how to boil the bark of the white cedar and make a tea rich in vitamin C. Thanks to the knowledge of the Native peoples, many of Cartier's crew recovered.

The early period of contact between the Europeans and the Native peoples was generally friendly. They traded with each other. The Europeans were eager to obtain furs from the Native peoples. In return the Native peoples bargained for metal knives, copper kettles, guns, and steel traps. They were quick to learn the usefulness of these new goods. They were experienced traders.

Gradually, contact changed the ways of life of both groups. Some changes were positive. The Europeans learned how to adapt to the Canadian environment from the Native peoples. They adopted many Native inventions such as the birchbark canoe, pemmican, and the snowshoe. Some explorers were fascinated by the Native governments, their beliefs, and their arts.

The Native peoples also learned to use the new goods the Europeans brought. With the goods, they found new ways to hunt, cook their food, and make new things. Members of each group respected the skills and knowledge of the other.

But not all changes were positive. As the Native peoples became more involved in the fur trade, they grew dependent on the goods they could get from the traders. Gradually some old Native ways of doing things were forgotten. Skills were neglected and sometimes lost completely.

Many Native people also caught European diseases such as smallpox and measles. So many died that their numbers were drastically reduced. Changes were also taking place in their values and beliefs. The Native peoples had their own religions. But European missionaries tried very hard to turn the Native peoples toward Christianity. The Europeans believed that their religion was the only true one. They believed they were saving the souls of the Native peoples.

The Native peoples were losing control of their own lives. Contact with the Europeans was changing their whole way of life. They were becoming more and more dependent on European goods and European ways. Strange diseases were killing off their people. They were told that some of their most basic beliefs were wrong and should be abandoned.

Thousands of Europeans continued to flood into Canada. They were settlers who wanted to clear the land of its forests and farm. They were bringing a new way of life–a new culture. The settlers wanted ownership of the land they cleared. The Native peoples did not have the same idea of ownership. To them, the land was there for everyone to use–for people, the animals, and the spirits. The Native peoples and the settlers had very different ideas. They did not always understand each other.

The Native peoples helped early explorers such as Jacques Cartier and his crew survive in Canada. This painting shows how the Native peoples told Cartier of the cure for scurvy.

In many parts of Canada, Native peoples were persuaded or forced into giving up most of their land to settlement. The government gave them money and promised goods such as farming equipment and livestock. They moved onto small tracts of land reserved for them. Today some Native peoples feel they were cheated. Little was given in exchange for their lands and the terms of the treaties were not always honoured. In some parts of Canada, no treaties were ever signed.

Life on the reserves brought more changes. The Native peoples could not continue their lives as hunters and gatherers. They were encouraged to earn a living by farming. Native children were expected to go to school and learn English or French. Children were often punished at school for speaking their own language.

In 1876 the Government of Canada passed the **Indian Act**. The government believed that Natives should gradually learn to live like settlers. Until they were ready to do so, the Act made the government responsible for them. The Indian Act decided who was a legal "Indian." It set up the Department of Indian Affairs as a branch of the government. It appointed agents across the country. These people were responsible for looking after the interests of the Native peoples and teaching them how to become settlers. The Native peoples were not consulted in the preparation of the Indian Act.

The Indian Act did not apply to all Native peoples. Today, only about 324 000 Native people come under it. These people are called **Status** or **Registered Indians**. In western Canada they are called **Treaty Indians**. If you were one of the people covered under the treaties, you and your descendants became Status Indians. Your name and number was placed on a list in Ottawa called the **Indian Register**.

Native people whose names are not on the Indian Register are **Non-status Indians**. There are about one million of them. They may be Native peoples whose ancestors did not sign a treaty with the government. Sometimes this was because they refused. In other cases they did not sign a treaty because they were not present when the government representative came. They may also be people whose ancestors gave up their status for the right to leave the reserve and live elsewhere.

Until recently, there was another way a Native person could become Non-status. A Native woman who married a non-Native lost her status. However, if a non-Native woman married a Status Native, she was recognized as a Status Native! As you will discover later in this chapter, this was recently changed.

Native peoples have charged that, under the terms of the Indian Act, they are being discriminated against. In fact, many Native people would like to see the Indian Act scrapped and the treaties either re-negotiated or declared illegal according to the Charter of Rights and Freedoms.

Discrimination means treating people unfairly on the basis of their sex, skin colour, or background. When we name-call and try to make people feel inferior because of their skin colour, for example, we are discriminating against them. When we put restrictions on their housing, jobs, or education, that too is discrimination. Read the following news item about discrimination.

DISCRIMINATION THRIVING NATIVE LEADER CHARGES

The Toronto Star
February 21, 1989

Squaw. The word evokes a grimace from Linda Jordan as she describes the discrimination faced by Native women.

"I've walked down the street in Ottawa and had young people call me a squaw," the Native leader says quietly. "When I was growing up, it happened all the time.

I continually felt inferior to others because of my skin colour. There was a lot of name-calling."

As head of the Native Women's Association of Canada, the political voice of thousands of Canada's most disadvantaged people, Jordon hears a lot of similar stories.

A Native justice inquiry under way in Manitoba was told last month that Native women facing trial often plead guilty–even when they're not–because they are depressed and worried about losing their families.

One big problem facing Native women is job discrimination, says Jordan.

The 1986 census shows status Indian women earned on average only $8200 a year, compared to $12 600 for other women.

And only 26 per cent of status Indian women had jobs, while half of all other Canadian women worked outside the home.

A Native rally for self-government. Many Native peoples feel that they should have the right to determine their own future.

1. Give examples of discrimination from the article.
2. Why do you think people discriminate?
3. Why would Linda Jordan continually feel inferior?
4. Why do Native women often plead guilty even when they are not?
5. How do people act when they are discriminated against?

Today a new phase in the history of the Native peoples has begun. It has been called the **re-birth** or **re-awakening** of Native Canadians. Native peoples are speaking out about the way they have been treated in the past and the conditions under which they have had to live. They have formed nation-wide organizations to discuss common problems. They are telling the world how Native peoples

are treated unfairly in Canada. They are demanding fair settlement of their many land claims and treaties. Native peoples are asking Canadians to recognize and respect their contributions to Canada.

Many Native peoples no longer want to be called "Indians." "Indians" is a European term. It was probably first used by Christopher Columbus when he arrived in Central America and thought he had reached Asia. He called the people he met "Indians." Today Canada's Native peoples call themselves the First Nations or the Native peoples. These terms recognize that they were the first inhabitants of North America.

Native Canadians want to preserve their traditions and ways of life. They are determined to decide for themselves what part they will play in Canadian life. They want to control their own future.

In the next part of this chapter, you will look at some of the current issues concerning Native peoples. An **issue** is a problem or question that people try to resolve. But there is often no easy way to answer the question or solve the problem. It is important to look at the issue from all sides.

Issue: Are Native Women Treated Unfairly?

1876

The Indian Act is passed by the Canadian government. It sought to define the rights and privileges of status and non-status Natives. However, not everyone was happy with it. Increasingly, over time, it came to be viewed by some Native women as discriminatory.

1973

Jeannette Corbière-Lavell, an Ojibwa woman from Manitoulin Island, married a non-Native. In 1973 she loses a court battle to have her status as an Indian restored.

Jeannette Corbière-Lavell, the Native woman who initiated revisions to the Indian Act regarding the status of Native women.

1975

The National Committee on Indian Rights for Women, established in Ottawa, defines "Indian woman" to mean any woman of North American Indian ancestry, regardless of marriage.

In Mexico at the United Nations world conference for International Women's Year, Mary Two-Axe Earley speaks out. She is a Canadian Mohawk who has lost her status after marrying a non-status man.

1979

Joe Clark, prime minister, tells a group of 100 Native women from Quebec that "the Indian Act is a disgrace" and will soon be changed.

1985

Section 12 1(b) of the Indian Act is declared inoperative by the Government of Canada under terms of Bill C-31. Native women who have married non-Native men do not lose their status.

NATIVE RIGHTS FIGHTER WINS BACK HER STATUS

By Denys Horgan
The Globe and Mail
July 5, 1985

The dream of Mary Two-Axe Earley's life will come true this morning.

After battling the federal government since 1968, her status as a Mohawk Indian will be restored today.

Not a day too early, in her opinion.

"Now I'll have legal rights again. After all these years, I'll be legally entitled to live on the reserve, to own property, die and be buried with my own people," Mrs. Earley said in a telephone interview from the Kahnawake (formerly Caughnawaga) reserve near Montreal last night.

Her restored status, the result of recent amendments to the Indian Act, will be celebrated at a ceremony in Toronto attended by Minister of Indian Affairs and Northern Development David Crombie.

Now 73, Mrs. Earley's problems began when she married a non-Indian in 1938. Under the law at that time, she lost her Indian status.

When her husband died in 1969, Mrs. Earley returned to the reserve, but she was threatened with eviction in 1975. The eviction notice was withdrawn.

In 1967, she founded Equal Rights For Indian Women and the following year she led a deputation to the Royal Commission on the Status of Women. The deputation was "to protest that our rights, our birthright, had been taken away," she said last night.

Amendments to the Indian Act given royal assent last week, while strengthening the jurisdiction of Indian governments by recognizing their right to control membership, at the same time eliminated discrimination against Indian women who marry non-Indians.

1985 INDIAN STATUS STILL BRINGS CONFLICT

Ending discrimination against women difficult for Ottawa say Indian Bands
The Toronto Star
November 1, 1985

Marlyn Kane

The new law has opened many conflicts as Indian bands grapple with the spectre of thousands of friends and relative strangers trying to move on to already crowded, poor reserves.

And Indian Affairs Minister David Crombie says his department wasn't prepared for the wave of applications for reinstatement, or to counter what Native women say is confusion about exactly what rights and benefits they have gained.

And Marlyn Kane, the aggressive president of the Ottawa-based Native Women's Association of Canada, says, "It's a mess and it didn't take a brain surgeon to predict this is what would happen."

Most Canadians don't appreciate the scope of Bill C-31, which they see as a simple matter of righting a historic wrong against Indian women.

But the new law, in a move to put more self-control in the hands of the country's 587 Indian bands, does not mean all those with restored status will automatically become members of their band of origin. Only women who lost status through marriage will be added to their original band membership lists.

Band membership is more than an honour. It means a share in the common ownership of the individual band's land, programs and resources, which can vary from meagre assets in the majority of cases to substantial land and resource holdings, such as those of some oil-rich bands in Alberta.

Crombie's department estimates that 70 000 people may be eligible for reinstatement, an admitted "guesstimate."

The struggle continues. . . .

Looking at the Issue

1. Review the meaning of the following terms and enter them in your dictionary:

   discrimination
   Indian Act
   Status Indian
   Non-status Indian
   reserve

2. How has the Indian Act created problems for Native women?

3. Explain some of the steps Native women have taken since 1971 to correct the problems created by the Indian Act.

4. Imagine you are someone like Mary Two-Axe Earley who has been involved in the struggle for a long time. Explain how you would feel when your status was restored.

5. What problems still exist for Native women today? Think back to the article about Linda Jordan to help with your answer.

Issue: How Can the Social and Economic Conditions Faced by Many Native Peoples Be Improved?

Making a Living

It is difficult for Native peoples to make a living on most reserves. Usually Native peoples chose land that was good for hunting. Only 20 percent of land on reserves in Canada is suitable for farming. However, on reserves with better farm land, Native peoples are successful farmers. The Blood of Alberta are a good example.

Other Native peoples used to make a living on the reserves trapping animals for their furs and fishing. Recently, the world price paid for fur has dropped and animals are becoming scarce. Fishing has also suffered because pollution has poisoned many lakes and streams.

Most reserves are located far from cities. On the reserves, there is just not enough work to provide jobs for everyone. As a result, many Native peoples are unemployed. Often they must leave the reserves and move to the cities to find work. Sometimes families are separated and it is more difficult for the people to keep their own culture.

Some Native people find good jobs in the cities. Many work as teachers, artists, lawyers, or office workers. In Toronto, a group of actors, musicians, writers, and dancers has come together in the Native Earth Performing Arts Company. They tell of their culture through plays and music. There are also other similar groups in communities across the country.

Housing

Some Native peoples live in modern housing with excellent facilities. Many others live in homes that have no bathrooms, central heating, electricity, or telephones. These are things most other Canadians take for granted.

About 26 percent of Native homes have only space heaters, cook stoves, or other devices for heating. Only 9 percent of non-Native homes are without central heating.

In Canada, about 60 percent of all houses in rural, cottage, and remote areas have running water, sewage disposal, and indoor plumbing. About 40 percent of Native houses have all these facilities.

Many Native persons enjoy a fine standard of living, as this photo of a Native person's home on the Westbank Reserve near Kelowna, British Columbia shows. However, as a group, Native people experience much higher rates of poverty, unemployment, and poor health than most Canadians.

Health

Native illness, death, and accident rates are about three times the Canadian average. What are some of the factors that lead to health problems among Native peoples?

- overcrowded, poorly equipped homes
- inadequate nutrition
- polluted water supply
- lack of proper sewage disposal facilities
- reserves are often a long distance from medical and hospital services
- alcohol abuse

Native Peoples Find Solutions

The best solutions are those that come from the Native peoples themselves, rather than from the government. In the past the government has tried to manage the affairs of the Native peoples. But the Native peoples do not want to be treated this way. Like other Canadians, the Native peoples feel they should be free to do what they think is best for them.

Many good businesses have been started in Native communities. Some have been aided by loans from the Indian Economic Development Fund. Examples include tourist resorts, wild rice production, bush airlines, craft industries, and shoe-making.

Other businesses are devoted to preserving Native cultures, languages, and ways of life. West Coast artists, for example, are producing carvings, prints, and jewellery using traditional designs. Cultural centres have opened on many reserves. There are also two Native publishing companies in Canada–one in Manitoba and one in British Columbia.

Stoney Natives at Morley, Alberta have opened a Wilderness Centre. Its purpose is to teach non-Natives about Native culture, philosophy, and religion. Visitors live in tipis and are taught survival skills and ancient legends.

Major resource development projects are another source of opportunity for Native peoples. Some of these projects are located near reserves. In northwest Alberta the Dene Tha Band developed their own construction company. This company will help with the Norman Wells oil field expansion and pipeline project.

This Native group in northern Quebec runs an air transport service.

Native people have actively promoted their culture and rights through educational programs, newsletters, conferences, festivals, and other programs.

Looking at the Issue

1. List some of the social and economic problems faced by Native peoples.

2. Suggest some reasons why Native peoples choose occupations such as:

  a) hunting and trapping

  b) tourist resort management

  c) teacher or lawyer

  d) cultural centre management.

3. a) What factors contribute to health problems among Native peoples?

  b) How have Native peoples worked to solve some of these problems?

  c) Design posters to celebrate some of these successful projects.

4. Find out about projects, businesses, or cultural centres run by Native people in your area.

Issue: Should the Canadian Government Settle the Land Claims of the Native Peoples?

Today in newspapers and on television Native peoples are speaking out. They want the Canadian government to settle their land claims. They are trying to work out a better deal for their people.

Native leaders say their ancestors were cheated. They are concerned about the treaties signed with the government of Canada. There were many of them. Treaties One to Eight, signed between 1870 and 1899, covered most of the territory west of Lake Superior to the Rocky Mountains and north to Great Slave Lake.

A **treaty** is an agreement between two nations or groups of people. In the treaties between the Native peoples and the government, the Natives believed that they had granted the government the right to use the land, not own it. In return, the Native peoples were to receive some money, supplies, reserves, hunting and fishing rights on the reserves, and other rights.

But promised supplies did not always arrive and rights were not always upheld. The Native peoples also believe that the money they received was often not a fair amount. The land on some reserves is very poor. Today, the Native peoples want to work out a fairer deal. They believe the terms of the treaties have been broken many times.

About half the Native peoples of Canada are not covered by any treaties. Their ancestors never signed treaties with the government. Native groups of Quebec and the Northwest Territories never surrendered their lands to the government.

JANUARY 27, 1977
MOST OF ALGONQUIN PARK TO BE IN LAND CLAIM PLANNED BY INDIANS

OCTOBER 4, 1980
MICMAC INDIANS LAY CLAIM TO QUARTER OF NEWFOUNDLAND

JUNE 30, 1982
INDIANS TO SETTLE CLAIM: RECEIVE $1.5 MILLI

APRIL 30, 1984
INDIANS WANT PAYMENT FROM OTTAWA FOR ISLANDS AND PARK IN GEORGIAN BAY

MAY 7, 1987
NATIVE CLAIM TO BC TRACT IS "FIRST" SEEKING OWNERSHIP AND JURISDICTION

JULY 23, 1988
INDIANS VOTE 59–0 TO ACCEPT PACKAGE IN YUKON LAND DEAL

SEPTEMBER 6, 1988
NATIVE CHIEFS LECTURE PM AS PACT SIGNED

OCTOBER 15, 1988
INDIANS, ALBERTA "FAR APART" IN BID TO SETTLE LAND CLAIM

MARCH 24, 1989
TEMAGAMI INDIANS SET TO BLOCK LOGGING RO

DECEMBER 9, 1989
INUIT WIN AGREEMENT ON HUGE LAND CLAIM

They have no legal documents to prove it, but they believe they have the first right to the lands. They were the first inhabitants. Their right as the first inhabitants is known as their **aboriginal right**. They demand that the government settle their claims to the land and pay for the right to use it.

Native Peoples Find Solutions

PM SIGNS LAND PACT AND GETS A HISTORY LESSON AT CEREMONY
By Matthew Fisher   *The Globe and Mail*   September 6, 1988

Prime Minister Mulroney and Dene Nation President William Erasmus signing the land claims agreement.

Rae-Edzo NWT–Prime Minister Brian Mulroney was given a stern lesson in Canadian history from the Native perspective yesterday before he signed an agreement in principle giving the Dene and Metis of the Western Arctic $500 million and 181 230 square kilometres of Crown land.

As about 1000 Dogrib, Slavey, Chipewayan and Cree Indians listened intently in front of a Roman Catholic mission beside Great Slave Lake, the President of the Dene Nation, William Erasmus, told Mr. Mulroney that for thousands of years before white men arrived, the Dene had decided how they should live in their corner of the world.

"Explorers you call great men like Hearne, Franklin and Mackenzie were helpless," said Mr. Erasmus who is Dogrib. "They were like lost children and it was our people who took care of them."

In his 30-minute speech, which was translated into four aboriginal languages, Mr. Erasmus said Natives view treaties with the federal government reached around the turn of the century as "agreements between nations."

But "almost every term of the treaties has been broken," Mr. Erasmus said. As a result Natives led miserable lives that often led to alcoholism and suicide, he said.

When it finally came his turn to speak, Mr. Mulroney said the agreement in principle he had travelled 4000 km from Ottawa to sign represented a historic "day of justice . . . for the Dene and Metis and all Canadians.

"This is about redeeming promises and getting on, together, with the task of building a more united and prosperous Canada," the Prime Minister said in his brief speech.

INUIT WIN AGREEMENT ON HUGE LAND CLAIM

The Toronto Star   December 9, 1989

Ottawa (CP)–The Inuit and the federal government have made a major breakthrough toward resolving a massive and long-standing land claim in the Northwest Territories.

Pierre Cadieux, the Indian affairs minister, announced an agreement in principle yesterday that would see Inuit in the central and eastern Arctic receive more than 260 000 square kilometres of land.

That's an area almost four times the size of New Brunswick and represents the largest claim ever negotiated.

The 17 000 Inuit, who are represented by the Tungavik Federation of Nunavut, would also receive $580 million in financial compensation.

The Inuit, 80 per cent of the population of the claim area, have been negotiating with Ottawa for 11 years.

"It's basically what we've been looking for," said Paul Quassa, chief negotiator for the Inuit. "We're very satisfied with it."

Cadieux described the package as fair and reasonable and expressed hope it would be ratified quickly by cabinet, the territorial government and the Inuit.

The agreement would then be signed and work would begin on a final deal.

The Inuit will also continue negotiations with the territorial government on their dream of dividing the vast northern region to create a separate jurisdiction of Nunavut, an Inuit word meaning homeland.

Special parcels of land within the central and eastern Arctic–a vast area of rolling tundra covered by snow eight months of the year–have not yet been selected.

The western boundary of the area follows the treeline in a northwesterly direction from Hudson Bay at the Manitoba-N.W.T. border to the Beaufort Sea. The area also includes Baffin Island and other northern islands.

Cadieux said a decision on dividing the territory will be settled by northern residents in a future plebiscite. "Within the next six months there will be discussions as to how this should be done," the minister said.

The agreement would give the Inuit sub-surface rights on 36 260 square kilometres of their land. . . .

Looking at the Issue

1. In what parts of Canada are Native peoples making land claims?

2. Imagine that you are a Native Canadian. Give reasons why your people have claim to the land.

3. In what areas have land claims been successfully settled? What were some of the terms that were worked out?

4. Should treaties that did not give the Native peoples a fair deal be redrawn? Explain why or why not.

Skill Building: Examining a Current Issue

Most people watch the news on television. A television clip of a news story lasts only about thirty seconds. To find out the details of a story, you often have to turn to newspaper accounts. Newspapers and magazines provide much more information about current issues. To understand an issue, you first need to collect information on it. Then you can examine it more carefully and try to form your own opinion.

Step 1: Collecting Information

1. As a class, list current issues concerning Native peoples. Suggest issues that are different from the ones you have looked at in this chapter. For example: Native rights to trap animals

2. Individually or in small groups, choose one issue from the list. Collect newspaper and magazine articles on the issue. Try to find at least three articles.

3. Make a scrapbook to organize your articles. Paste the articles or photocopies of them on the left-hand pages of the scrapbook. On the right-hand pages, write summaries of each article. Use an organizer that will identify the main ideas and supporting statements in each article.

Let's practise with an example. Read the following article carefully.

TRADITION UNDER ATTACK

Groups in Europe and Canada are campaigning against our country's oldest industry

There are 50 000 Native trappers in Canada committed to a way of life that Native peoples have followed for centuries. Today, this traditional lifestyle is under attack from a powerful anti-trapping movement in Europe. This movement is even gaining a foothold in southern Canada.

In the mountainous wilderness of the Yukon, Native trapper Art John is concerned about the people who would put a stop to his livelihood. Mr. John, now in his 60s, got his first lynx when he was only ten years old; he's been trapping ever since.

Trapping is a demanding occupation which requires a great deal of effort and knowledge. Many days, Mr. John is on the trapline from daylight to dark. He respects the animals he traps, and says it took many years to learn to be a successful trapper. The persistence and hard work last year brought Mr. John an income of $18 000.

While Mr. John recognizes that he may be more successful than the average Native trapper, who makes less than $5000 a year, he stresses the importance of trapping for Native communities. "Native people like trapping," Mr. John says, "they live from that. Without it, how could we survive?"

Trappers make up about 3% of the Yukon's population, among Native communities the percentage is higher. Trapping is crucial to many Native people who have few other economic opportunities. The Council for Yukon Indians recently published a report on trapping which challenges the anti-trapping movement, terming it "a devastating threat to our continued existence." Other Canadian groups, such as Indigenous Survival International, are also putting forward the Native point of view on the issue.

Native groups challenge the claim that trapping is an inhumane and poorly managed use of animals. Art John agrees. "Native people are careful," he says. Mr. John uses mostly conibears, a trap that is designed to kill an animal instantly, rather than the leg-hold type, which can cause an animal to suffer a lingering and painful death. Also, he carefully monitors the animal populations on his trapline. This year, he is not trapping marten on a part of his territory so the population can rebuild itself. This sort of management makes sense to Mr. John, because his trapping is not a short-term job for him; it is his life.

Yet, it seems that anti-trapping groups will not give up their fight. Should their lobby succeed, fur coats, and the trappers that produce the pelts, may soon be only memories.

Sitting in his cozy log cabin, Mr. John ponders the future. "The Indian," he says, "was the first on this land. It's a good life when you stay in the bush, but if Native people move into town full-time, it would be different." These differences he implies would not be good ones.

For Native peoples, the end of trapping would be one more blow directed against a traditional way of life that depends on the land and the animals that live there.

4. What is the main idea in this article? Can you identify the supporting statements? Complete the organizer below in your notebooks.

Article: Tradition Under Attack

___

MAIN IDEA

___

THE NATIVE PEOPLES OF CANADA SHOULD BE ALLOWED TO CONTINUE THEIR CENTURIES-OLD PRACTICE OF TRAPPING.

SUPPORTING STATEMENTS

___

a. it is their livelihood
b. Natives respect the animals they trap
c. some Native peoples have few other opportunities for making a living
d.
e.
f.
g.

Step 2: Examining an Issue

Now you are ready to examine an issue more closely.

1. Re-examine the articles in your scrapbook. State the problem or issue in the form of a question.

For example: Should Native peoples be allowed to continue their centuries-old practice of trapping?

2. There is no simple answer to any issue. Every issue has both positive and negative sides. Set up an organizer like the one below to summarize the positive and negative sides of the issue. Use the information you gathered in your scrapbook to help you summarize the two sides. Add your own ideas as well.

Issue:	Positive side (Yes)	Negative side (No)
Should Native peoples be allowed to continue their centuries-old practice of trapping?		

3. Review the positive and negative points in your organizer. What do you think? Try to come to your own decision on the question. How difficult was your decision?

Native Contributions

The Native peoples are an important part of Canada's founding heritage. They have made many contributions to Canadian life. You will see some of these contributions in your own community by just looking around you. Others may not be so obvious. These often have to do with beliefs and values.

Look at a map of Canada. Try to identify all of the Native place names.

There are many. "Canada" is a Native word. Four of our provinces have Native names. Communities, lakes, and rivers also remind us of Canada's Native heritage. You will find places such as Miramichi, Nipigon, Winnipegosis, Temiskaming, and Ottawa. Other names are Native words translated directly into English or French. Find Moose Jaw, Medicine Hat, White Horse Plains, and Pembina Hills, for example.

We see the Native influence in our

Native peoples have made an important contribution to contemporary arts such as theatre. This photo is a scene from "Diary of a Crazy Boy," written by John McLeod and directed by Tomson Highway and Rene Highway of Native Earth Performing Arts.

language as well. Did you know that caribou, chipmunk, moose, coyote, racoon, skunk, and woodchuck all come from Native words? Other common words and phrases are also of Native origin. We have caucus, canoe, pow-wow and Indian summer.

Countless medicines originated with the Native peoples. Think about common foods as well. Corn, beans, squash, pumpkins, and maple syrup all owe their origins to the Native peoples. Corn is the most important. Today, corn is eaten by millions of people around the world and is an important feed for countless animals. The Native habit of flaking the kernels and roasting them has been adapted into quick, nutritious breakfast foods today. And popcorn has become a Canadian tradition.

Native modes of transportation have played an important role in our history. The early explorers and traders quickly recognized the value of the birchbark canoe in the Canadian environment. The canoe made it possible to travel swiftly over long distances and to explore the water highways of the Natives. The Inuit dogsled was imitated in the North. Canvas and fibreglass models of the Inuit kayak are being made today. Native snowshoes and toboggans were copied by the Europeans. They were used along well-established Native paths throughout our early history.

Native clothing was also quickly adopted. Many examples can still be seen today. We have adopted mocassins, leggings, buckskin shirts and jackets, and the parka of the Inuit. All are well suited to life in the Canadian environment.

We can see Native influences in designs as well, from modern jewellery to housing. The army's Sibley tent is an adaptation of the tipi. The Quonset hut is also a Native design. Though the structure appears flimsy, it stands up to strong winds and heavy rains.

Many aspects of Native cultures have influenced Canadian culture. But it is important to recognize that Native cultures are very diverse and each is a rich and vital culture in its own right. Native peoples are preserving and expressing their own cultural heritage in their art, literature, music, and politics.

Today, Native legends and history, preserved through storytelling, are appearing in print. Native themes and heroes are celebrated in books and plays.

Native art and sculpture have also achieved worldwide recognition. Artists such as Norval Morrisseau, Jackson Beardy, Daphne Odjig Beavon, Allen Sapp, Bill Reid, Robert Davidson, and Edward Poitras are known internationally. Native crafts such as the quillwork baskets of the Micmac and fine woodwork of the Pacific Coast Natives are all highly prized.

Music and dance have always been important in the lives of the Native peoples. They were an essential part of ceremonies such as the Sun Dance on the Plains and the potlatch on the Pacific Coast. The music and the dance have been kept alive in the traditional way. Native artists such as Buffy Sainte-Marie, Susan Aglukark and Kashtin have also brought this rich heritage to popular music, as well as to folk and country styles.

Native leaders such as Elijah Harper, Phil Fontaine, Ovide Mercredi and Ethel Blondin-Andrew are speaking for their people on the political front.

One of the most important contributions of the Native peoples is their view of life. Today we are increasingly concerned about issues such as pollution and the destruction of the natural environment. The problem grows more frightening each day.

Conservationists remind us of the values of the Native peoples. They remind us that the Native peoples lived in harmony with nature. Natives believe that men and women are part of nature. They are one with the forces of the land, air, water, vegetation, and wildlife. We must respect these forces and learn to live with them, rather than destroy them. The earth belongs to no one person, but provides for all.

Artist Bill Reid's sculpture "The Raven and the First Men." Many Native artists like Bill Reid have become known internationally for their work.

Activities

Looking Back

1. Define each of the following words and enter them in your dictionary.

   Indian Act
   Indian Register
   treaty
   aboriginal right

2. Why was the early period of contact between Native peoples and Europeans generally friendly? Why did things eventually change?

3. What changes did life on the reserve bring for the Native peoples?

Using Your Knowledge

4. Today we celebrate a re-birth or re-awakening among Native Canadians. What does this mean? Give examples.

5. The Native peoples complained that the Indian Act treated them like children. Why did they feel this way?

Extending Your Thinking

6. Did the government buy the land in your community from the Native peoples? If so, find out the price paid and decide whether it was a fair price. If it was not a fair deal, should the terms be renegotiated?

7. Write a letter to a local newspaper outlining your ideas on one of the following:
   a) the rights of Native women
   b) conditions under which some Native peoples must live
   c) Native land claims.
   Send a copy of your letter to your Member of Parliament and ask for a response.

8. Find out if there is a Native craft store or gallery nearby. Plan a field trip to view and appreciate Native arts and crafts.

9. Choose a prominent Native Canadian. Find out about that person's contribution to Canadian life. Present your findings to the class. You could choose from the following list or select someone else you have heard about.
   a) Roberta Jamieson   **c)** George Clutesi   **e)** Tom Longboat   **g)** Daphne Odjig
   b) Norval Morrisseau **d)** Pauline Johnson   **f)** James Gladstone   Beavon

UNIT THREE

The Community of
New France

CHAPTER 12

Early Exploration and Settlement

The Norse on the coast of America.

Early Explorers of North America

Today huge passenger jets cross the Atlantic Ocean in a few hours. With pressurized cabins, powerful engines, and computerized instruments they have little difficulty making the long journey between Europe and North America. But think back a thousand years. Then wooden sailing ships, with crews of adventurous sailors, pushed westward from Europe. They journeyed until at last the shores of Newfoundland and Labrador rose out of the mists. By 986 they had reached North America.

Who were these daring explorers who braved the cold, rough Atlantic? They were the Norse–or Vikings as we sometimes call them. Originally they came from Norway, Sweden, and Denmark. They left their overcrowded homelands in search of new places to settle. They reached England, Scotland, and Ireland first in about 800. By about 860 they had arrived in Iceland. A little more than a hundred years later, they had crossed the ocean to Greenland and North America.

The Vikings told of their adventures in stories called **sagas**. One saga, the *Flatey Book*, was written about 1300. It tells of a voyage made in the year 1000. A Viking named Leif Ericsson sailed west of Greenland and then sighted land again after several days at sea.

In the background were great glaciers, and all the land between the sea and the glaciers was like one great rock. The country seemed worthless. Leif said, 'I will give this country a name and call it Helluland' [the land of flat stone].

Then they returned on board and sailed to a new land, cast anchor and went ashore. This land was low lying and wooded. Wherever they went there were wide stretches of white sand and a shallow slope up from the sea. Then Leif said, 'This land will be named Markland' [woodland].

–From *The Vikings* by Jon Nicol

For a long time historians knew about Viking journeys only from their sagas. Then in 1960 the first remains of a Norse settlement were found at L'Anse aux Meadows, Newfoundland. The area around L'Anse aux Meadows is like Markland described in the *Flatey Book*. Archaeologists uncovered two great houses similar to Norse houses found in Greenland.

Leif may have ventured even farther south, perhaps as far as Nova Scotia or Massachusetts. He named another area Vinland, where he reported finding wild grapes and wheat. The exact location of Vinland is still a matter of guesswork. Very little additional evidence of Viking settlement in America has been found.

Silks and Spices

In Europe, stories of the Norse explorations were forgotten. Europeans were dreaming of land to the east. China and India were the sources of spices and silk. These were the treasures that Europeans longed for.

What a difference spices made to the food Europeans ate! At that time, meat and fish had to be preserved with salt. There was no refrigeration. Pepper and cloves brought new flavours to even the saltiest meat and fish. Nutmeg, cinnamon, and ginger made cakes, puddings, and bread much tastier and more enjoyable. And think of the difference to clothing! Dresses could be made of smooth colourful silk instead of dull rough wool. Trousers and jackets could be made of soft thick velvet.

Everyone in Europe wanted silks and spices from East Asia. Getting them was another matter. First the goods had to be transported across the deserts and mountains of Asia. On the backs of camels and mules they were hauled to the Mediterranean Sea. There they were loaded aboard ships and sent to the busy ports of Venice and Genoa. Then they went on by riverboat or mule train to the market places of Europe. Every country they passed through charged a tax on the goods. After such a long and expensive journey, no wonder only the rich could afford the silks and spices of Asia!

If only these riches could be brought all the way from China by sea. But no sailor would dare make the journey. People believed that the sea boiled at the equator. Anyone who crossed it would be burned black. They also believed terrible tales of sea monsters that swallowed whole ships when they ventured too far from land.

Then in the late 1400s, two great inventions changed navigation–the **compass** and the **astrolabe**. The compass had a needle that always pointed north. A sailor could tell direction even when clouds covered the moon and sun. The astrolabe allowed sailors to steer by the

An astrolabe. This astrolabe is a copy of one found near Cobden, Ontario in 1867. It is believed to have belonged to a French explorer in the seventeenth century.

stars. With these two inventions, it was possible to sail farther from the sight of land.

Ideas were also changing. People had believed the earth was flat. Now they began to believe that the ancient Greeks were right when they said the earth was round. They noticed that masts of approaching ships came into view before the whole ship could be seen. Surely this proved that the earth was round, not flat. Why not try sailing west, around the earth, to East Asia?

Europe Looks West to Asia

In 1492 Christopher Columbus sailed west from Spain to find the sea route to Asia. But instead of Asia, Columbus found Central and South America. Instead of silks and spices, he returned to Spain with ships full of silver and gold. With this new found wealth, Spain was the envy of all other European nations.

Spanish explorers were also the first Europeans to find a route into the Pacific Ocean. Ferdinand Magellan sailed along the coast of South America in 1519. He found a passage into the Pacific Ocean and named it the Strait of Magellan. The Spanish had come upon a southwest passage to Asia.

The English also tried to find kingdoms as rich as those the Spanish had found in Central America. John Cabot set out from England in 1497. After forty-two days he landed on the northeast coast of America. He claimed the land for the King of England and called it New-Found-Land. There was no thought that the Native peoples already living there might have a claim to the land. Though the English failed to reach Asia, they found other riches — vast supplies of cod fish.

Would people be satisfied with cod fish when they were searching for silks and spices, gold and silver? At this time many people in Europe did not have enough to eat. Fish was also a substitute for meat on Roman Catholic holy days and most Europeans were Roman Catholics. Fish were so plentiful off the coast of North America that they could be caught by dipping baskets into the sea.

France Enters the Race for New Lands

The King of France was jealous of the Spanish and English successes. The French had been so busy with wars that they had made no effort to explore for new lands and wealth. Now King Francis I was ready to send French ships to America. His rivals, Spain and England, must be beaten! France must be the first to find a more direct way to Asia. King Francis chose Jacques Cartier of St. Malo for the task. Cartier believed he could find a northwest passage to Asia.

Cartier's First Voyage

King Francis outfitted Cartier with two ships and sixty-one sailors. He ordered Cartier to explore the coast of Newfound-land and the waters beyond it. On 20 April 1534, Cartier set sail from St. Malo.

Newfoundland was reached after just twenty days. At the northern tip, Cartier threaded his way among the icebergs. He sailed through the Strait of Belle Isle into the Gulf of St. Lawrence. He was sure he had found the passage they were looking for! Cartier knew from the movement of the water that there must be a great river ahead.

Imagine the excitement of the crew. If one of the sailors had kept a journal, this is what he might have written. The account is based on facts from the voyage.

Jacques Cartier.

In our excitement we jumped down into small boats and made for the shore. As we explored up and down the coast [Labrador], we grew more and more disappointed. Everything was bleak. There were no riches here. Sadly, Captain Cartier summoned us back to the main ships and we steered south.

After some time we sighted land that looked more promising. It was green and thickly covered with trees [Prince Edward Island]. We sailed on for a little while and came to a huge bay [Bay of Chaleur]. The captain gave order to land at a spot where a giant rock juts into the sea [Gaspé].

We were overjoyed to set foot on land after so long a sea journey. We waded ashore and claimed this land in the name of our beloved King Francis. One of our first acts was to set up a huge wooden cross. On the top of the cross we wrote these words:

'Vive le Roi de France!' [Long live the King of France!].

Cartier and his crew at Gaspé in 1534 claiming the land for France. What might the Native peoples think of Cartier's claim?

At Gaspé Cartier met a group of Iroquois. With their chief, Donnacona, they had come to hunt seal. The Iroquois appeared to be experienced traders and bartered their furs with Cartier. But Cartier was more interested in exploring than trading. A few days later he was ready to continue his exploration of the Gulf.

Cartier knew it was important to have Native guides who could speak a little French. He also knew that King Francis would be impressed if he could see Native people from the new land. Cartier captured two of Donnacona's sons to take back to France. In return, he gave the Iroquois shirts, red caps, clothing, and other presents. He promised Donnacona that he would return with his sons.

Cartier set sail from Gaspé and headed north and then east. He sailed around the eastern end of Anticosti Island. Twice he missed the entrance to the great river that led into the heart of North America. But winter was coming. It was time to return to France.

On this first voyage Cartier had found neither gold nor spices. He had not discovered the passage to Asia. However, he had found a way into the waters west of Newfoundland. He hoped to persuade King Francis to allow him to return the next year.

Cartier's Second Voyage

The following year, 1535, Cartier was back. This time he came with three ships and 110 sailors. As he promised, he brought back Donnacona's sons. As they neared Anticosti Island, the Native youths became very excited. They pointed to a way past the island and into a river. They called it "the way to Canada." By "Canada" they meant Stadacona, their village near present-day Quebec City.

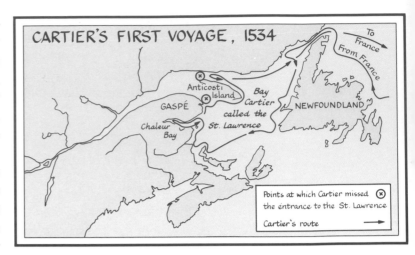

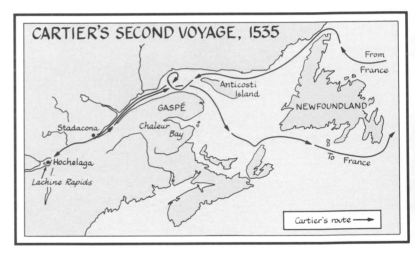

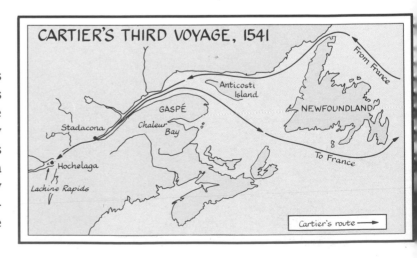

Cartier made his way carefully up the river, zigzagging from shore to shore. On 7 September 1535 he reached Stadacona. In time, Cartier referred to all of the area under Donnacona's control as the "province of Canada." Within fifteen years "Canada" was appearing on maps as the whole area along the north and south banks of the St. Lawrence River.

The Iroquois did not want to help Cartier sail farther up the River of Canada. Perhaps they wanted to make sure that he stayed with them at Stadacona. Perhaps they feared that the inexperienced French explorers would not survive in the wilderness. The reasons are not clear. They told Cartier of dangers that could befall him, but Cartier was determined. He set out in his smallest ship and in thirteen days had reached the Native village of Hochelaga, now Montreal.

Hochelaga was surrounded by a wooden fence to protect it from enemy attack. It was built on a hill Cartier named Mount Royal because of the wonderful view of the river. He wrote:

As far as the eye can reach, one sees that river so large and wide and broad. We were told that, after passing the rapids, one could navigate that river for more than three moons. And they showed us that along the mountains to the north there is another large river [Ottawa River] which comes from the west.
      –From Cartier's Journal

Cartier was beginning to understand the vastness of the new land. As he travelled up the river, he reached rapids and could not go on. There were no Native guides to help him. Later these rapids were called the "La Chine" rapids. "La Chine" means China. The French still dreamed of finding the passage to the Far East. Cartier turned back to Stadacona where he decided to spend the winter.

Picture what that first winter in Canada must have been like. It was a nightmare! The Great River of Canada froze. The snow was piled shoulder high. Worst of all, Cartier's men fell ill from scurvy. They had no fresh fruit or vegetables. The men's limbs became sore and swollen, their teeth loosened, and their mouths filled with sores. One by one they died and were buried in the snow drifts. By the middle of February, only 10 of the crew of 110 remained in good health.

The sick had almost given up hope when Cartier learned of a cure from the Natives. They showed Cartier how to boil the crushed bark and needles of the white cedar. They told him that the sick should drink the mixture and put the pulp on their diseased limbs. Almost everyone recovered. Cartier wrote in his journal, "If all the doctors in France had been here, they could not have done as much in a year as this did in six days."

When spring came, Cartier and his crew were anxious to return to France.

Cartier's ship La Grande Hermine.

But Cartier knew he would have to put on a good show for the King if he hoped to return. He had been gone all winter and lost twenty-five men. His plan was to capture Donnacona and some of his followers. He hoped that Donnacona's tales of the River of Canada would convince the King that Cartier should explore it.

This second journey of 1535-36 was much more important than the first. On the return to France Cartier found the strait separating Newfoundland from Cape Breton. He realized Newfoundland was an island. He had found the great river that led to the heart of North America. He called it the St. Lawrence. He had also passed many rivers that flowed into the St. Lawrence. These could be used as highways to build a French empire. At the same time, he had spent a winter in Canada and survived!

At first all went well in France. Donnacona had learned some French. Reports say he told the King of a wonderful land rich in gold beyond Hochelaga. The King was impressed. This time he agreed not only to another voyage, he wanted to found a colony. These rich lands should be secured for France.

Then Cartier's plan went sour. The King appointed an important noble, Sieur de Roberval, to be in charge of the expedition. It was not good enough to have a sea captain represent the King in the "New World." Cartier was to serve only as Roberval's guide. Then more trouble struck. Donnacona died in France. The Native people at Stadacona would naturally be suspicious and upset when Cartier returned without their chief.

Cartier's Third Voyage

In 1541 Cartier set out for Canada ahead of Roberval. This time his crew was made up of criminals who had been pardoned when they agreed to settle in Canada. Not many people could be persuaded to leave their homes for a strange, wild land. The little group spent another terrible winter in Stadacona. The Iroquois were angry that Donnacona was missing and did not believe Cartier's story that Donnacona had married in France.

Cartier's crew did find large quantities of what they believed to be gold and diamonds. They headed for France to announce this excellent news. In the gulf, they met Roberval and the other ships coming from France. Cartier was ordered to go back to the winter settlement, but he slipped away in the night. The minerals he took back to France turned out to be nothing more than quartz and iron pyrites–**fool's gold**. Roberval tried to establish a settlement in Canada, but he was defeated by sickness and the harsh winter.

The first attempt to create a French community in Canada had failed. Cartier had found no gold. The shorter route to Asia was still a mystery. The Native peoples were becoming increasingly uneasy. But Jacques Cartier had mapped the Great River of Canada. One day this river would lead to the riches of the interior. For now the French were discouraged from attempting any further colonization. Sixty years passed before they again seriously considered colonizing New France.

Reasons for Settlement

Fish and Furs

Every spring hundreds of small boats left Europe and sailed across the Atlantic. All summer they fished off the coast of Newfoundland and then returned home for the winter. At first few boats went into shore for any long period of time.

Since the fishing crews were away for months at a time, the fish had to be preserved. They were cleaned immediately on board the ship and packed in layers of salt. This way of preserving the fish was known as the **green method**. But salt was expensive. Fishing crews began to adopt another method. They took their catch into shore to dry it.

The crews salted the fish lightly and then left them to dry in the sun on large wooden racks. In four or five days the fish were hard as boards and much lighter. Three times more dried as fresh fish could be carried home in the hold of a ship. Cooks in Europe said that dried fish tasted better too. All they had to do was soak it in water and it filled out again like a sponge. There was lots of money to be made in cod.

Natives who lived nearby watched the crews at work on the shore. They also came to trade. Thus the fishing crews were the first Europeans to trade with the Native peoples. The Natives were especially interested in the sharp metal knives used to cut off the fish heads.

What did the Europeans want in return? They wanted furs. Fashion experts in Europe were saying that to be stylish, women should line their cloaks with fur. European gentlemen were demanding hats made of fine beaver felt. Hats were so important that a rich man often left his hat in a will, as we might leave stocks, bonds, and jewellery today.

The fishing crews found that the Native peoples would bring piles of their finest beaver pelts. To the Native peoples, beaver pelts were plentiful and not especially valuable. In return they bargained for knives, copper kettles, and other new and wonderful goods. Trading had advantages for both sides. Knives and kettles were common, inexpensive items to the Europeans. In exchange they received furs worth ten to twenty times a knife or kettle.

When spring came, French traders raced each other to get to New France. Those who arrived first would get the best furs from the winter hunt. Then some decided that it would be better to stay in New France all winter. They would then always be close to the Native peoples and their supply of furs. In that sense the fur trade helped to bring settlement to New France.

By 1600 the French began to look west again with new interest. Fish and furs could earn fortunes. Perhaps Canada was important after all.

Drying and salting cod on the shore.

EARLY EUROPEAN EXPLORERS OF THE AMERICAS

986
Norse explorers reach the northeast coast of North America.

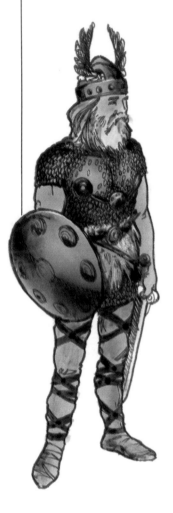

1492
Christopher Columbus explores parts of Central and South America for Spain. He does not find the route to East Asia but returns with gold and other riches.

1497
John Cabot sets sail on his first voyage for the King of England. He sails again in 1498. He explores the coast of Newfoundland and the rich fishing grounds called the Grand Banks.

1513
Balboa from Spain lands in Panama. He crosses the peninsula and is the first European to see the Pacific Ocean.

1519
Ferdinand Magellan sails for Spain and heads south along the coast of South America. He finds a strait at the south end of the continent and sails through it into the Pacific Ocean.

1534
Cartier plants a cross at Gaspé and claims the land for King Francis I of France.

1535
Cartier's second voyage takes him as far as the Native villages of Stadacona and Hochelaga on the St. Lawrence.

1541
Cartier makes his third voyage with Roberval to establish a settlement. The colony fails and Cartier returns with only fool's gold.

1583
Sir Humphrey Gilbert claims all of Newfoundland for England.

1603
Champlain makes his first voyage to New France. In 1604 and 1605 he helps establish the settlements at Ste. Croix and Port Royal in Acadia.

1608
Champlain builds the Habitation at Quebec.

From the late 1500s, explorers including John Davis, Henry Hudson, William Baffin, Sir John Franklin, and Robert McClure continued to search for a Northwest Passage to Asia through the Arctic. All were unsuccessful. Not until 1903-06, almost 400 years after the first attempts, did a ship sail through the Northwest Passage from the Atlantic to the Pacific.

The Time for Settlement Has Come

The King of France decided it was time to settle the banks of the Great River of Canada. Settlement would establish France's claim to the land. Other nations were beginning to build colonies in the New World. France must not be left out. French settlers could also make friends with the Natives and trade for furs.

But the King would not pay the huge costs of building the settlements. Instead he offered to bargain with a rich fur trader. In return for bringing settlers to New France, the King would grant the trader a **monopoly** of the fur trade. A monopoly meant that the merchant was the only one allowed to trade in the territory. All of the profits would be that trader's alone.

The First Settlements in Acadia

One of the first traders to receive a monopoly was a nobleman named de Monts. De Monts tried to build a settlement in Acadia, the Atlantic region of New France.

In June 1604, de Monts and his mapmaker Samuel de Champlain chose a small island at the mouth of the Ste. Croix River on the Bay of Fundy. In the summer it seemed like a good choice. But when winter came harsh winds swept down the valley and across the unprotected island. The settlers huddled in freezing cabins as the temperature dipped. There was very little wood to burn. Most of the nearby trees had been cut down to build the cabins.

Food was also a problem. There was nothing to eat but salt meat and frozen cider. With no fresh vegetables, the settlers fell one by one to the terrible disease of scurvy. By spring, only half of them were still alive.

The first winter in Acadia had taught them a hard lesson. But de Monts was not ready to give up. In the summer of 1605 the settlers moved across the bay to a well sheltered harbour. They named the new settlement Port Royal. A nearby forest provided building materials and firewood. The settlers constructed a large weather-proof building with a sheltered courtyard. They planted wheat and vegetable gardens. The hunger, cold, and sickness of the previous winter were not quickly forgotten.

To keep up the settlers' spirits in winter, Champlain organized a club. He called it L'Ordre de Bon Temps, which means the Order of Good Cheer. Every two weeks, one of the settlers acted as host for a special evening. It was this person's job to plan and cook a great feast. At supper the host put a big gold chain around his neck and led the settlers to the table. Each person carried a platter of food. Sometimes the platters held roasts of moose, duck, goose, rabbit, bear; or porcupine. Beaver tail was considered a great delicacy. Sometimes the plates were heavy with fresh fish caught through the ice. There were huge loaves of fresh baked bread and often some sort of dessert.

The French sometimes invited the Native chiefs to the feasts. At one feast the Micmac chief Membertou tasted the European food called bread for the first time. Often there was music and singing, and occasionally short plays. In 1606, Marc Lescarbot wrote a playlet called "The Theatre of Neptune." It was the first play performed in Canada.

The Order of Good Cheer worked wonders. The settlers' spirits were high that winter. Their diet was much better and scurvy was greatly reduced. The colonists had shown that they could survive a winter in Acadia.

Unfortunately, bad news arrived from France. The King decided to cancel de Monts's monopoly. In 1607 Port Royal was abandoned and the settlers sailed back to France.

One of the original settlers, Baron de Poutrincourt, was not ready to give up. Three years later he returned to Port Royal with settlers and a priest. In the following years there were frequent conflicts with the English settlers to the south. But slowly a farming community grew up around Port Royal and along the coast.

These settlers were the ancestors of the Acadian population that still lives in the provinces of Nova Scotia and New Brunswick.

The French had discovered, however, that Acadia was too far from the centre of the fur trade. They needed to locate along Cartier's Great River of Canada in the heart of fur trade country.

Things had changed along the Great River since Cartier's day. The towns of Stadacona and Hochelaga had disappeared. The Algonkins and the Montagnais were living along the north shore of the St. Lawrence River now. The Iroquois had moved farther south into the valleys of the Richelieu and Mohawk rivers.

A re-enactment of the Order of Good Cheer at Port Royal. What foods have been prepared and how are they being eaten?

A portrait of Samuel de Champlain.

Champlain: The Father of New France

Samuel de Champlain was chosen to found the first French settlement along the St. Lawrence. Champlain was an experienced soldier, explorer, and geographer. He had travelled to the West Indies and written a book with extraordinary maps and drawings. For his work the King of France had named him the Royal Geographer. Champlain had also helped found Ste. Croix and Port Royal. Now he would help to build the first permanent settlement along the St. Lawrence. For his role in founding Quebec, Champlain would be known ever after as the "Father of New France."

Champlain's Habitation

In the summer of 1608 Champlain sailed up the St. Lawrence. He chose a site for his village where the river narrowed and where there was an excellent harbour. It was the old site of Stadacona, the Iroquois village. Champlain called the place Quebec, from the Algonkian word *Kebec*, meaning "narrows." The settlement was to be a home, a warehouse, a fort, and a trading post. Champlain called it the **Habitation**. It stood close to the river with a high cliff behind it so that it would be easy to defend. It was protected all around with wooden fences. Like many castles, the Habitation also had a moat with a drawbridge.

Skill Building: Using an Historical Document

To solve a mystery, you examine all the available evidence. One of the best sources of evidence is an eyewitness–someone who was there when an event took place. Eyewitnesses can give you a first-hand account.

Artifacts and documents such as old newspapers, diaries, letters, census records, old maps, and sketches are all first-hand evidence. They were prepared by people who lived at the time of the events. Historians call all first-hand accounts **primary** or **original sources**.

To solve the mystery you might also talk to people who heard about events from an eyewitness. They could give you a second-hand account. Second-hand accounts in history include books and articles written about the past. They are called **secondary sources**. A book written today about early explorers of North America, for example, is a secondary source.

Write the headings "Primary Sources" and "Secondary Sources" in your notebook. Place the items in the following list under the correct headings.

Cartier's journal

a recent book called *Champlain: The Father of New France*

Champlain's map of Ste. Croix

a settler's letter to a relative in France

a Micmac legend

a bone comb found at an archaeological dig

a television program on life in New France

your textbook *Community Canada*

Primary sources are interesting because they help historians see what a real person in history was thinking and feeling. Historians try to think as the writer thought. They try to understand the person's feelings and concerns.

You can learn how people in the past thought and felt by studying primary sources too. Here are some steps to follow when you examine a document:

1. Read the document carefully.

2. Determine the event in history that the document is talking about. Does it relate to the topic you are studying?

3. Decide if the document is reliable.
Who was the author?
Was the author present at the event?
How soon after the event was the document written?

4. Look up the meaning of any unknown words or phrases.

5. Look for information the document can give you. What questions does it answer?

6. Try to describe the feelings or attitudes of the author. What can the document tell you about the author and the period?

Now let's examine a real document. Read Champlain's description about how the settlers built the Habitation. Study the sketch Champlain drew.

I employed a part of our workmen cutting down the trees to make a site for our settlement, another part in sawing planks, and another in digging the cellar and making ditches. . . . The first thing we made is the store-house, to put our supplies under cover. . . . After the store-house was finished I continued the construction of our quarters, which contained three main buildings of two stories. All the way round our buildings I had a gallery made . . . and several platforms where we put our cannons.

–From *The Works of Samuel de Champlain*

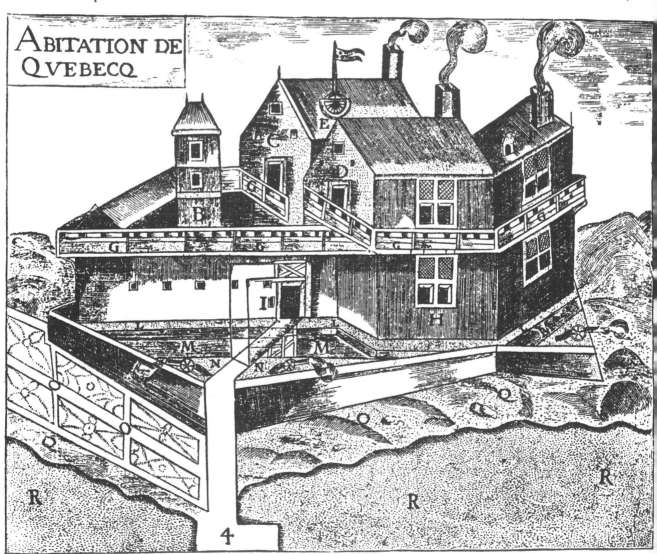

1. Write the title, author, and date of the document in your notebook.

2. Note the event the document is describing.

3. Describe how you know the document is reliable.

4. a) What was the settlers' first task?
b) What was the first building they constructed? Why?
c) What buildings were constructed next? Explain why these were most important to Champlain.

5. Examine the sketch of the Habitation. Check the key and find each building on the sketch. Look up these unfamiliar words: sundial, forge, galleries, moat, pier. Write a sentence to explain each one.

6. What other information can the sketch give you? Here are some interesting questions:

a) Why might Champlain feel the Habitation needed a forge? What might the settlers make there?

b) Why were there gardens around the Habitation?

c) What use was a sundial?

d) What were the fortifications like?

7. What do these documents tell you about Champlain's concerns when he built the Habitation? Why do you think Champlain drew the sketch?

Champlain's sketch of the Habitation at Quebec, 1608.

Key to the drawing:
A: *Warehouse/storerooms*
B: *Pigeon house*
C: *Building for arms and for workers to live*
D: *More lodgings for workers*
E: *Sundial*
F: *Forge and workers' lodgings*
G: *Galleries all the way around*
H: *Lodging for Champlain*
I: *Gate with drawbridge*
M: *Moat all the way around*
N: *Platforms for the cannon*
O: *Gardens*

Soon Champlain ran into trouble with his settlers. They grumbled about the mosquitoes and the hard work. They were afraid they would die in this terrible place. Champlain barely escaped from a plot to kill him. When he heard of the mutiny he took swift action. The ringleaders were given a fair trial. One man was condemned to be hanged and the others were sent back to France in chains.

Then winter struck. The water froze in the tea kettles. Scurvy killed twenty-eight settlers. By spring only Champlain and seven others were alive.

From the experience of that first winter at Quebec, Champlain learned an important lesson. The colony could only survive if it had a steady supply of food, building materials, and trade goods from France. But most of all, Quebec needed more settlers.

Champlain made many trips back to France. He tried to convince the King and the merchants that permanent settlers and supplies were needed for the colony. But the merchants were afraid that settlers would interfere in their trade with the Natives. They also did not want the settlers to clear the land and drive out the beaver. As a result, only a trickle of settlers came to the colony. In spite of all Champlain's efforts, the population numbered only sixty-five by 1627.

What sort of people made good settlers for New France? What supplies would they need in the colony? Pierre Boucher came to New France in 1635. In his book, written in 1664, he gave some answers to these questions:

The people best fitted for this country are those who can work with their own hands in making clearings, putting up buildings. . . .

It would be well for a man coming to settle, to bring provisions with him for at least a year or two years if possible, especially flour, which he could get for much less in France and could not even be sure of being always able to get for any money here. . . .

Most of our settlers are persons who came over in the capacity of servants, and who, after serving their masters for three years, set up for themselves. They had not worked for more than a year before they had cleared land on which they got in more than enough grain for their food. . . .

Poor people would be much better off here than they are in France provided they are not lazy; they could not fail to get employment.

–From a book by Pierre Boucher

Champlain Allies with the Native Peoples

Champlain was anxious to keep on friendly terms with his Native neighbours. The few French living in Quebec were greatly outnumbered by the Native peoples. Also, Champlain realized how much help the Native peoples could be in the fur trade. They knew where and how to trap the beaver. They were expert canoeists and could use the rivers as highways to bring furs to Quebec.

In 1609 the Algonkins and Montagnais tested Champlain's friendship. They asked him to join an attack on their enemies, the Iroquois. Champlain agreed. They set out in canoes up the Richelieu River to a large lake they named Lake Champlain. In the evening they met 200 Iroquois paddling toward them. The Iroquois quickly made for the shore and hacked down trees to build a fort. The invaders lashed their canoes together, but stayed on the water. All night the two parties hurled insults at each other. In the morning the fight began.

The Algonkins and Montagnais went ashore with Champlain and two other French settlers. Each settler was armed with a gun called an **arquebus**. The Iroquois swarmed out of their fort to meet the invaders. Champlain stood in front of his Native allies. He fired the arquebus and killed two Iroquois chiefs. He himself was wounded in the neck by an arrow. The other two French fired from the woods where they were hidden. In alarm, the Iroquois turned and fled into the woods. That day was a great victory for the Algonkins, Montagnais, and their new French friends. The following year Champlain helped to defeat another group of Iroquois near the mouth of the Richelieu River.

By siding with the Algonkins and the Montagnais, Champlain took a decisive step. That day the French became the

Champlain with the Algonkins and Montagnais against the Iroquois in the Battle of 1609. This drawing is from Champlain's works.

enemy of the Iroquois. The Iroquois turned south to make friends with the English who had settled in the Hudson valley. For the next 150 years the pattern of partnerships with the Native groups was set. It would be the French, the Algonkins, the Montagnais, and their friends the Huron against the English and the Iroquois.

Champlain the Explorer

Champlain also continued his explorations of the country. In 1615 he set out with Algonkin guides on a long canoe trip up the Ottawa River, past Morrison Island, along the French River, and into Georgian Bay. From there the group headed south to the homeland of the Huron. Champlain mapped much of the area he explored.

While in Huronia, Champlain was asked to join a war party. The plan was to attack the Iroquois south of Lake Ontario, near Syracuse. In September Champlain travelled with 500 Huron through the Trent River system into Lake Ontario. The Natives hid their canoes on the south shore of the lake and went the rest of the way on foot.

This time it was not a great victory for Champlain and his Native allies. Although the Huron stayed until the snow began to fall, they could not capture the Iroquois fort. Champlain was wounded in the leg and had to be carried back to the canoes in a basket on a Native's back. Champlain spent that winter with the Huron and did not return to Quebec until June 1616.

On Christmas Day 1635, Champlain died in Quebec. He had worked with the colony for twenty-seven years. He had been its governor and supporter. He would be missed.

Activities

Looking Back

1. Define the following words and enter them in your dictionary.

saga	fool's gold	arquebus
compass	monopoly	primary source
astrolabe	habitation	secondary source
green method		

2. What evidence suggests that the Norse reached North America?

3. Identify these places and locate them on a map:
   a) the peninsula where Cartier erected a cross
   b) the Great River of Canada
   c) Stadacona
   d) Hochelaga
   e) "the large river that comes from the west."

4. Why were Europeans so eager to get to Asia?

5. List Cartier's major accomplishments. Organize your answer under the headings: First Voyage, Second Voyage, Third Voyage.

6. Describe the first French settlements in Acadia. What problems did the settlers have? What were their successes?

Using Your Knowledge

7. There were many reasons why explorers came to North America. Explain the importance of two of the following:
   a) the search for a Northwest Passage to Asia
   b) competition among nations in Europe
   c) fish
   d) furs
   e) desire for new lands to settle.

8. a) Locate France and China on a globe. Look for the Northwest Passage that would allow sailors to travel between the two countries.
   b) What would be the advantages of a Northwest Passage over other routes? What would be the disadvantages?

9. Why did Cartier believe he had the right to claim the new land for France? Why would the Native peoples see it differently?

10. a) Have you ever traded anything? Why?
    b) Why would the Native peoples be attracted to the trade items the French offered?
    c) Why were the French attracted to the items the Native peoples offered?

11. Reread the advice Pierre Boucher gave to new settlers. Would you give the same advice to someone who wants to settle in Canada today? Why or why not?

Extending Your Thinking

12. a) Imagine you are Cartier. Introduce Donnacona's sons to King Francis. Tell the King about the lifestyle of the Natives you have met.
    b) Imagine you are King Francis. What questions would you ask the Natives?
    c) You are Donnacona's sons. Describe how you feel about Cartier, France, and the King.

13. Write and present a short play to illustrate the problems colonists at Port Royal or Quebec encountered during the winter.

CHAPTER 13

Fur Traders and Missionaries

One sunny day in early June 1626, two merchant ships arrived on the St. Lawrence from France. A priest, Charles Lalemant, described the events.

These two ships bring all the merchandise which these Gentlemen use in trading with the Indians; that is to say cloaks, blankets, nightcaps, hats, shirts, sheets, hatchets, iron arrow heads, swords, picks to break the ice in winter, kettles, prunes, raisins. . . . In exchange the ships will carry back the hides of the moose, lynx, fox, otters, martens, badgers, and muskrats; but they deal principally in Beavers in which they find the greatest profit.

The day of their arrival they erect their huts and the Indians arrive in their canoes. The second day the Indians hold a council and present their gifts. Gifts are always given when people visit each other. The French give presents then to the Indians. The third and fourth day the Indians trade and barter their furs for blankets, hatchets, kettles, capes, little glass beads, and many similar things. It is a pleasure to watch them during this trading. When it is over they take one more day for the feast which is made for them, and the dance. Early the next morning the Indians disappear like a flock of birds.

–From *The Jesuit Relations*

Fur trading at Montreal.

THE SIX
ELEMENTS
OF THE
FUR TRADE

What was Charles Lalemant describing?
What goods were traded?
Which animal fur was most prized?
Describe the ceremony that took place.

The Fur Trade

Lalemant was describing the fur trade. The fur trade in New France depended on six key elements: Native peoples, beavers, fashions in Europe, coureurs de bois, birchbark canoes, and merchants.

Native Peoples

The Native peoples were essential to the fur trade. They had trapped the beaver for food and pelts long before the Europeans arrived. They knew the lakes and streams where the beaver lived. Many were expert trappers.

In 1723 a traveller described two methods the Natives used to kill the beaver. One way was a simple trap made with a heavy log balanced high on the end of a stick. The traps were baited with the beaver's favourite food. When the animal started to eat, even the slightest movement brought the log crashing down on its head.

A different method was used in the winter. Then the fur was thickest and best. A Native chopped a hole in the ice opposite the entrance to the beaver's lodge. A net was placed in the hole. Another Native then broke into the top of the beaver's lodge. When the animal tried to escape, it swam into the net. The hunter then killed it quickly with a blow to the head. A moment's hesitation and the beaver could gnaw the net to pieces. The beaver's bite was also dangerous. With those sharp teeth it could cut through a hunter's arm.

As the fur trade became established, the Huron developed the idea of working as "middle traders." The Huron lived in the region of the Great Lakes just northwest of the St. Lawrence. They knew that the Cree beyond Lake Superior had furs

that had not reached the St. Lawrence. They also knew that the French merchants had goods the Cree wanted. Why shouldn't the Huron bridge the gap?

In their fleets of birchbark canoes the Huron headed north and west on the rivers and lakes. They peddled knives and blankets among the Cree and brought back furs for the French merchants. They ran kind of a "trucking service" along the river highways of New France. But the Iroquois became concerned with the Huron's important place in the fur trade. In a bloody war during 1649 the Iroquois wiped out most of the Huron nation. Others would have to fill the gap in the fur trade.

Facts About the Beaver

Today the beaver is Canada's national emblem. This fact tells us something about its importance in our history. The fur trade in New France depended on the beaver. It was the most prized fur.

THE CANADIAN BEAVER (CASTOR CANADENSIS)

· belongs to the family of rodents along with mice, rats, porcupines, and squirrels

· fur grows in two layers; a coarse, reddish-brown outer fur and a smooth, downy under fur

· adult weighs approximately 30 kg

· excellent swimmers and can stay underwater for up to 15 minutes

· flat, black tail shaped like a paddle is slapped on the water to warn others of danger

· builds dams in slow-flowing streams to create ponds where it can build its lodge

· entrance to the lodge is underwater; ramps lead up to the beaver's living quarters

· feeds on bark and twigs of birch, aspen, poplar, and willow trees

· four sharp, curved front teeth are used to gnaw through wood

· teeth grow continuously; gnawing prevents them from becoming too long

Father LeClerq, a Jesuit priest, recorded the following statement from a Native:

In truth the Beaver does everything to perfection. He makes for us kettles, axes, swords, knives, and gives us drink and food without the trouble of cultivating the ground.

-From *New Relation of the Gaspesia*

1. How did the beaver provide all of these things for the Native peoples?
2. What problems could the Native peoples face if the supply of beaver ran out?

Fashions in Europe

The fur trade in New France depended upon Paris fashions for its success. The market demanded specialty furs such as ermine and fox. These were used to trim the robes of kings, wealthy nobles, and church officials. Europeans also wanted to buy deer and moose hides because they made excellent leather. But more than anything else the Paris market wanted beaver fur. Some beaver pelts were used for wraps and boots, but most were made into the ultimate item of fashion–the beaver hat.

Fashion designers demanded the pelts known as **castor gras** for their hats. Castor gras means "greasy beaver." These pelts were worn by the Native peoples for a time before they were sold. The long top hair of the pelts was rubbed away. Oil and sweat from the Natives' bodies matted the soft underhair. Castor gras made the finest felt for hats.

Wealthy and not so wealthy people purchased the beaver felt hats in great numbers. Some even went into debt to buy a beaver hat. It was a **status symbol**, an important sign of a person's high rank in society.

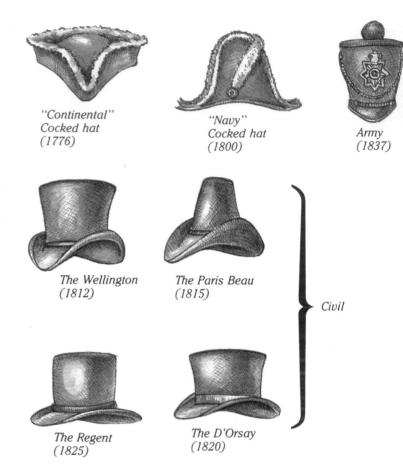

"Continental" Cocked hat (1776)

"Navy" Cocked hat (1800)

Army (1837)

The Wellington (1812)

The Paris Beau (1815)

The Regent (1825)

The D'Orsay (1820)

Civil

Coureurs de Bois

When the Huron disappeared from the trade routes, the French had to go west to collect furs from the Natives. Some jumped at the chance to get away from the dull life on the farm or in the towns. They went into the woods and made friends with the Natives. Sometimes they lived with the Natives for months at a time. From them they learned the skills of handling the canoe, searching out the finest pelts, and surviving in the wilderness. They traded and brought furs to the merchants of Montreal and Quebec. Basically all they needed was a loaded musket, a birchbark canoe piled with goods to trade, and a knowledge of the woods. People called them **coureurs de bois**–"runners of the woods."

Clerical (Eighteenth century)

Styles of beaver hats. The fashion for beaver hats in Europe was a driving force behind the fur trade in New France.

THE FIRST COUREUR DE BOIS

The first coureur de bois in New France was Étienne Brûlé. He was only fifteen when he arrived in 1608 with the first group of settlers at Quebec. Two years later Brûlé begged Champlain to let him go and live among the Natives. Champlain agreed and the seventeen-year-old Brûlé set off to live with the Algonkian chief, Iroquet.

Brûlé became the first French person to learn Native languages and customs. He acted as an interpreter for Champlain as they journeyed up the Ottawa River into Huron country around Georgian Bay.

After these adventures Brûlé was never again content to live for long periods at Quebec. Life in town was simply too dull. It couldn't compare with the excitement of racing a birchbark canoe through the rapids or joining a hunting party to trap beaver.

Brûlé travelled through areas where no French person had ever been. He visited each of the five Great Lakes and followed Native trails from present-day Toronto along the shores of Lake Ontario to Niagara Falls. Without Brûlé Champlain would have had difficulty completing his maps of the vast new continent.

Étienne Brûlé worked with the fur merchants of Montreal and Quebec. They paid him to encourage the Native peoples to bring their furs to the French. Since he spoke their languages and understood their ways, Brûlé gained the friendship and respect of the Native peoples.

Many times during his life, Brûlé faced death. Once he was captured by some Seneca, enemies of the Huron. He was tortured and would have been killed. Reports say he managed to escape by persuading his captors that an approaching thunderstorm was a sign from the spirits that he should live. Brûlé found his way back to Huron territory through hundreds of kilometres of wilderness.

In the end some Huron killed Brûlé in the summer of 1633. No one knows why. Perhaps Brûlé had insulted or betrayed them. There is no record for the reason of the first coureur de bois's death.

The lives of the coureurs de bois were full of risk, loneliness, and sometimes violence. As a rule they travelled in threes. A tarpaulin served as a sail for the canoe when the wind was behind them. It also doubled as a tent for shelter at night. Coureurs de bois carried very little food with them. They preferred to use the space in the canoe for furs and trade goods. They lived mostly on game and fish from the woods. When desperately short of food, coureurs were known to boil and eat their moccasins!

By 1678 there were about 600 coureurs de bois in New France. The total population of the colony was then only about 9000. The coureurs de bois played a vital role in the fur trade. They acted as interpreters for the Native peoples and the merchants. As friends of the Natives, they helped to ensure a constant supply of furs at French forts. In their constant search for more furs, they explored the interior of North America.

Not everyone approved of so many settlers leaving the farms for the woods. Government officials and church leaders wanted the coureurs to stay at home, have large families, and develop the settlements.

To solve this problem, the governor of New France passed a new law. Traders had to have permits and only a limited number of permits was issued. Those who had trading permits were called the **voyageurs**. However, in spite of this new law, hundreds of coureurs de bois continued to operate. Besides, if the Natives could not take their furs to the French, they would trade them to the English. Like them or not, the fur trade needed the coureurs de bois.

Étienne Brûlé at the mouth of the Humber River. Brûlé travelled over a vast area trading with the Native peoples.

Voyageurs shooting the rapids. Large canoes like this one carried furs on the waterways well into the nineteenth century.

Birchbark Canoes

For years the Native peoples had travelled through the Canadian waterways in their birchbark canoes to trade, fish, and hunt. When the fur trade began, they used their canoes to deliver the precious furs to the trading posts along the St. Lawrence. Later, Europeans learned to handle the canoes almost as expertly as the Natives. Then birchbark canoes took French fur traders into the heart of the continent.

The birchbark canoe rode the backwoods waterways with ease and speed. Freight canoes could be up to 12 m long. They could carry a crew of six to twelve and a cargo of 2300 kg. Imagine how many beaver pelts these great canoes could carry!

Normally the traders knelt in the canoes as they paddled, but an expert could stand up and pole in the rapids. When the rapids were too dangerous to run, the canoe could be pulled along the bank. Sometimes the traders had to portage or carry the canoe and goods over land. Even then two people could carry a canoe upside down on their shoulders while others brought the supplies and paddles.

At night the canoe was unloaded and tied to small wooden stakes driven into the ground. This was a necessary precaution because a sudden gust of wind could hurl the fragile craft against a rock or tree.

Canoes could be damaged easily and this was their major disadvantage. Sharp rocks could spell disaster. But crews always carried a supply of tools and spruce or pine gum to make minor repairs on the spot.

Canoes were propelled by the quick continuous stroke of narrow paddles. A freight canoe with a large crew and cargo could cover up to 140 km with the current in an eighteen-hour day! Without canoes and the skill of the Native peoples in handling them, the fur trade could never have expanded so quickly and widely.

Merchants

Many French and French-Canadian merchants took advantage of the new opportunities in the colony. They bought goods in France and shipped them to the colony to trade for furs. The goods were stored in warehouses at Montreal and Quebec. These towns were ideally located on the St. Lawrence River–the major highway of the fur trade. Natives brought canoe-loads of furs to Montreal and Quebec from the rivers and lakes of the interior.

Merchants transported the furs back to France and sold them. They took risks but they most often made a handsome profit. As long as the fur trade thrived, the merchants were the most powerful people in New France.

Clothes, blankets, tools, guns, gun powder, and brandy were popular trade items with the Native peoples. Guns made hunting easier and meant even more furs for the next year. The Natives favoured blankets made of white, blue, or red cloth edged with black stripes. They were very particular about the blackness of the stripes. They felt English blankets were best. To keep their business, French merchants bought their supplies of blankets in England.

Brandy caused the most trouble. The Native peoples were not used to the effects of alcohol. People in the colony agreed that alcohol was destroying the lives of many Native people. The Church urged the traders to stop supplying brandy to the Natives. But if the French refused to trade brandy, the English might take their trade away by offering rum to the Native peoples. Rivalry between the English and the French in the fur trade was intense. To keep their trade, the French continued to sell brandy to the Natives.

Beaver pelts and goods were used as money in New France. You can see how the trade worked from this table of exchange:

12 beaver pelts buys 1 gun
4 beaver pelts buys 4.5 L brandy
2 beaver pelts buys 10 fish hooks
1 beaver pelt buys 0.25 kg coloured
glass beads

Fur Traders or Colonists?

For years, the fur trade was the lifeblood of New France. For France it was the only real source of wealth coming in from the colony. Fur traders also helped to unroll the map of North America. On their travels they added more and more territory to the French empire.

Between 1608 and 1640 the fur trade grew quickly. But the population of New France did not. A century after Cartier, fewer than 500 people lived in all of New France. The tiny population was grouped around the towns of Quebec, Montreal, and Trois Rivières. The fur-trading companies seemed interested only in making a profit. They were not fulfilling their promise to bring colonists.

In 1627, King Louis XIII gave the monopoly to a new fur-trading company–the Company of One Hundred Associates. It promised to bring in thousands of settlers and help them get started. But years later, there were few new colonists. Those who had come complained that the Company refused to provide them with farm supplies. It seemed the merchants preferred to fill their ships with trade goods rather than ploughs and farm animals. The colonists also complained that the Company did nothing to protect them from Iroquois counter attacks.

The fur traders argued that they had tried to bring settlers. In 1628, the first shipload of settlers and supplies had been captured by the English when war broke out. And it was difficult to persuade new settlers to come. They heard of the hard work, loneliness, and danger of Iroquois attack. Some preferred to face poverty in France rather than risk their lives in a wild land.

France would soon have to make up its mind who should control the colony. Would it be settlers or fur traders? Others would also have a voice in the direction of the colony. The Church had become a powerful force in New France. In New France, the Church was the Roman Catholic Church.

Missionaries in New France

Every summer thousands of tourists turn off Highway 12 near Midland, Ontario to visit Ste. Marie Among the Hurons. Ste. Marie is a reconstructed Roman Catholic mission. It was originally built in 1639 in the heart of Huron country.

More than 350 years ago Roman Catholic priests from France went to work among the Native peoples. They were called **missionaries**. Many were members of a religious community known as the Society of Jesus, or **Jesuits**. Missionaries believed it was their duty to bring the Christian religion to the Natives. At that time almost all the people in France were Christians, though today there are many different religions in France and Canada. The missionaries came to New France with the permission and blessing of the King. They helped to found settlements in North America.

The first missionaries lived in the Huron longhouses. In 1639 they built their own village, Ste. Marie, on the east bank of the Wye River. With the help of carpenters and masons from Quebec, they constructed a church, a small hospital, kitchens, and workshops for a blacksmith, a carpenter, and a shoemaker. There were also simple living quarters for the missionaries and the **donnes**, the skilled crafters who volunteered their help. At times during the year, a few soldiers also stayed at Ste. Marie.

Today life at the mission of Ste. Marie Among the Hurons is re-enacted for visitors.

Everyday Life

What was life like for a missionary in New France? The missionaries left important written reports about their work among the Huron. These reports are called the *Jesuit Relations*. From them we know a great deal about life at Ste. Marie from 1639 to 1649.

The life of a missionary in New France was neither easy nor comfortable. The missionaries made many long and difficult journeys into the wilderness. It took about twenty-eight days in a canoe to make the 1000 km journey from Quebec to Huronia. The Jesuits divided Huronia into a number of districts. Each was cared for by two priests who lived in a Native village.

At each mission village a church was built and religious services were held for the Huron. Some "Black Robes," as the Natives called them, travelled among the villages teaching, preaching, and visiting the longhouses. Missionaries and fur traders often journeyed together. The coureurs de bois wanted furs. The missionaries wanted to bring Christianity to the Natives.

The missionaries tried to learn the Huron language and win the Natives' friendship with kindness. But progress was slow. Few Huron became Christians.

The End of Ste. Marie

From the beginning the Huron spiritual leaders, called shamans, were opponents of the priests. Can you understand why? They knew that if their people became Christians, they would have to abandon their traditional beliefs. The shamans blamed the Jesuits for troubles that befell Huronia. The missionaries had told the people that their prayers could bring rain and heal the sick. When it failed to rain or when a smallpox epidemic broke out, the Christians were held responsible. The missionaries knew they were living in constant danger, even among their allies the Huron.

A more serious threat came from the Iroquois. Since the days of Champlain, the Iroquois had competed with the French and Huron in the fur trade. Both sides fought and ambushed the other's fur-trading parties. Stories of Iroquois raids on Montreal intensified and in 1648 the Iroquois launched an offensive against Huronia.

In July 1648 the Iroquois overran the mission station of St. Joseph, resulting in the capture of 700 Hurons and the death of one priest. In the following year, two other missions were captured. The Jesuits decided to abandon their mission at Ste. Marie.

The remaining Huron decided to accompany the Black Robes back to the St. Lawrence in 1650. The retreat marked the end of the Jesuit mission at Huronia and a victory for the Iroquois in this phase of their ongoing war with the French-Huron alliance.

Work Among the Settlers

From the earliest days of the colony, the Roman Catholic Church played an important role. The desire to bring the Christian religion to the Native peoples helped to found communities in the New World.

Montreal, for example, also started as a mission post. On a summer afternoon you can hear tour guides in the Place d'Armes tell the story:

The soldier on the monument is Maisonneuve, who founded this city in 1642. With him he brought priests, nurses, and teachers. They belonged to an organization in France called the Society of Our Lady. Their purpose was to help the Native peoples by introducing them to the Christian religion. They called this little settlement Ville Marie.

As the population of New France grew, priests were also needed for the French settlers. The first priests came from France, but soon the Jesuits opened a school in Quebec. There they educated boys from the colony and trained some to be priests.

Priests called **curés** travelled among the tiny settlements of New France. They baptized babies, prayed for the sick, buried the dead, and looked after the spiritual needs of the colonists. Often the priest was the best educated person in the community and also acted as a teacher. He was responsible for registering births and deaths and often drew up wills and recorded business dealings for people who could not read or write.

Religious Women

Religious women also played a vital role in the life of New France. Christian women, called nuns, journeyed from France to establish schools and hospitals in the colony. They cared for the poor, the elderly, and the Native peoples. Three of the most important women in New France were Marie de L'Incarnation, Jeanne Mance, and Marguerite Bourgeoys.

MARIE GUYART: QUEBEC'S FIRST SCHOOL MISTRESS

Marie Guyart was born in 1599, the daughter of a master baker in Tours, France. As a child she had religious visions and longed to be a nun. When she was seventeen her family forced her to marry against her will. Two years later her husband died, leaving her with a young son.

For years her religious visions continued. She saw a far-away land and was convinced it was Canada. She believed that God was calling her to go there and "build a house for Jesus and Mary." The visions also told her she would meet a great friend who would help her with her work in Canada. She left her son in the care of a sister and entered an Ursuline convent. In 1636 she met Marie-Madeleine Peltrie, a French woman of enormous wealth. She knew instantly that Madame Peltrie was the great friend of her vision.

There were only 200 people living in Quebec in 1639 when Marie Guyart and Madame Peltrie, three other nuns, and three nurses arrived. After unpacking, the women set to work. They established their convent in a crude two-room shelter. Marie Guyart was the first Superior of the Ursuline Nuns in New France and became known as Marie de L'Incarnation. Three years later the convent burned, but the nuns simply rebuilt it. This time they erected a large stone convent, the most imposing structure in New France at that time.

The Ursuline school in Quebec was for Native and French girls. They were taught reading, writing, housekeeping, and the Christian religion.

For the next thirty years Marie de L'Incarnation dedicated her life to educating the young women of New France. She also spoke out strongly against the wrongs she saw around her. She was against the practice of trading brandy to the Native peoples. We also know a great deal about life in the colony from over 7000 letters Marie wrote to her friends and family.

The arrival of the Ursuline nuns at Quebec in 1639.

Jeanne Mance

JEANNE MANCE: CO-FOUNDER OF MONTREAL

Two years after the Ursuline nuns came to Quebec, Jeanne Mance arrived with her own mission. It was to found a hospital. Her plan was to join the soldier Maisonneuve and a few other colonists in a new settlement up river from Quebec. The site they chose was at the junction of the St. Lawrence and Ottawa rivers, where Montreal stands today. Ville Marie, as it was then called, was close to the northern edge of Iroquois country.

Jeanne Mance was one of the most able women of her time. Born in 1606, she felt called at an early age to serve in Canada. She had little money of her own, but her powers of persuasion helped her secure funds from some wealthy women of France.

The new settlement of Ville Marie was built like a fort to protect it from the Iroquois since peace between the French and the Iroquois seemed unlikely. There were walls around it and inside a windmill, a few houses, and Hôtel-Dieu, Jeanne's hospital. There were only forty colonists in the beginning.

The Iroquois discovered this new French outpost on the St. Lawrence. Then watch had to be kept.

During the first battle with the Iroquois in 1643, several colonists were killed and a number wounded. The wounded were among the first patients cared for by Jeanne Mance. A priest reported, "No sooner was the hospital finished than there appeared plenty of sick and wounded to fill it." In the years that followed, the Hôtel-Dieu cared for many more patients, French and Native.

At least twice Jeanne returned to France to raise money for the hospital. She also gained support for Ville Marie and encouraged settlers to come from France. Jeanne became godmother to more than seventy children born in Ville Marie. She watched the growth of the town she had helped to found with pride. By the time of her death in 1673, Montreal had a population of 1500. It had become the most important centre of the fur trade. Eight hundred fur-laden canoes came each year from the interior of Canada.

MARGUERITE BOURGEOYS: MONTREAL'S FIRST SOCIAL WORKER

Marguerite Bourgeoys was thirty-three when she arrived at Montreal in 1653. As a nun she had spent most of her life helping the poor and sick. When Sister Marguerite heard stories about New France, she felt she could do some good there.

Marguerite Bourgeoys

Her first pupils in Montreal were gathered in a stable loaned to her by Maisonneuve. The girls were taught reading, writing, sewing, and other useful handicrafts. Women in New France had to be able to make most of what they needed. At night the pupils slept above the stable in a loft. It was a humble beginning.

Marguerite Bourgeoys's social work included looking after the orphan girls who arrived from France. She helped them to find husbands in the small colony. She also encouraged other women from the colony and France to join her work. She founded a group of nuns called the Congregation of Notre Dame. These nuns did not stay in their convent as most nuns did at that time. They went out into the community to help others. They travelled up and down the St. Lawrence founding schools, teaching, visiting, and helping the colonists.

Marguerite Bourgeoys died in 1700 at the age of eighty, but her order of nuns survives today.

Skill Building: Preparing a Personality Profile

Marquis de Montcalm

It is exciting and informative to read about people in history. Books about people's lives are called **biographies**. You may also find letters or diaries written by people about their experiences. These can give you a first-hand view of what they thought and felt. The letters and diaries are primary sources. Biographies are secondary sources.

From these sources, you can develop a personality profile. A personality profile is an outline of a person's character and accomplishments. To be interesting, it should tell about both strengths and weaknesses, failures and successes. It should conclude by suggesting some reasons for the person's importance in history.

Here is how you can develop a personality profile:

1. Set a focus for the profile. Develop key questions you want to answer. For example:
What people or events influenced this person's life? How?
What were the person's strengths and weaknesses?
What were his or her major accomplishments?
What difficulties or problems had to be overcome?

2. Use your questions to create focus headings for an organizer.
For example:

Personality: Samuel de Champlain–"Father of New France"

Influences
Strengths
Weaknesses
Major Accomplishments
Difficulties

3. Locate various sources of information. Look for biographies, letters, diaries or journals, and reports about the person.

4. Make a point-form summary of the information you collect under your focus headings.

5. Decide on the person's most important contribution.

6. Use the point-form summary to write a personality profile in paragraph form.

Choose an important man or woman who lived in New France. Prepare a personality profile. Consider the following: Cartier, Champlain, Marie de l'Incarnation, Jeanne Mance, Marguerite Bourgeoys, or others you will read about in the next chapters.

Activities

Looking Back

1. Define the following words and enter them in your dictionary.

   castor gras   Jesuits
   status symbol   donne
   coureur de bois   curé
   voyageur   biography
   missionary

2. Review the six key elements in the fur trade. For each element ask: Could the fur trade have developed without it? Why or why not? Give two reasons for each element.

3. Why did the missionaries come to New France? What role did they play?

Using Your Knowledge

4. When Champlain first visited the St. Lawrence River in 1603, he was impressed by the birchbark canoe. This is what he wrote:

   Their canoes are some eight or nine paces long, and a pace and a half broad in the middle and sharper toward both ends. They are very subject to overturning, if one knows not how to guide them, for they are made from the bark of the birch tree, strengthened within with little half circles of wood, well and beautifully framed. The canoes are so light that one man can carry them easily.

   a) Name one advantage of the canoe Champlain mentions.
   b) Name one disadvantage.
   c) In the hands of an experienced canoeist, how could this disadvantage be turned into an advantage?

5. **a)** Explain how each of the following made the work of the missionaries difficult in New France:
   i) Native beliefs and religion
   ii) the shamans
   iii) problems of language
   iv) their own beliefs and different way of life
   v) the Iroquois—French rivalry.
   b) How did the Native peoples view the missionaries? Explain.

Extending Your Thinking

6. The beaver was almost eliminated in Canada by over-trapping. What rules apply to trapping beaver in your area? How do people feel about the fur trade and trapping wild animals today?

7. Imagine you are a coureur de bois living among the Native people.
   a) Explain how you make your living.
   b) Describe your lifestyle.
   c) Tell something about your adventures in the interior and your trips to Montreal or Quebec.
   d) What does your family think of your lifestyle? Why?
   e) Why do you think the coureurs de bois are important for New France? Include drawings to illustrate your story.

8. Imagine you are one of the following people in New France.
   a) coureur de bois
   b) fur-trading merchant
   c) farmer
   d) Huron trader
   e) missionary
   f) government official

   Who do you think should have control in New France–fur traders or settlers? Why? Role play your answer for the class.

9. Write a diary entry to describe the experiences of one of the following:
   a) an Iroquois
   b) a donne at Ste. Marie
   c) a nun in Jeanne Mance's hospital or a curé
   d) one of the first settlers at Montreal.

CHAPTER 14

Organizing the Community of New France

Louis XIV—The Sun King

King Louis XIV. The Sun King ruled France and its colonies from 1661 to 1715.

Louis XIV became King of France at the age of five! For the next eighteen years his ministers ruled in his name. Finally in 1661, Louis was ready to take control. He adopted as his emblem the sun, the centre of the universe. He was determined to be at the centre of everything that happened in the French empire. Louis XIV ruled France for the next fifty-four years.

Imagine it is 1663. One morning a courtier at Versailles steps forward bravely and requests an audience with the Sun King.

Excuse me your gracious Majesty, but I have just returned from New France. I observed serious problems that your most powerful Majesty should know about. Here is a list of the problems I observed:

1. The number of people in the colony is very small. It is estimated that, from 1608 to 1661, only 1260 settlers arrived. This is an average of only about 24 each year!
2. The French–Iroquois rivalry puts the settlers at risk.
3. Very few settlers come to farm the land. The fur traders discourage farming.
4. The fur-trading merchants seem to be interested only in making money, not settlement.
5. New France is on its last legs. The colony is dying from neglect.

A New Government for New France

Louis XIV decided to act. He wanted the control of New France to be in his hands, not in the hands of the fur merchants. More important, he was determined to build a great French empire in America. The Sun King decided the rule of the Company of One Hundred Associates was over. In 1663, New France became a royal colony governed by the King and his ministers. The King provided money, settlers, and a plan.

Under the new system of government, three officials acted on behalf of the King in New France–the governor, the bishop, and the intendant. The governor was responsible for the safety of the colony. The bishop was in charge of overseeing its churches, missions, hospitals, and schools. The intendant had the most important job because he was responsible for the day-to-day operation of the colony. He looked after trade, the transportation system, industry, and law and order. These three officials were assisted by a Sovereign Council. The Council had five members who were appointed each year.

Jean Talon–The Great Intendant

A small group of settlers gathered on the wharf at Quebec in 1665 to welcome the new intendant. As Jean Talon stepped off the ship they saw a forty-year-old man, with shoulder-length brown curls underneath an expensive beaver hat. They would soon discover that Talon was an energetic and able man. He would help to put the colony on its feet.

Talon lost no time. One of his first acts was to conduct a census. He wanted an accurate count of the people in the colony, their names, ages, and occupations.

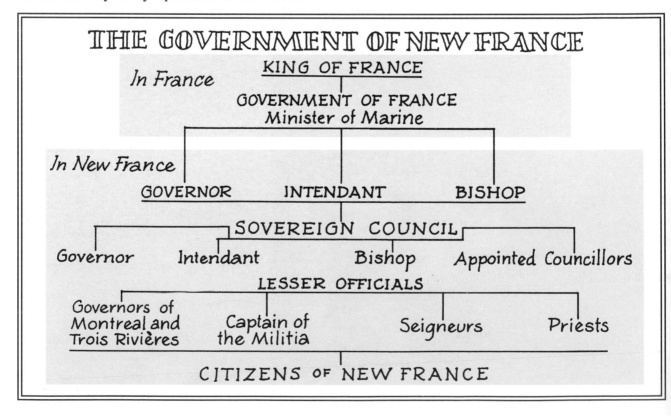

THE GOVERNMENT OF NEW FRANCE

In France

KING OF FRANCE

GOVERNMENT OF FRANCE
Minister of Marine

In New France

GOVERNOR   INTENDANT   BISHOP

SOVEREIGN COUNCIL

Governor   Intendant   Bishop   Appointed Councillors

LESSER OFFICIALS

Governors of Montreal and Trois Rivières   Captain of the Militia   Seigneurs   Priests

CITIZENS OF NEW FRANCE

Skill Building: Using Census Statistics as a Source of Information

Today the Canadian government counts the population every ten years. This count is called the **census**. A census tells us more than just the total number of people in the country. It indicates how people make their living, their ages, and other useful information. Talon's census in 1666 was one of the first taken in Canada.

When you examine any census information:

1. Identify the title, source, and date of the census statistics.

For example: Canadian Census, Dominion Bureau of Statistics, 1941

2. Identify the categories or types of information presented.

For example: occupations, ages, number of women in the work force

3. Focus on the category that relates to your topic.

4. Develop conclusions or general statements based on the statistics.

For example: 1. The majority of the population live in the city rather than the country.
2. Thirty percent of the population is over the age of seventy-five.

5. Choose the best way to present your conclusions. You could use words, charts, or graphs.

Let's examine some of the statistics from Talon's census of 1666.

Some Facts from the Census of 1666

Males	2 034
Females	1 181
Total population	3 215
Colonists under age 16	1 250
Colonists over age 81	4
Seigneurs	63
Carpenters	36
Stone masons	32
Shoemakers	20
Tailors	30
Teachers	3
Storekeepers	18
Coopers	8
Armourers	4
Gunsmiths	7
Hatters	7
Joiners	27
Millers	9
Ropemakers	6
Servants	401
Ship Captains	22
Slaters	1
Weavers	16

Note: Farmers and members of the clergy, nobility, and government were not included in Talon's list of occupations and trades.

-From Ottawa Dominion Bureau of Statistics

What conclusions can we draw about the community of New France from these statistics? Consider the following questions:

1. What kinds or categories of statistics are presented?

2. Compare the number of males in the colony with the number of females. What do the statistics tell you?

3. What age were the majority of colonists?

4. Why did the census figures of 1666 cause the French government to worry about New France?

5. Examine the list of occupations. Look up any unfamiliar words. Seigneurs were landowners who managed the farms of New France.
a) Which occupation had the highest population in the colony? Why do you think this was so?
b) Organize the information in the list under these two headings:
   Occupations that numbered more than 25
   Occupations that numbered less than 25
c) Compare the two lists. Which occupations were most numerous? Can you suggest why? Suggest some reasons for the small number of teachers.

Talon travelled throughout the colony talking to people and gathering information. He wanted to find out why New France was not prospering. Everywhere he heard the same complaint. The war with the Iroquois made the people afraid. It wasn't safe to go hunting or fishing, or even out into the fields. Talon immediately wrote to France for soldiers.

Colonial Defence

Shiploads of professional soldiers from the Carrignan-Salières Infantry Regiment soon arrived. About 1300 were sent from France under the leadership of the Marquis de Tracy. De Tracy set out to build a chain of forts from the St. Lawrence to Lake Champlain to block the Iroquois route into New France.

De Tracy marched his army up the Richelieu River into Iroquois territory. Tremendously outnumbered, the Iroquois retreated. De Tracy proceeded to burn their villages and crops. During the following winter, many Native people died of starvation. During the French–Iroquois wars, many innocent people on both sides suffered.

The following July, representatives of the Iroquois met at Quebec and made peace with the French. The peace lasted for the next eighteen years. De Tracy returned to France with some of his army, but more than 400 soldiers accepted discharge, took a grant of land, and settled in New France. Now there were experienced soldiers living on farms along the St. Lawrence.

Les Filles du Roi

Talon's next task was to find female settlers for the colony. The census had shown that there were twice as many men as women. The young women he brought were called **filles du roi** or "King's daughters." This term originally applied to orphan girls who lived in the king's orphanages. But not all were orphans. Many came from large, poor families and might have viewed New France as an opportunity to better their future. Each young woman brought a dowry to help her start her married life — an ox, a cow, two chickens, two barrels of salt beef, and a purse of money.

Can you imagine how the filles du roi felt when they arrived? The following imaginary letter will give you an idea.

The arrival of the filles du roi at Quebec. How were they received? How would you have felt as one of them?

Québec le 12 juillet 1668
Ma chère tante Hélène:

At last we are here in Quebec. What a voyage–forty-two filles du roi with nuns, all of us sailing to the New World. What would be waiting for us at the end of the voyage?

Imagine how excited and nervous we were as we got off the boat. People were crowded on the docks trying to catch sight of us. They seemed friendly. It was strange to think that one of these men might be my future husband. We were whisked away to the convent to rest from the journey.

The next day the young men began calling at the convent. The nuns questioned them closely. How much land had they cleared on their farms? Did they have a house ready? Did they drink liquor?

When Mother Superior had talked to Robert she called me in. "Marie-Anne," she said, "this is Robert. He is from Normandy, the same part of France you are from. He is nineteen, four years older than you, and is already well established with a good farm on the Île d'Orléans. I think you could be well suited to each other."

I must admit, dear aunt, that at first I was quite disappointed with Robert. But during the last few days he has been visiting me at the convent. We have had a chance to talk and get to know one another and I believe him to be a good person. I think we will get on well. Robert's farm sounds very nice and it is right on the river, not too far from Quebec. So I have decided to accept his proposal.

Tomorrow, I am off to the Île d'Orléans. Soon I shall be settled in a home of my own! Wish me luck.

Your niece,
Marie-Anne

Between 1665 and 1672, more than 1100 young women arrived in the colony. Within fifteen years the population had increased from 3215 to almost 10 000.

Talon had other plans to increase the population. Parents who did not marry their daughters by age sixteen or their sons by twenty were fined. On the other hand, young men and women who married early received a special gift of money from the King. To encourage large families, a special allowance was paid to those who had more than ten children.

Farming and Industry

Talon also wanted to develop agriculture in New France. Settlers who lived on the farms were called **habitants**. Talon encouraged the habitants to spend more time clearing and cultivating the land rather than hunting and trapping. While the colony was in the hands of the fur traders, farming was discouraged. Trapping had been more profitable.

On his own farm Talon tried out new strains of grain and seed. He wanted to know which crops would grow best in Canada. He made sure that cattle and livestock, including horses, were brought into the colony. His goal was to make the colony completely self-sufficient in grain and beef production. In other words, Talon wanted to be certain that enough food was produced in the colony to make it independent of France.

Talon had ambitious plans for the development of industries along the St. Lawrence. With financial help from France he started a shipbuilding yard and iron works. He expanded the fisheries and opened a shoe factory and a brewery. He encouraged spinning so that wool from sheep in New France could be made into fine yarns for clothing. In a letter to Louis XIV, Talon boasted that he was "clothed from head to toe with goods made in New France."

Talon did not remain long in the colony. He returned to Versailles in 1672 and became a personal secretary, colonial counsel, and wardrobe advisor to the King. Without his attention, most of the economic projects Talon had started in New France withered and died.

Talon studying plans at the new shipbuilding yard.

Law and the Community

The intendant was responsible for law and order in New France. Laws were the same as those used in Paris, France. The collection of laws was called the Custom of Paris.

The highest court was the Sovereign Council, which dealt with all serious cases. Lower courts handled matters such as traffic and fire regulations. The landowners, called **seigneurs**, sometimes acted as judges to solve disputes between farmers.

Punishment for crimes was harsh. A person suspected of a crime was presumed guilty. Men were locked up in the royal prisons. Women were guarded by a nun in the Hôpital-Géneral. At the trial, the accused was expected to prove his or her own innocence. The judge pronounced the sentence.

A thief could be sentenced to death. He or she was hanged and then the body was burned and thrown into a ditch. Executions were held in front of the townspeople to warn them of the punishment for breaking the law.

People convicted of lesser crimes were also held up as examples. On one occasion, several important citizens were accused of breaking the laws regarding alcohol. They were found guilty and condemned to thirty days in prison. Every day they were marched into the marketplace before the townspeople. They were made to sit on the back of a wooden horse. Signs were hung around their necks proclaiming their crimes. Meanwhile, the townspeople hurled insults at them.

Count Frontenac – The Most Important Governor

This statue of Governor Frontenac stands in Quebec City. It celebrates an event in 1690 while Frontenac was governor of New France. English soldiers sailed up the St. Lawrence and tried to capture Quebec. They sent a messenger to the governor demanding that he surrender the town. Frontenac drew himself up to his full height and answered the messenger this way, "I will not write an answer to your master on paper. Tell him the mouths of my cannons will deliver my reply."

What does this event tell you about

Frontenac is pointing at the mouth of a cannon in this statue. Why?

Frontenac's character? People said that he was conceited and bad-tempered. But trained as a soldier, Frontenac was experienced on the battlefield. He had the courage and experience the colony needed in a military emergency.

Shortly after his arrival in 1672, Frontenac assembled 400 soldiers and volunteers. They travelled up the St. Lawrence in a great procession of canoes to a site close to Kingston, Ontario. Frontenac had called a group of Iroquois to meet him there. He gave the Natives gifts, put on feasts, and for four days held discussions with their chiefs. All the time Frontenac's soldiers and volunteers were building an armed fort. The fort was completed in a very short time.

Frontenac asked the Iroquois to come to Fort Frontenac instead of going to the English at Fort Albany to sell their furs and get supplies. He promised that the goods at the French fort would be cheap. And would not the journey also be shorter and less dangerous for the Iroquois? As long as Frontenac was governor, there was no armed conflict between the French and Iroquois. Each side knew and respected the other.

Expansion and War

Fort Frontenac was the first in a long line of forts that marked out the French empire to the south and west. Frontenac strongly encouraged expansion into the territory of the Ohio and Mississippi rivers.

But the intendant opposed the extension of the fur trade into the Ohio valley. He preferred the settlers to stay on the farms. Frontenac frequently argued with the other officials in the colony. He also disagreed with the bishop's strong view

that brandy should not be traded to the Natives. Frontenac insisted that fur traders had the right to trade brandy if it was necessary to obtain the furs. Finally King Louis XIV grew weary of the squabbling among his ministers. Frontenac was ordered back to France.

War broke out again between the French and Iroquois. England and France were at war with each other in Europe. The rivalry between them and their Native allies in America also intensified. The English and the Iroquois were still allies and fought against the French in New France.

On 5 August 1689, during a driving hailstorm, a battle was fought between the French and the Iroquois at the settlement of Lachine near Montreal. The next day the village was in ruins. There were heavy losses on both sides.

Concerned, Louis XIV turned again to the aging Frontenac. Louis called Frontenac before him and reportedly said, "You are a proven leader...I am sending you back to Canada where I expect that you will serve me as well as you did before." By 1689 Frontenac was back as governor of New France.

In the meantime, the Iroquois launched an offensive against the farms along the St. Lawrence. They were highly mobile, while the settlers stayed in their farms to fight.

Governor Frontenac organized a military raid against the Iroquois in 1696. He set off south and west with a force of 2000 French soldiers and their Native allies. In the territory of the Onondaga and Oneida, the invading army found nothing but deserted villages. Nevertheless, Frontenac ordered the crops in the fields and storehouses burned. The Native villages were completely destroyed. Although Iroquois people starved that winter, they fought to a draw and survived.

Eventually the French and Iroquois signed a peace treaty in 1701. The Iroquois agreed to remain neutral in any war between the English and French. Frontenac was not present to witness this treaty. He had died in Quebec City in 1698.

Fourteen-year-old Madeleine de Verchères was one of many people from both sides caught in the midst of the French-Iroquois wars.

WHAT WAS NEW FRANCE?

What was this place called New France? Today it is the province of Quebec. In the 1600s, the French territory called New France covered about one-third of North America. In the years that followed, it had different names: Quebec, Lower Canada, Canada East, and finally again, Quebec. Examine the maps below. What was the area of present-day Quebec called in each map? How did the size of the territory change?

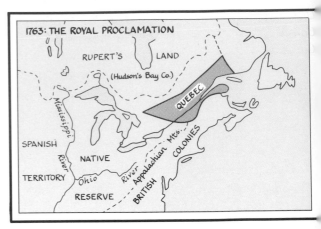

In 1763, France gave up the colony of New France to Britain. The British called it Quebec.

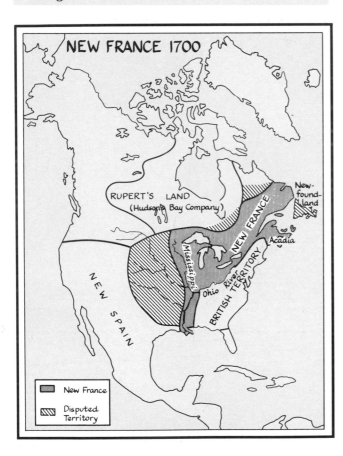

In the early 1700s, France had claim to about one-third of North America and called the region New France.

Quebec was split into two colonies. The French-speaking colony on the lower St. Lawrence River was called Lower Canada. The English-speaking part on the upper St. Lawrence became Upper Canada.

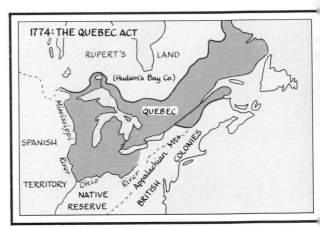

In 1774, Britain expanded the territory of French-speaking Quebec to include the Ohio valley.

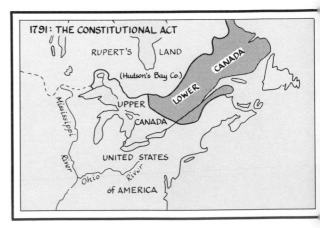

Upper and Lower Canada were reunited. Lower Canada was renamed Canada East and Upper Canada was renamed Canada West.

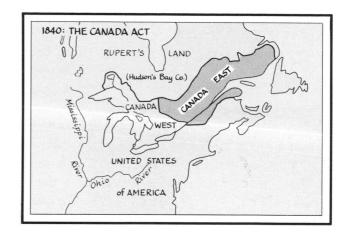

Canada East joined Nova Scotia, New Brunswick, and Canada West at Confederation. Canada East became known as the province of Quebec.

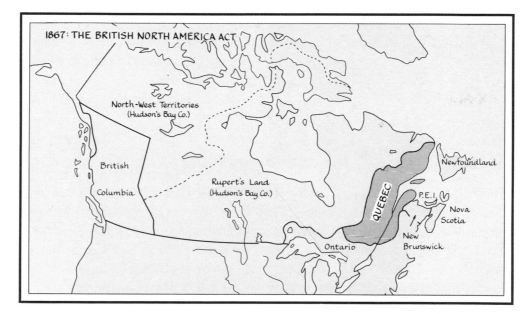

Quebec today is Canada's largest province. Nine out of ten Canadians of French origin live in the province. Quebec is the only region in North America where French is the language of the majority.

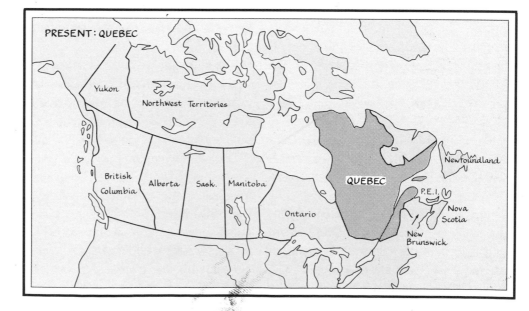

BISHOP LAVAL–THE MOST POWERFUL CHURCH LEADER

The Roman Catholic Church had a great deal of influence in New France. The bishop was the head of the Church. He also had a strong voice in the government since he was a member of the Sovereign Council. The Church looked after schools, hospitals, and the poor. It was also the single biggest landowner in the colony. The people of New France were almost all Roman Catholics and attended church regularly. They looked to the Church for guidance. It had an influence on their values, behaviour, and daily lives.

From 1659 to 1671 François de Laval was the bishop of New France. These were some of his major accomplishments:

1. Organized New France into religious districts called parishes and appointed priests to perform religious services such as weddings and burials
2. Strongly opposed trading brandy to the Native peoples and confronted Governor Frontenac on this issue
3. Established a school for priests in Quebec so that the colony would not be dependent on priests from France
4. Supported primary schools for boys and girls and trade schools for cabinet makers, sculptors, painters, and gilders
5. Encouraged more advanced education at the Jesuit College and Ursuline convent in Quebec
6. Strongly encouraged family life and traditions and insisted on upright behaviour from all the people
7. Demanded that the Church be allowed to collect a tax called a **tithe** from all the people; the money was to help pay the costs of building churches and supporting the priests.

The Seigneurial System

Since the days of Champlain there had been seigneuries in New France. **Seigneuries** were large tracts of land varying in size from 16 to 160 km^2. The King or governor granted these plots to landlords called seigneurs. The seigneurs parcelled out sections of the land to settlers known as habitants. This landholding system was modelled on the system used in France.

The seigneuries extended along the St. Lawrence River and its tributaries. There were very few roads in New France and the rivers were the major highways. Each seigneury needed frontage on the river.

Look at the map on page 215. You can see that the seigneuries were long narrow rectangles. They extended far back inland from the rivers. In 1760 about 200 seigneuries were spread along the St. Lawrence, Richelieu, and Chaudière rivers.

From the St. Lawrence it must have appeared to travellers that New France was a village strung out along the river. Behind the little row of houses were the long, thin fields and then nothing but wilderness. Eventually, when the river lots were filled up, a second row of seigneuries developed with no frontage on the river.

Who Were the Seigneurs?

Who were chosen to be seigneurs? Seigneurs were usually wealthy, important citizens. Some were retired military leaders. Others were members of religious orders that owned land in the colony. The seigneurs had many important duties. The first was to bring settlers to clear and settle the land. In this way they were responsible for finding suitable future citizens for New France. They were expected to set a good example for the habitants by going to church regularly and managing their own farms wisely. When important officials visited, the seigneurs were called upon to entertain them suitably. Often the seigneurs also acted as judges to settle disputes among the habitants. Above all, seigneurs had to be absolutely faithful to the King.

In 1663 about half of all the seigneurial land was held by women. Some were members of religious communities that owned land. Others had been left to manage the land alone when their husbands died.

What were the duties of the seigneurs once they received the land? The following letter tells you something of what a new seigneur might expect.

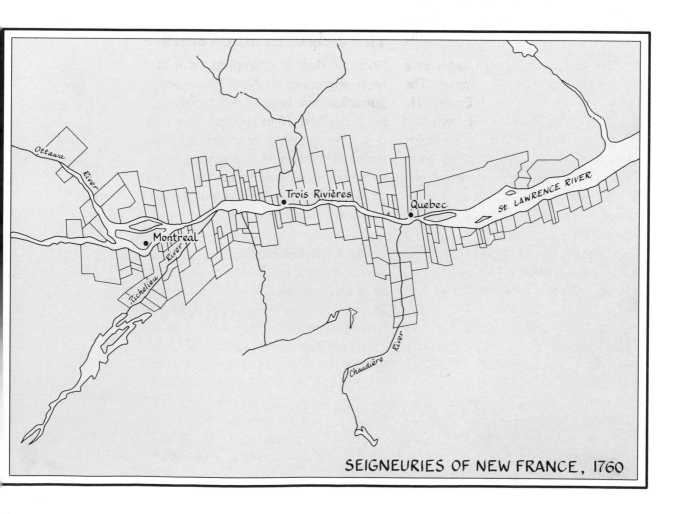

SEIGNEURIES OF NEW FRANCE, 1760

Québec
le 1 juin 1669
Mon cher ami:

Today is the proudest day of my life! This day I received my seigneurial land grant from His Majesty, King Louis XIV.

Yesterday I arrived at Quebec after a long journey to receive my grant. I removed my sword and spurs and knelt before the governor to swear my loyalty to the King. I promised to perform all my seigneurial duties. The governor warned me that the seigneury can be taken away from me if I fail to carry out my promises. Then the governor bade me rise. He shook my hand warmly and addressed me as Monsieur Le Seigneur!

In a few days my family and I will set out in a canoe along the river to visit our land. We will choose a part of the land for our own farm. I have engaged local carpenters to help us build our barns and manor house. It will be a fine sturdy house, built of stone, and with a high wooden fence around it. In case of Iroquois attack, God forbid, all the habitants will be able to take shelter there.

In time I must also build a small church or chapel and a mill where the habitants can grind their wheat into flour. I will also construct an outdoor bake oven for bread.

Soon we will start to divide the seigneury into farms. I am anxious to see the habitants build their homes and clear and till the soil. Jean and Hélène, two of the habitants, have a daughter who is about to be married. Jean and Hélène will divide their farm so that the new young couple will have some land of their own. They will be happy to have their parents and neighbours nearby to help them get started. Each family will have a home along the river.

I will write again soon.
Your friend,

Jean-Claude

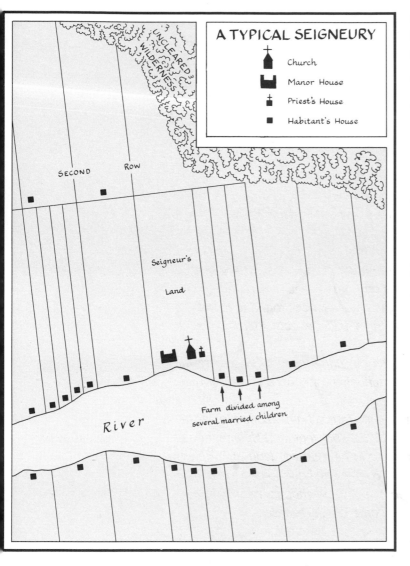

A TYPICAL SEIGNEURY

† Church
⊔ Manor House
† Priest's House
■ Habitant's House

UNCLEARED WILDERNESS

SECOND ROW

Seigneur's Land

River

Farm divided among several married children

could be appointed to certain government positions in the colony. Their sons could become officers in the army.

The Habitants

The habitants could make a good living on the seigneuries. They built their own log homes on the banks of the river. They cleared and worked their fields and produced enough to meet their needs. They were expected to be loyal to the seigneur and had their own duties to perform.

Habitants were expected to pay the seigneurs taxes called **cens et rentes**. These were fixed when the land contract was made. But the taxes were not extraordinarily high and could usually be paid in goods from the farm. Habitants might pay with a fine pig, some sacks of wheat, or a few chickens.

The habitants promised to work in the seigneur's fields three days each year, usually during planting and harvest. They also promised to take their grain to the seigneur's mill to be ground into flour. They paid the seigneur for the use of the flour mill, usually one-fourteenth of the grain they ground. Some contracts stated that the seigneur must be given a portion of the fish caught in the river in front of the seigneury. The seigneur was also given some of the wood cut on the property. As long as the habitants performed their contract duties, they could stay on the seigneury and had the protection of the seigneur. Family and neighbours were also close by to help in times of need.

The seigneurial system remained part of the life of New France for 200 years. But New France did not become the great farming colony that Louis XIV and Talon wanted. A government survey in 1711 showed that while some seigneuries were prosperous and well developed,

Each year seigneurs reported to the King on the number of land grants they had made and the amount of land that had been cleared. They also had to report any minerals found on their land. These were considered to be the property of the King. All the oak trees also belonged to the King and could not be cut down without permission. Oak was thought to be the best wood for shipbuilding and making fine furniture.

The seigneurs held an honoured position in society. They had a special place to sit in the local church and prayers were said for them at Sunday mass. Seigneurs

many others were largely uncleared and unsettled.

In fact by 1700, Louis XIV had almost lost interest in New France. From 1688 France was at war almost constantly. There was no time or money to spend on developing the colony. But the habitants and seigneurs continued to work together on the land. They had developed a distinctive way of life in the colony away from France. Traces of the long, narrow farms can still be seen today along the shores of the St. Lawrence.

A painting of a typical seigneury near Quebec.

Activities

Looking Back

1. Define the following words and enter them in your dictionary.

   census   seigneur
   fille du roi   habitant
   tithe   cens et rentes
   seigneuries

2. What problems led Louis XIV to establish a new government in New France?

3. Describe the territory of New France in the early 1700s. How is it different from Quebec today?

4. Examine the map of a typical seigneury on page 217.
   a) Describe the shape of the farms.
   b) Where are the habitants' homes located? Why?
   c) What will happen to the farms after two or three generations have lived on them?

5. Review the rights and obligations of the seigneurial system. On a chart like the one below, list the obligations of the seigneur and the habitant.

What the seigneur promises the habitant	What the habitant promises the seigneur

Using Your Knowledge

6. Decide which official in New France should deal with each of the following situations. Explain your answer.

a) Word has just reached Quebec that a small band of Iroquois have attacked a seigneury 20 km up the river.

b) Citizens and priests have complained that coureurs de bois are providing large amounts of brandy to the Native peoples.

c) The colony is desperately short of settlers.

d) Two habitants, neighbours on their seigneury, are squabbling about fishing rights in the river.

e) A thief has broken into the seigneur's house and stolen a silver candlestick.

f) An epidemic of influenza has broken out in the town and there is an urgent need for nurses and doctors.

7. How did Talon try to solve the problems revealed in the census of 1666? Was he successful? Explain your answer.

Extending Your Thinking

8. Imagine you are Marie-Anne writing back to tante Hélène in 1670. Two years have passed since you arrived as a fille du roi. Tell of your experiences in your new life on the Île d'Orléans.

9. Prepare a personality profile for one of the following:

a) Louis XIV
b) Talon
c) Frontenac
d) Bishop Laval
e) Madeleine de Verchères.

CHAPTER 15

Everyday Life in New France

THE SUGAR BUSH–A PIONEER REMEMBERS

In early spring we looked forward to making maple sugar. It meant fresh maple candy and fun for the whole family. We chose a place for boiling the sap in the centre of the sugar bush. The children helped to collect a huge supply of firewood for the boiling. Fires had to burn steadily day and night. We begged our parents to let us stay in the sugar bush all night to tend the fires.

The sap was boiled in big iron kettles. Parents, friends, and relatives all helped to carry the sap from the trees to the boiling kettles. Grandpère had a wooden yoke slung across his shoulders with a pail hanging from each end full of sap. Papa had the ox and sleigh to bring barrels of the sap from the wooden troughs under the trees.

The sap was boiled until it became a thin syrup almost ready for "sugaring off." Jeanne often brought her fiddle and there was music and dancing right there in the sugar bush. Even the smallest children came out armed with spoons and ladles for a taste. To test the syrup, we let drops fall on the snow. If they hardened, the syrup was ready. The hardened drops were wonderful to eat.

Later the syrup was poured into wooden moulds and left to harden into blocks of sugar. Grandpère, like most habitants, carved the sugar moulds into fancy shapes such as hearts, houses, animals, and books.

Tapping maple trees to make sugar was an event that marked the coming of spring for the habitants.

Life on a Seigneury

Sugar-making

Sugar-making in the spring was a festive time for the habitants. The whole family took part. Usually by mid-March the tapping of maple trees was well under way. It was hard work for the next few weeks but it was enjoyable and marked the end of the long winter.

The French settlers learned about sugar-making from the Native peoples. There are references in the *Jesuit Relations* to "maple water" running from the trees. It was reported that the Natives "split the tree they called *micktan* to get from it a juice, sweet as honey or as sugar."

French settlers soon developed their own way to tap the maple sap. They drilled a small hole in the south side of the maple tree. Then they drove a hollow wooden tube into the hole and let the sap drip into wooden containers. The sap ran best on sunny days after frosty nights.

An average family made 50 or 60 kg of maple sugar from their own trees each spring. Some families made much more and sold it in the towns. Very little cane sugar, like that we use today, was available in Canada at that time. Maple sugar therefore added a very welcome bit of sweetness to the habitants' foods.

Working on the Farm

Wheat was the most important crop on habitant farms and was planted in spring. It was needed for bread which was eaten at every meal. An average man ate almost 1 kg of bread every day. This would equal two full-size loaves of the bread we eat today.

Each year the habitants tried to clear a little more land for planting crops. It was hard work and almost all done by hand. Trees were chopped down with axes. The trunks and branches were sawn into logs for the fireplace. Stumps were burned or pulled out if the farmer was lucky enough to own a team of oxen. If not, the stumps were left in the fields and the crops were planted around them. Rocks and stones had to be picked up one by one and hauled away. Some were used for fences or for building fireplaces and foundations of homes.

Summer brought days of hard work for all members of the family. Men and women rose at dawn and worked until nightfall in the fields. Hay for the animals had to be brought in and a huge vegetable garden always needed tending. Peas, beans, onions, carrots, and cucumbers were grown. Children also had special farm chores. One of their daily tasks was to weed and hoe the garden. On days when the weather was bad, axes and scythes had to be sharpened, cart wheels greased, and hand tools repaired.

A habitant man and woman. Their clothes were almost all homemade. The high leather moccasins and leather jacket worn by the man show the influence of the Native peoples.

Preparing for Winter

Autumn was the time to get ready for the long winter ahead. Fruit was dried or made into jam. Supplies of vegetables were put down into the cool root cellar below the floor boards. Bacon, pork, chicken, venison, moose meat, and wild ducks and geese were stored away too. The meat was placed outside to freeze and then packed into barrels. When the habitants wanted to eat the meat, they simply thawed it over the stove. Eels from the river were salted and stored in barrels as well. They were a favourite delicacy of the habitants.

Men and boys repaired the house and barns to make sure they were snug for winter. They also cut and hauled great loads of firewood. There was no shortage of wood, but it was back-breaking work to haul it out of the bush. The family had to stock enough wood before the snow became too deep for the ox to pull the sleigh.

During the winter when the countryside was covered with snow, the habitants made their furniture or did a bit of hunting. Ice fishing was also a popular pastime. The habitants would chop two holes in the ice. Then they stretched a net between the holes across the direction of the current. Fish caught in the nets were a welcome addition to the winter diet.

Daily Chores

Besides the seasonal jobs, there were many daily chores to be done. Lucky families had at least one cow to be milked. The cream was churned into butter by hand. Winter and summer, water had to be hauled from the river for

---

STORIES FROM GRANDMÈRE AND GRANDPÈRE

Telling stories was an important form of entertainment in New France. In the days before television and radio, it helped to pass the long evening hours. When few could read and books were scarce and expensive, it was also a way of passing on folktales and customs.

The Dreams of Hunters

I'd like to tell you that once there were three gentlemen and their cook who went hunting in the woods. After hunting all day without eating, they had killed only one partridge. They said: "Let's keep this partridge for breakfast. It will be for the one who has the finest dream."

The next morning: "What did you dream?" they asked each other. One of them replied: "Me, I dreamed that I was married to the most beautiful princess in the world." The others said: "Ah, you had a fine dream." "Me," said another, "I dreamed of the Holy Virgin, that I saw her in all her beauty." The third: "Me, I dreamed that I was in heaven, where I saw the good God himself."

The cook added: "Me, also, I had a fine one. I dreamed that I had eaten a partridge, and I see that my dream is true because I can't find it this morning."

–From Folktales of French Canada

cooking, drinking, and bathing. Something as simple as washing the family clothes was a major undertaking. Pail after pail of water had to be carried to the house and heated in huge kettles over the fire. When the river froze in winter, blocks of ice were sawn out, dragged back on sleighs, and melted for water.

Every day there was wood to be chopped. Young boys were expected to keep the woodbox stocked at all times. Even in the summer, wood was needed to build fires for cooking.

At dusk work stopped. Families went to bed early, usually right after the evening meal. Candles were expensive and didn't provide enough light to work by. Sometimes the family gathered together for storytelling before they went to bed.

Building a Home

Most of the early houses on the seigneuries were built of wood. Wood was cheap and readily available. It was also a better insulating material than stone. A stone house could be very cold, though it was better protected against fire. Stone houses were also more expensive to build and most belonged to the seigneurs.

How did the habitants build their first homes? It was back-breaking work. Often neighbours and relatives would come from near and far to help. The habitants first had to haul stones from the fields to build a foundation. Then squared timbers were laid one on top of the other. A mixture of sand, lime, and water made mortar. The mortar was used to fill the spaces between the timbers and hold them together. The ends of the timbers were fitted carefully into the upright corner posts. This was called the **pièce-sur-pièce** method of construction.

The roof of the house was usually a series of overlapping planks. Later the habitant might add cedar shingles. Roofs were always very high and steep so that the snow would slide off easily in the winter.

A huge fireplace in the middle of the house was the only source of heat for the early home. If you look at the early house in the picture on page 224, you can see that the chimney is in the middle of the roof. Fire was a constant danger, however, and the habitants had to be extremely cautious at all times. If fire did break out, they could do little but haul buckets of water from the river to try and put it out.

Windows tended to be small. Glass was very expensive so the habitants used oiled skins or greased paper for the windows. These allowed a soft glow of light to pass through but they could not see through them. Most windows also had shutters to keep out wind and rain.

The habitants painted the outside walls with whitewash so that the house looked neat and clean. Houses on a seigneury were more or less alike but they were sturdy, well-insulated, and reasonably comfortable. You can still see later examples of these sturdy, steep-roofed homes in Quebec today.

Pièce-sur-pièce construction. The ends of the squared timber were fitted into upright cornerposts.

A typical habitant home. Why is there a ladder on the roof?

Settling in

Let's look inside a typical habitant home. As you step through the door, you come into the large main room of the house. The family spends most of its time in this room. It serves as a kitchen, living room, and dining room. There is a red glow in the fireplace and a stew is simmering in a black kettle over the coals. Pots, pans, kettles, and other cooking utensils hang around the fireplace. On one side a deep bake oven is built into the bricks. The habitant woman is making apple pies. She lights a roaring wood fire in the oven. Later she removes the ashes and then places the pies inside while the bricks are still hot. An iron door on the oven keeps in the heat. The fresh-baked pies smell wonderful.

You notice that there isn't much furniture in the house. A table, a few chairs with woven rush seats, benches, a cupboard, shelves for buckets, and a spinning wheel are the basics. Most of the furniture is made by the family with wood cut on the farm. Pine and yellow birch grow thick around the house. They are good

for making furniture because they can be cut into long, knot-free planks.

The furniture is stained dark brown or painted with homemade paint. The favourite colours seem to be red, blue, and dark green. The habitant woman tells you that she made the red paint by mixing fine red earth from their fields with linseed oil and skim milk.

The bare wooden floor boards must be cold in winter. No wonder the habitants have thrown rugs woven from rags on the

The main room in a habitant home. Can you identify the main pieces of furniture?

A habitant bedroom. Notice the wooden clogs, called sabots, by the bed.

There is a four-poster bed in this bedroom. You feel the mattress. It seems to be filled with straw. Mattresses were also filled with chicken or duck feathers, goose down, or sometimes even milkweed. In the cupboard are animal skins and heavy quilts to pile on the beds in winter.

Food

What were the habitants' foods? Bread and meat were the most important foods. The habitants preferred outdoor ovens for baking bread because these were much larger than the fireplace ovens. Sometimes the habitants paid a small fee to use the seigneur's bake oven. Most though built their own ovens a few metres from their kitchen door. The bake oven was made of stones, mortar, and clay. It had a roof for protection from the weather. Usually the oven was fired up once or twice a week and several huge round crusty loaves were baked at one time. Each loaf weighed about 2 kg.

floors. You also see a beautiful hooked rug with an intricate design. The rugs add warmth and colour to the room.

Next you step into the bedroom. A candle table, cupboard, and bed are the main furniture. You learn that the earliest beds in the colony were called **cabanes**. They look like large cabinets with doors made of planks. The bed is built right inside. The habitants could keep warm inside. There was no stove in the bedroom. Cabanes were no longer used when stoves became more common.

An outdoor bake oven with a roof to protect it from the weather.

Most habitants ate four meals a day. They rose before dawn and tended to chores for one or two hours before breakfast. Then they sat down to a hearty breakfast of milk, bread, and pancakes. Lunches were carried out to the fields at noon and again at about four o'clock if the workers were too busy to come into the house.

The main meal of the day was eaten at about eight o'clock, after the evening chores were finished. It was usually soup, baked beans, some kind of meat or fish, and of course more bread. The habitants usually drank milk, cider, or homemade beer made from wheat or corn. Vegetables were eaten with enthusiasm, especially when they were fresh from the garden. Strangely enough the habitants did not eat the potato. They called it "the root" and looked down on it with contempt. In a letter written in 1737, the Mother Superior of the Hôtel-Dieu described a time of terrible food shortages when the people were forced to eat "the buds of trees, potatoes, and other foods never meant to be eaten by human beings."

The meal usually ended with some kind of dessert. It might be as simple as a slice of bread sprinkled with maple sugar and covered with fresh cream. It could be fresh fruit or preserved fruit baked into a pie. Maple syrup pie was also a favourite.

The Role of Women

A woman of New France, like pioneer women everywhere, shared in the farm work completely. She helped in the fields with the planting and harvesting. She cared for a huge vegetable garden and stored its produce for the winter. She helped to feed the livestock and chickens and milk the cows.

Women also needed many skills to help manage the home and farm. Careful planning was needed and almost everything was made from scratch. There were few nearby shops, no boxes of mixes or tins of ready-made goods. Women spun yarn and wove cloth. They made most of the clothing for the family as well as curtains, rugs, towels, and blankets. They made paints and helped to build the furniture for the homes.

Many women in New France were also experts at such specialized tasks as making soap and candles. They made candles in the autumn after the winter meat had been butchered. First the **tallow**, or hard fat of the animals, was melted down in a

HABITANT PEA SOUP

500 g	dried peas
1	onion, chopped
1	carrot, grated
2	sprigs of parsley, chopped
1	bay leaf
10 mL	salt
200 g	salt pork or salty bacon
3 L	cold water

Soak peas in water overnight. In the morning, bring to a boil and add the onion, carrot, and salt. Reduce heat to a simmer. Add parsley, bay leaf, and salt pork to the soup. Simmer for 3-4 hours. Add more water if necessary.

large pot. The pot was placed on the floor between two chairs. Two long poles were laid over the backs of the chairs. Candle rods were placed crosswise over the rods. Over each candle rod, six pieces of coarse cotton wick were hung.

The candle rod with its six wicks was dipped into the melted tallow for the right number of seconds. Then it was placed back on the poles. When all the wicks

Making candles by the dipping method. Pioneer women in New France and Upper Canada (as you will see later) were skilled in candle-making by this method.

had been dipped, it was time to start all over again. Many dippings were needed to make candles the required thickness.

Cool air helped to harden the tallow. Small boys were often given the task of standing outside holding the candle rods. Girls usually helped their mothers by holding the other end of the dipping rod.

Candle-making was a messy, painstaking process. But a habitant woman, with help from her family, could make 200 candles in a day.

Colonists on the seigneuries were a long way from the hospitals of Montreal and Quebec. When a family member was sick, parents sat up night after night with the patient. Many women knew the folk remedies. By their care they tried to nurse the sick back to health.

A woman in New France who could read and write would teach her children these skills too. Before schools were built in the country, most children were educated in the home.

In the towns, women helped to manage the trade shops and businesses. For example, one woman named Madame Legardeur de Repentigny, founded a small cloth and textile factory in Montreal in 1704. It stayed in operation until 1713. In 1749, the widow Fournel obtained the trade rights in an area that stretched from Sept-Îles to Île Aux Coudres and covered the immense lowlands of Lac Saint-Jean. She had the right to trade clothes, blankets, tools, guns, gunpowder, and brandy with the Native peoples in exchange for pelts.

The Church in Everyday Life

Many social activities centred around the church. Most habitants attended church regularly on Sundays and on the frequent holy days of the year. They believed it was their duty to worship God.

The church was an important meeting place. People came together with friends and neighbours and exchanged news. Important announcements from the governor and bishop were read at church. In the days before radio and newspapers, all news had to be passed on by letter or word of mouth.

Some of the most important festivities in the colony revolved around the church. Christmas celebrations, for example, were directly related to the Christian religion. On Christmas Eve children went to bed early. Then they were awakened for the sleigh ride through the snow to midnight mass at church. Heavy bearskin rugs kept them warm. Sleigh bells jingled in the cold frosty air.

Out of respect and honour, the seigneur was the first to enter the church and the first to leave. Midnight mass was followed by a huge meal. Christmas Day was spent quietly, perhaps singing some old French carols. The homemade gifts were not exchanged until New Year's Day.

Social Life on the Seigneury

Both the habitants and the seigneurs of New France worked hard. But there were times for fun and relaxation when the work was done. On 11 November all the habitants gathered at the manor house to pay their rent. Harvest was over and the crops were safe in the barns. Now it was time to settle the accounts.

All afternoon the paths to the manor house were busy. Habitant families brought sacks of wheat, chickens, ducks, and bags of wool. They were received in the largest room of the manor house. There the seigneur made entries in the big account book. When the habitants had paid their rent, they knelt to ask the seigneur's blessing. Then they were treated to refreshments. After enjoying a huge supper, all danced to the music of the fiddle until the roosters began to crow!

Another colourful day in the year was **May Day**. May Day celebrated the coming of spring. Habitants planted a maypole decorated with streamers on the front lawn of the manor house. It was a tall spruce tree stripped of its branches except for a few at the top. The priest blessed the maypole and then the seigneur stepped forward amid shouts of "Vive le Roi, vive le seigneur!" The seigneur accepted a ceremonial glass of brandy and then blasted the maypole with his musket! Everyone took a turn at shooting the maypole until it was blackened. Then all danced around the pole.

Afterwards the seigneur invited everyone into the manor house for a meal. What a meal it was! Fresh and smoked meats, tourtières, eels, baked beans, pies, and maple sugar candy were all enjoyed. It was a fine way to welcome spring and the new crop year.

TOP: *Planting the maypole. The decorated pole was often raised in front of the seigneur's house.*

BOTTOM: *A village dance. There was time for recreation when the chores were done.*

Skill Building: Recognizing How the Roles of Family Members Have Changed

The family was very important in New France. Parents, children, grandparents and even aunts, uncles, and cousins often lived near one another and worked together. They could depend on each other in times of need. Families are still very important today. But the roles of family members have changed over time. For example, fifty years ago few women worked at jobs outside the family home. Today many women work both inside and outside the home. They work in businesses and professions, schools, and industries. The role of women in the family has changed dramatically.

A **role** is the part someone plays in society. It includes the person's jobs or duties. Changes have occurred in the roles of all family members. To investigate how these roles have changed, you could use a comparison organizer.

1. Draw up a comparison organizer like the one that follows. List the roles of family members down the left column of the organizer. These are your criteria. List the items you will compare across the top of the organizer. In this case, you will compare two periods in history—New France and Canada today.

Roles of Family Members	New France	Canada Today
Men		
Women		
Young girls		
Young boys		

2. Locate and record information for each role on your organizer. Check your library for books. Look for pictures or illustrations as well.

3. When your organizer is complete, write a sentence to summarize the most important change in each family role.

4. Suggest reasons for the changes.

5. Compare your notes with a partner. Did you come to the same conclusions about the major changes in family roles?

6. Evaluate your decisions. Check that they were based on facts rather than opinions and that they were free of bias.

Everyday Life in the Towns

Not all the colonists who came to New France were farmers or fur traders. Some came from cities and towns in Europe. When they arrived, they carried on their trades and professions as skilled craftspeople, shopkeepers, priests, or doctors in the towns of New France. A few were rich nobles who were officials of the government. One in every four persons lived in town. The main towns were Quebec, Montreal, and Trois Rivières. In Acadia, many small settlements and towns had grown up around sites such as Port Royal and later Louisbourg.

Quebec

In 1750, 8000 people lived in Quebec. The little settlement had grown since Champlain first built the Habitation in 1608. Growth had been slow but steady. By 1750 Quebec was bustling with life. Perched on a cliff high above the St. Lawrence River, it controlled the traffic on the great highway of Canada.

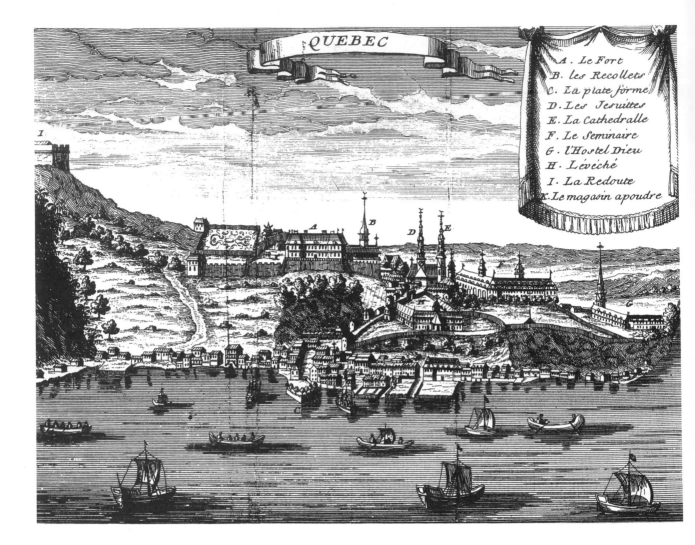

QUEBEC

A. Le Fort
B. les Recollets
C. La plate forme
D. Les Jesuittes
E. La Cathedralle
F. Le Seminaire
G. l'Hostel Dieu
H. L'évéché
I. La Redoute
x. Le magasin apoudre

A view of Quebec in the 1730s. Can you identify the important buildings and their purpose?

Quebec turned toward France and linked the colony to the home country. The town had an excellent natural harbour and it was by ship that contact with France was maintained. There was great excitement in the spring when the sails of the first ships were spotted coming up the river. Their arrival meant news from relatives and friends. It meant long-awaited supplies would fill the shops. There would be new faces as boatloads of colonists arrived. There might also be new troops to help defend the colonists. Officials from France might bear the latest orders from the King.

Quebec was actually made up of two towns, Lower Town and Upper Town. The two parts were quite different. Lower Town was located on the riverfront where the ships docked. It was the trade and business centre of Quebec. Inns for travellers and warehouses that held the furs bound for France were located there. Along the narrow dirt streets were the shops of artisans and traders. The market was also located in Lower Town. On market day the streets were especially busy. Habitants carted in their produce and the townspeople gathered to buy vegetables, meat, fish, cheese, and eggs.

Workers, tradespeople, and merchants often lived with their families right above their stores. Fire was a constant danger in Lower Town. Houses were built very

A stone house in Quebec, built in the seventeenth century. Why were the chimneys built so tall above the roof?

A carriole. In winter, the people of New France often travelled in these horse-drawn sleighs.

A calèche. These two-wheeled carriages were common on the streets of the towns in New France.

close together. Huge piles of firewood in the courtyards and against the houses made the town a woodpile ready to catch fire. When fires started there was very little the townspeople could do.

As early as 1664 there were strict rules for fire prevention. Townspeople were ordered to have chimneys cleaned regularly. Fire escape ladders had to be installed against the houses and on the roofs. People were permitted to have only a small amount of gunpowder in their houses. Smoking in the bedrooms of inns was strictly forbidden. At the first sound of the fire bell, citizens were expected to rush to the scene with leather buckets full of water.

One solution to the fire problem was to build more stone houses. Stone masons cut and prepared the stones over the winter. When the weather warmed up, they could begin building the stone walls of the homes. Most stone houses in Quebec were three stories high. Roofs were made of cedar shingles. Chimneys were built tall to reduce the risk of a fire starting on the roof.

The buildings in Upper Town were grander than those in Lower Town. The skyline was dominated by the governor's mansion, known as the Château St. Louis, by the Jesuit seminary, and by important churches. The buildings were made of stone and were large and impressive.

The governor, bishop, military officers, wealthy citizens, and priests and nuns of the religious orders lived in Upper Town. It was said that the women of Upper Town were as stylish as women at Versailles in their silks and laces. One visitor in 1755 described the men of Upper Town Quebec as vain and pompous. They too loved to be dressed in the latest Paris fashions. Men carried swords and wore wigs and beaver hats.

In summer the rich trotted about the streets in elegant two-wheeled carriages called **calèches**. The calèches were light and fast. Their large wheels were well suited to the muddy roads of the town.

In winter people travelled in the **carriole**–a horse-drawn sleigh somewhat larger than a calèche. Rich people could have upholstered seats and fur rugs to keep warm as they dashed about town. So popular were carrioles that in 1716 officials had to post the first traffic regulations:

We forbid all persons, drivers of carrioles as well as those on horseback, to allow trotting or galloping while the congregation leaves church.

Montreal

While Quebec turned toward France, Montreal faced the interior of North America. It was 250 km up river from Quebec and much closer to the frontier of the colony. It had been founded as a religious community, but progress in converting the Native peoples to Christianity had been slow. The town grew most quickly when the fur trade developed.

Montreal was the natural centre of the fur trade. At first the traders gathered there for the annual fur fair. Later, voyageurs assembled their huge fleets of canoes there for trips to the interior. As the fur trade prospered, other businesses followed. Merchants and traders came to supply the needs of the voyageurs. Contractors, builders, and masons arrived to build warehouses and homes. There were also labourers and skilled craftspeople of every kind. As the community grew wealthy, banks developed to handle the finances of the fur trade.

While Quebec had its polished high society, Montreal remained a frontier town. Visitors from Europe found that people in Montreal were less "stuffy" and friendlier. Citizens seemed to mix more freely no matter what their social class or occupation.

Looking at the streets of Montreal in 1750 you would see the four foundation stones of New France. The constant presence of soldiers reminded the citizens of their long struggle with the Iroquois. Black-robed nuns and priests were testimony to the early beginnings of the town as a Christian community. Coureurs de bois and Native people drifting in and out were a symbol of the prosperous fur trade. And habitants from nearby seigneuries with their ox carts of farm produce showed the importance of agriculture. Soldiers, religion, furs, and agriculture–these were the four foundation stones of New France.

Notre-Dame Street in Montreal, 1786. By the 1780s, the town was bustling with activity.

Transportation in New France

The St. Lawrence River was the main highway of New France. It linked Acadia, the main towns of Quebec, Trois Rivières, and Montreal, and all the seigneuries along the shores of the river. In summer people travelled up and down the river in birchbark canoes. Heavy loads were transported on a freight raft called a **cajeu**. The cajeu was made of rough pieces of wood nailed together. With sails it could be used to carry loads of grain, furniture, or even cattle. Since a cajeu was too heavy to be portaged around rapids, it was left on the river at these spots. Travellers going in the opposite direction were free to use it.

Even when the river froze in winter it could still be used as a highway. Home-made sleighs with runners were pulled by horses over the ice. Poor families who did not own a horse used dog teams to pull their sleighs. Sleighs had no covering so travellers were well bundled up in their warmest clothes. They were tucked in under blankets and furs. Sometimes heated logs were placed on the floor of the sleigh to prevent frozen toes or feet.

Snowshoes and toboggans were also used for winter travel. Both could be made from materials at hand in the forests. Without snowshoes it was almost impossible to travel far in deep snow. But a coureur de bois wearing snowshoes, with his toboggan tied to his belt, could travel through the bush easily and quickly.

There were very few roads in New France. It was not until 1734 that a rough road was opened between Montreal and Quebec. Even then, the fastest and most comfortable way to travel was still by water. The roads that existed were not much more than rough winding paths. In wet weather and in winter they were impassable.

Seigneurs were responsible for the upkeep of roads through their seigneuries, but the habitants were often unwilling to work on the roads. Road-building took them away from their fields and as long as everyone had access to the river, who needed roads? It was not until the second row of seigneuries developed away from the river that roads became necessary.

A cajeu carrying freight on the St. Lawrence. Why does this cajeu have both sails and oars?

Activities

Looking Back

1. Define the following words and enter them in your dictionary.

   pièce-sur-pièce construction   May Day   cabane   calèche
   carriole   cajeu   tallow   role

2. In what ways did the lives of the habitants follow the seasons?

3. What steps were taken to control fires in the towns of New France?

4. Describe in your own words the "four foundation stones" on which New France was built.

5. Why were the sleigh and the canoe so important to the people of New France?

Using Your Knowledge

6. Imagine you are a teenager in a habitant family. Describe a day in your life. Be sure to include details about work and leisure activities, clothing, food, and schooling, if any. What will your future occupation likely be? How much choice do you have?

7. Create a timeline of a day's activities for a habitant man, woman, or child on a seigneury.

8. Look at the picture of a habitant main room on page 224.
   a) Identify as many objects in the room as you can.
   b) Find out how each object was used. What was each made of?
   c) Explain your findings to a partner. Give him or her a tour of the room.

9. Imagine a busy street in Lower Town Quebec. Describe:
   a) what shops you might find there
   b) what the buildings look like
   c) where the people live
   d) a typical day's activities on the street.

10. Compare life in Upper Town and Lower Town Quebec. Use a comparison organizer in your answer.

Extending Your Thinking

11. Find out more about habitant handicrafts such as furniture, rugs, sugar moulds, homemade clothing, candles, and sleighs or carts. Create a picture mural to illustrate and explain the crafts.

12. Suppose you had to put together a time capsule of everyday life in New France. What would you include? Why?

13. Construct a model of an early habitant farmhouse or a seigneury.

CHAPTER 16

Conflict and Change

The Battle of the Plains of Abraham.

Most of the inhabitants of Quebec were asleep. It was well past midnight. But along the river west of the town something suspicious was going on. Twenty-four hand-picked British soldiers had landed at the foot of the cliffs.

The French believed that no army could ever attack them at Quebec. The cliffs were too high and incredibly steep. But the British General James Wolfe had other ideas.

The sharp-eyed Wolfe had observed women washing clothes along the riverbank. Later the clothes were seen drying at the top of the cliff. Obviously there was a way up the cliffs. Wolfe intended to use it! Now, clinging to roots and branches, the first British soldiers started to scale the cliffs. Everything depended on silence, darkness, and surprise.

At one point a French sentry heard an unexpected sound and called out, "Who goes there?" The reply came back in perfect French, "Provisions from Montreal." There followed a quick blow to the head, a half-strangled cry, and it was done. Not a shot had been fired. The British were in control at the top of the cliffs. Only thirty French sentries had been guarding the heights.

The death of General Montcalm. "I am glad I shall not live to see the surrender of Quebec," he said.

A signal light was flashed to the river. Hundreds of British soldiers had been waiting in flat-bottomed boats for the signal. Now they started landing on the shore and scrambling up the cliffs. The place where they climbed is now called Anse au Foulon. By dawn there were more than 4400 British troops on the heights. They were gathered in battle formation on an open field called the Plains of Abraham. They were 3 km from the town of Quebec.

The French General Montcalm had not slept well. He was uneasy about the British troop movements he had observed these last few days. Now he was taken completely by surprise. "I see the British where they ought not to be," he exclaimed. "We must give battle and crush them before midday." Montcalm decided that if he waited any longer the British could lay siege to Quebec. At eight o'clock that morning he led three divisions out of the gates and onto the Plains of Abraham.

At ten o'clock the French army advanced. The British had been told to hold their fire until the enemy was within musket range. Then the order was given: Fire! British muskets rang out. Before the smoke had cleared the British reloaded and fired again. French soldiers fell in heaps. When General Wolfe gave the order to charge, the French army retreated to the town.

By noon the battle of the Plains of Abraham was over. General Wolfe was one of the 655 British soldiers killed. As he lay dying on the field it is said that he heard a messenger cry, "They run, they run!" "Who runs?" the general whispered. "The enemy runs away," came the reply. Then General Wolfe turned on his side and murmured, "I die happy!"

General Montcalm was also hit by a bullet. He was carried back into the town fatally wounded. His doctor told him he did not have long to live. "I am glad," said Montcalm, "I shall not live to see the surrender of Quebec." A few days later Quebec was handed over to the British.

The skull of Montcalm, kept at the Ursuline Convent in Quebec City.

Rivals: Britain Versus France

Why did Britain and France clash at Quebec in 1759? What events led up to this battle? Who were the opposing leaders and what were their strengths and weaknesses? Why did New France finally fall to the British?

Today France and Britain are friendly neighbours. People travel freely between the two countries. In the twentieth century the British and French fought side by side in two world wars. They have worked together on giant projects such as the development of the Concorde supersonic jet.

But relations have not always been friendly. In earlier days Britain and France were sometimes bitter enemies and at war. They were rivals for trade, especially the rich fur trade of North America. They were also rivals for colonies in many parts of the world. They practised different religions. Most British were Protestant; most French were Roman Catholic. They were also rivals for military and naval power.

In 1756 the Seven Years' War broke out in North America. It was the result of long-standing tensions in Europe. But the war also spread to other parts of the world. The British and French fought each other in Europe and India as well as North America. Their colonies all over the world were battlegrounds.

In North America, Britain and France were in conflict in three main areas. First, they had often clashed in the Atlantic areas of Newfoundland, Nova Scotia, and Acadia. These regions had been exchanged during peace talks like pieces in a chess game.

In 1720 France had decided to build a huge fortress at Louisbourg on the barren shores of Cape Breton Island. No expense was spared. Hundreds of workers were sent out from France. Louis XV complained about the skyrocketing cost of the fortress. But France was nevertheless determined to defend its last bit of territory in the Atlantic region. Louisbourg would protect the rich fisheries and guard the entrance to the St. Lawrence.

The second area of conflict was in the north and west. In 1670 the British had founded the Hudson's Bay Company. Forts were built where major rivers flowed into Hudson and James bays. The British hoped to convince the Native peoples to bring their furs to these forts, rather than to the French forts to the south.

The French responded to the challenge. They sent expeditions northwest to Lake Superior and south along the Mississippi River. Louis Jolliet and Cavelier de La Salle explored these areas and established forts to control and protect the French fur trade.

During the 1730s and 1740s, Pierre de La Vérendrye and his sons pushed westward. They established French forts as far

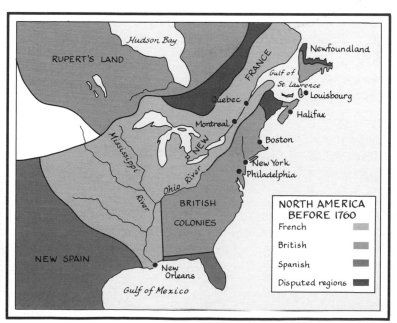

NORTH AMERICA
BEFORE 1760

French
British
Spanish
Disputed regions

west as the present-day city of Portage La Prairie in Manitoba. French trading posts also sprang up on Lake Winnipeg and on the lower Saskatchewan River. The French were intercepting the Native peoples and their furs before they got to the Hudson's Bay trading posts.

The third area of British-French conflict was in the Ohio valley. The coureurs de bois had explored this area extensively. They had established a chain of forts all the way from the St. Lawrence to New Orleans. English colonies along the Atlantic seaboard were feeling hemmed in. They needed new farmland for their rapidly growing population. They wanted the French out of Ohio country. The English were prepared to drive them out by force if necessary.

Which Side Had the Best Chance to Win?

Who would win in a war? Before the Stanley Cup playoffs, you can try to predict which team will win. You compare the strengths and weaknesses of the two teams. In warfare, you can also judge which side you think has the advantage. Look at the facts in the following chart.

1. List the advantages and disadvantages of both the French and the British. Decide which side has the best chance to win. Give reasons for your decision.

2. Look at the map of forts on page 239. Can you see any weaknesses in the British defences?

New France	British Colonies	
60 000	1 500 000	Population
vast territory to defend, stretching from the St. Lawrence to the Gulf of Mexico	territory stretched along the Atlantic seaboard and around Hudson Bay	Territory
a string of forts throughout their territory especially strong fortresses at Quebec and Louisbourg	some forts to protect their territory, especially along the Atlantic coast, e.g. Halifax these forts will help to keep supply lines to Britain open	Defences
large army of tough part-time soldiers who are very experienced in wilderness fighting, canoeing, and surprise attack	British colonists are not as experienced in wilderness warfare; colonists were more interested in farming and business than exploring and surviving in the bush	Military Experience of Colonists
largest and best army in Europe	largest and most powerful navy in Europe	Military Strength of Home Country
many excellent Native allies	Iroquois are the only Native allies	Allies
colonies are relatively poor and depend on France to provide food and supplies through the ports of Quebec and Montreal	rich, prosperous colonies whose farms and plantations, mills and factories can provide most of the needed food and military supplies	Supplies
Marquis de Montcalm, a highly experienced soldier and commander from France	General James Wolfe from Britain, with little experience in commanding a large army	Leadership

The Seven Years' War

9 July 1755 – The Ohio Valley

The opening shots in the war were heard in the Ohio valley of North America. Major-General Braddock was sent from England with 1500 regulars. His orders were to sweep the French out of the Ohio valley and capture forts Niagara and Frontenac. The idea was to cut the supply line between the St. Lawrence and the French forts in the interior.

What followed was a disaster for Britain. General Braddock fought as they did in Europe. He marched his soldiers along in lines. But the French and the Natives used **guerrilla warfare**. They hid behind trees and ambushed the red-coated British regulars as they marched. Although there were only 200 French soldiers and 600 Natives, it was a decisive French victory.

General Braddock was mortally wounded and 1000 British regulars were killed. The survivors retreated to their base in Virginia. The French captured some English guns and supplies, including some of the general's secret papers. These provided valuable information about future British war plans. In the Atlantic region, however, the situation was reversed.

A painting of the battle between Braddock's forces and the French. Why did the British have so many casualties?

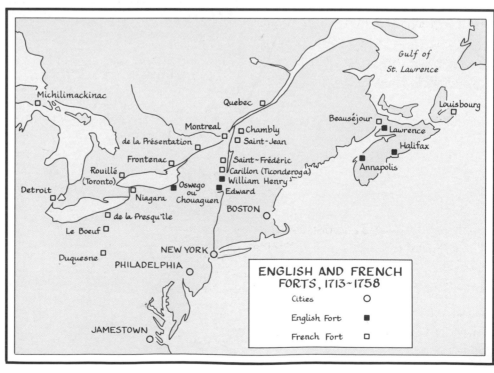

The Expulsion of the Acadians

The British governor Charles Lawrence of Nova Scotia was worried. He was troubled by what he called "the Acadian problem." Acadians were French-speaking Roman Catholics living in Nova Scotia, New Brunswick, and Prince Edward Island. Acadia had first been explored and settled by Champlain. Fought over by the French and British, it had changed hands many times. Now it belonged to Britain–and Britain and France were at war.

What troubled Charles Lawrence was this: What would happen if a large French fleet appeared off the coast of Nova Scotia? Could he trust the Acadians? Or would the population of 10 000 rise up against the British? If they did, there was no way Lawrence and a few British troops could hold Nova Scotia.

The Acadians were generally peaceful and hard-working farmers. But they had continually refused to take an oath of loyalty to the British King. Now in 1755, Governor Lawrence once more demanded that the Acadians swear an oath of loyalty. They must promise never to fight against the British King. When they refused, Governor Lawrence announced that all Acadians would be **expelled** from Nova Scotia. They would be moved, by force if necessary, to other British colonies far from the potential trouble spot in Nova Scotia.

British soldiers moved into Acadian villages. Homes, lands, and most possessions were taken from the Acadians. Men, women, and children were herded onto ships. When the broken-hearted Acadians looked back, they saw clouds of smoke hanging over their villages.

Ships carrying the Acadians made their way to Georgia, Maryland, Virginia, and

Acadians waiting on the shores for the ships that took them away from their homeland.

other British colonies. Some passengers died on the journey when ships sank on the high seas. Those who survived the voyage often found themselves living in misery and poverty. They dwelt now among strangers in places where they could not speak the language.

A few Acadians fled into the woods and made their way back to Cape Breton and Louisbourg. Others ended up in France, Louisiana, or Quebec. Six to eight thousand Acadians had been expelled from their lands.

After the war about 2000 Acadians returned to their old homes. They found English-speaking strangers on their farms and in their villages. They began the long and painful process of starting all over again.

Victories for Montcalm

In 1756 a new commander-in-chief arrived in New France. The Marquis de Montcalm was a highly experienced, professional soldier.

Montcalm began his career in New France with the quick capture of the powerful British fort at Oswego on Lake Ontario. He seized 4 British warships, 200 smaller boats, 70 cannons, and vast stores of ammunition. The elimination of Fort Oswego let the French breathe a little easier. Their fur-trading forts to the west were safer now.

The next year Montcalm went up the Richelieu River to the French fort at Ticonderoga. From there he successfully attacked Fort William Henry. He seemed to be on the verge of marching all the way to New York. The war was going badly for Britain in Europe and India. Now things were not looking well in North America.

A New British War Plan

Fortunately for the British, a new war plan was taking shape. The British government under Prime Minister William Pitt believed that the best strategy was to attack France in her colonies. Fresh troops were needed. Fifty thousand soldiers were poured into North America. New generals were appointed. Young men such as James Wolfe were promoted to carry out Pitt's plans for victory.

The British plan began to work. In 1758, Fort Duquesne in the Ohio valley was captured. This fort was the major

The burning of Fort Duquesne, 1758. One of the key French strongholds in the Ohio valley was gone.

symbol of French domination in the region. When the French commander saw that all was lost, he gave orders to blow up the fort. On the warm ashes the British built a stockade and named it Pittsburgh after William Pitt.

About the same time a large English army surprised the French at Fort Frontenac on Lake Ontario. When this fort fell, the British captured tonnes of winter supplies intended for the western fur posts. The gateway to the St. Lawrence was now in British hands. The British were in a position to move from the west toward Montreal and Quebec.

Meanwhile a huge British army was marching toward Montreal from the south. Although the French slowed down the advancing army at Lake Champlain, they were forced to fall back and protect Montreal.

The Fall of Louisbourg

On the Atlantic coast, other events were coming to a head. The British were determined to destroy Louisbourg once and for all. In June 1758, 160 British warships appeared off the coast. The British bombardment of the fortress began!

The British ships cut off the line of reinforcements, food, and supplies to the defenders of Louisbourg. As ammunition supplies dwindled in the fortress, the British were able to land soldiers and cannons on the shore. One of the first to leap ashore was James Wolfe. He would also soon lead the British attack on Quebec.

For forty-nine days the defenders of Louisbourg held on. Food was running out and people inside the fortress were starving. The walls of the fortress were crumbling under the daily cannon fire. The French fleet had not arrived and there appeared to be no chance of rescue. On 26 July Louisbourg surrendered to the British. This time the fortress was lost forever.

The destruction of Louisbourg was the beginning of the end for the French. The Gulf of St. Lawrence now lay wide open to the British navy. Quebec was in grave danger. What happened the following spring would be critical. Unless the French fleet was the first to arrive on the St. Lawrence with soldiers and reinforcements, Quebec was doomed. But the French fleet did not arrive. It was an English fleet that appeared first on the river in June 1759. James Wolfe came with 39 000 soldiers and 25 warships. With plenty of food and ammunition, the British prepared to take Quebec.

The restored fortress of Louisbourg. Today the fortress is an important heritage site.

The Siege of Quebec

From his camp on the Île d'Orléans, Wolfe could see Quebec protected by its walls and cannons. To the west was the St. Charles River and to the east was the Montmorency River with its spectacular falls 30 m higher than Niagara Falls. Between the rivers was the Beauport shore. This shore was heavily guarded by 14 000 French. During the summer Wolfe made an attempt to land his forces on the shore. But his small boats were driven back and his soldiers were blasted with grapeshot and musket fire.

In July Wolfe set up camp at Montmorency Falls. He hoped the French could be drawn into attacking him there. Although he waited for twenty-one days, no French attack came.

British batteries were established at Point Lévis. From there they could bombard Quebec. Their artillery could fire shells for 3 km.

Meanwhile, some British warships managed to dodge the cannon fire from the walls of Quebec. They passed the town and anchored up river to the west.

By September Wolfe was running out of time. Winter was approaching. Quebec was weakened because of the bombardment, but it had not fallen. Wolfe was desperate. He decided to make one more attempt to capture the town. This time he would scale the cliffs and attack Quebec from its weaker western side. It was a daring gamble. But when he found a path up the cliffs at Anse au Foulon, Wolfe knew he had a chance to make his plan work.

That day on the Plains of Abraham, one of the most important battles in Canadian history was fought. Wolfe defeated Montcalm, and New France fell to the British.

The End of French Rule

The next spring three English armies invaded the last French stronghold at Montreal. Eighteen thousand troops were involved in the attack. One army came up the St. Lawrence from Quebec, another came from Lake Ontario to the west, and the third came from the Richelieu River to the south. On 8 September 1760 Governor Vaudreuil surrendered New France to the British. The **fleur-de-lis**, which had flown over Quebec since the days of Cartier and Champlain, came down. French rule in North America had ended.

After the Conquest

You are a member of a school team that has won its way to the playoffs. Then in the crucial championship game, your team is defeated. How would you feel? Most people would feel sad, angry, disappointed, and frustrated.

What happened to the people of New France was far worse than losing a championship. They had lost control of their homeland! Quebec lay in ruins. Their farms were overgrown with weeds. There were foreign soldiers in their streets.

What was to become of them? Most of

QUEBEC, 1759

their leaders had returned to France. France seemed to have abandoned them. They knew that things were going to be very different for them now. To the French-Canadians, the British victory seemed like the worst possible disaster.

Imagine their reactions. What questions and fears might they have?

Habitant: What will happen to us? Will we all have to learn a new language? Will we be forbidden to speak French? Will I lose my land and my home?

French merchant in Quebec: France is no longer my home. I can't go back there now. All my roots are here. I am Canadien. I will not return to France.

Seigneur: France has abandoned us. It will be very difficult for us. I do not know if I will be able to keep the seigneury and help the habitants. We may all be scattered.

French official in Paris: I am glad to be rid of New France. It has always been a drain on French resources. The colony never did become self-supporting. Nothing there but a few hectares of snow!

Bishop: I worry about our holy religion. The English are not Roman Catholics. How will they treat us? Will they allow the people to keep their faith?

British merchant in the Thirteen Colonies: Now we have control of the fish, furs, and forests of most of the North American continent! We have a larger market for our goods.

British official in the Thirteen Colonies: At last the French threat from the north has been removed. Now the frontiers will be safe. The westward expansion of our colonies can begin.

British official in Quebec: What shall we do with these people? How can we rule people who speak a different language, practise a different religion, and live by different traditions and customs?

The **conquest** also presented problems for the British. It was true that Britain was in control of most of the North American continent. The wealth of furs, fish, and forests was theirs. There were also more customers to buy British manufactured goods.

But the British were not quite sure what

A view of Quebec after the siege of 1759. Buildings lay in ruins.

to do with the colonists in the new province of Quebec. At first the British plan was to try to change the Canadiens. They wanted the habitants to become British. Britain hoped that the French culture and language would soon disappear. They thought this would happen automatically as English-speaking settlers moved north from the other British colonies. But very few people in the south wanted to move to a colder climate where the best land was already taken up. Nor did English-speaking colonists want to live in a province where they would be outnumbered by the French.

The Royal Proclamation of 1763

The **Royal Proclamation of 1763** outlined the main objectives of Britain's first plan for Quebec.

1. The boundary of the new province of Quebec will be limited to the area along the St. Lawrence River valley and the Ottawa River valley.
2. Lands between the Ottawa, Ohio, and Mississippi rivers will be closed to settlement to protect the fur trade and the Native peoples.
3. The official religion of the province will be Protestant (not Roman Catholic).
4. English law will replace French law.
5. A British governor and his appointed council will rule the province.
6. English language schools will be established and run by Protestants.

The British government soon realized they would have to come up with a better plan for Quebec. The French culture would not easily disappear. Besides, there was trouble brewing in the English colonies to the south. The last thing the British needed was trouble with the French-speaking colony of Quebec. Therefore, in 1774, the British government passed the **Quebec Act**. The British wanted to keep the French-Canadians happy so that they would never attempt to break away from Britain.

The Quebec Act, 1774

These were the main terms of the Quebec Act:

1. The territory in the Ohio valley west of the Appalachian Mountains will belong to Quebec.
2. Seigneurs may continue to own their seigneuries and collect rents.
3. The French may continue to worship in the Roman Catholic religion and the Church may collect taxes.
4. There will be two kinds of laws: French civil law, which the people are familiar with, and English criminal law, with trial by jury.
5. Roman Catholics may be appointed to the governing council (this was forbidden in Britain).

Would the French be satisfied with the Quebec Act? If trouble broke out in Britain's Thirteen Colonies to the south, would the Canadiens remain loyal to Britain? The British did not have to wait long to find out. Within two years, the American Revolution had begun!

Quebec Today

French rule in North America ended in 1760. But the French influence will always be felt in Canada. Today more than five million French-speaking descendants of the early settlers live in the province of Quebec.

French culture survives in the people. They refused to be absorbed by British culture and traditions. They preserved their language, religion, and customs. They have continued to develop their own distinct Québécois way of life.

Skill Building: Examining Bias

Two students witness a fight. Yet each student's description of what went on is quite different. Why?

Remember that everyone has his or her own point of view or way of seeing things. People's points of view are shaped by their experiences in life, their family, up-bringing, friends, occupations, religions, interests, and even politics.

The two witnesses to the fight report from different points of view. One witness, for example, might be a close friend of one of the people involved in the fight. She is sympathetic to her friend. Her point of view is one-sided. She has a bias. The second witness may feel strongly that fighting and violence are wrong. That point of view is also a bias. It will influence how the person views the fight.

Have you ever wondered why two accounts of the same historical event can be so different? Each historian brings his or her own bias to the interpretation of the event. Read these two fictional accounts of the Battle of the Plains of Abraham. Answer the questions that follow.

1. In a sentence, describe the bias in each article.

2. Find two facts that both stories discuss but disagree on. Explain the differences.

3. a) Find words or phrases in the *Montreal Matin* article that describe the French side in very favourable terms.

b) Find words or phrases in the *Boston Times* article that describe the English in very favourable terms.

4. a) Find words or phrases in the *Montreal Matin* article that describe the English in negative or "loaded" terms.

b) Find words or phrases in the *Boston Times* article that describe the French in negative terms.

5. Explain how each newspaper's point of view could account for its bias in reporting the same story.

Boston Times
September 1759

Today wonderful news has reached us. The mighty French fortress at Quebec has fallen! Though greatly outnumbered by the French, superior British fire power and strategy have won the day!

From eyewitness accounts we learn that General Wolfe carried out a brilliant plan. Scaling the cliffs under cover of darkness, British troops easily over-powered a weak French force guarding the Heights.

Fortunately, Montcalm foolishly led his troops out to fight. They were lured from behind the safety of the stone barricades of Quebec. Had the French stayed in the town, we might not be celebrating such a joyous and easy victory.

Alas our brilliant General, James Wolfe, was mortal-ly wounded in the service of King and country.

Montreal Matin
September 1759

Today shocking news has reached us. Disaster has struck Quebec. General Montcalm and our brave brothers and sisters at Quebec have been overrun by a huge British army. After fighting bravely to the end Quebec has fallen.

From eyewitness accounts we learn that Wolfe advance party somehow scaled the cliffs from t￼ river. We believe this could only have been done w￼ the help of some traitor among our ranks. By daybr￼ thousands of snarling wolves were on the Plains.

General Montcalm wisely led the armies out f￼ behind the walls before the redcoats could entre￼ themselves in the fields. Alas, our brilliant Ge￼ was mortally wounded defending our be￼ homeland.

Activities

Looking Back

1. Define the following words and enter them in your dictionary.

guerrilla warfare	Royal Proclamation
expulsion	Quebec Act
conquest	fleur-de-lis

2. **a)** Locate the following places on a map.

Quebec	Louisbourg	Hudson Bay
Lake Superior	Mississippi River	Portage La Prairie
Lake Winnipeg	New Orleans	Ohio River
Fort Niagara	Fort Frontenac	Nova Scotia
Cape Breton	Halifax	Oswego
Ticonderoga	James Bay	Fort Dusquesne

   b) Explain the importance of Louisbourg, Fort Oswego, Fort Dusquesne, and Ticonderoga.

3. Why did the British believe it was important to conquer the French in the Ohio valley? Why was the destruction of Louisbourg "the beginning of the end" for the French?

4. Describe the natural advantages of the fortress at Quebec.

5. Study the map of the Battle of Quebec in 1759. Locate each of the following:
   a) the high steep cliffs west of Quebec
   b) the place where the British scrambled up the cliffs
   c) the open ground where the battle was fought
   d) Wolfe's camp on Île d'Orléans
   e) the French camp between the St. Charles and Montmorency rivers
   f) the location of the British guns used to bombard Quebec from across the river.
   Use these places on the map to describe the events of the battle.

Using Your Knowledge

6. Acadians have been described as people "caught between the French and the British."
   a) Did the Acadians deserve the punishment of expulsion? Explain your answer.
   b) Should they have been allowed to move to a French territory?
   c) Should they have been excused from swearing an oath of loyalty?
   d) The Acadians claimed they were neutral. Is it possible to be neutral in time of war? Explain your answer.

7. Who do you think was the better general, Wolfe or Montcalm? To answer this question, list the major decisions made by each general before and during the Battle of Quebec. Indicate which decisions were good ones and which were mistakes. Explain your answers.

8. Suppose you had been in the shoes of General Montcalm. What would you have done differently to defend Quebec? Be as specific as possible.

9. The Royal Proclamation and the Quebec Act were both British plans for governing the province of Quebec. How did they differ? Account for the differences.

10. Many battles were fought between the British and French during the Seven Years' War.
   a) Arrange the battles listed below in chronological order.

   Fort Frontenac   Montreal
   Fort William Henry   Louisbourg
   Quebec   Oswego
   Fort Duquesne

   b) Make a timeline from 1755 to 1760 and place each event in the correct year.
   c) Decide whether each battle was a victory for the French or the British. Highlight French victories with one colour and British victories with another colour on your timeline.
   d) In what year did the French begin to experience defeat? Suggest some reasons why.

Extending Your Thinking

11. It is 8 September 1760. Governor Vaudreuil has just surrendered Montreal to the British. Write an imaginary conversation between French-Canadian citizens of the town. The first sentence of your conversation is: "What do you think will happen to us now?"

12. Why, despite military defeat, has the French-Canadian culture survived so strongly to this day?

13. Find out about the French-speaking people in the Maritime provinces today.
   a) Where are they located?
   b) Do they call themselves Acadians?
   c) French-speaking people in Louisiana, USA are called "Cajuns." Suggest where this name may have come from?

14. If you have francophone teachers or other French-speaking people in your community, invite them to speak to your class about the French heritage and culture today.

UNIT FOUR

The Community of Upper Canada

CHAPTER 17

The United Empire Loyalists

Letters to Liverpool

After the Seven Years' War, the British controlled an empire in North America that stretched from the mouth of the St. Lawrence River to the Gulf of Mexico. The threat of the French had been removed. Britain was the most important European power in North America.

Yet, all was not well in the American colonies. The Thirteen Colonies had developed along the eastern seaboard of America at the same time that New France had been developing to the north. By 1763 the colonies had a total population of over 1 500 000. They had developed some prosperous industries. People began to feel that they did not need ties with Britain. Many began to resent the way they were governed by the home country.

Britain and the American colonies grew further and further apart between 1763 and 1776. Their differences ended in all out war. The American Revolution (War of Independence) raged on from 1776 to 1783. It led finally to the creation of the United States of America.

The following two letters tell of some of the problems in America. The letters are fictional, but the events they describe are real. The first letter is dated 1765. The second is dated a decade later. They are written by a colonist of New York to his cousin in Liverpool, England.

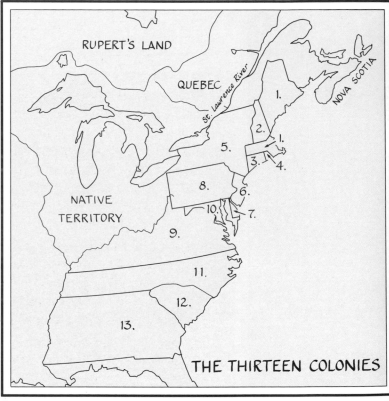

THE THIRTEEN COLONIES

NAME	DATE FOUNDED	REASONS FOR FOUNDING
NEW ENGLAND		
1. Massachusetts	1620	Religious freedom
2. New Hampshire	1623	Agriculture, trade, fishing
3. Connecticut	1635	Agriculture, trade
4. Rhode Island	1636	Religious freedom
MIDDLE COLONIES		
5. New York	1624	Agriculture, trade
6. New Jersey	1629	Agriculture, trade
7. Delaware	1638	Agriculture, trade
8. Pennsylvania	1682	Religious freedom, agriculture, trade
SOUTHERN COLONIES		
9. Virginia	1607	Agriculture, trade
10. Maryland	1634	Religious freedom, agriculture, trade
11. North Carolina	1653	Agriculture, trade
12. South Carolina	1670	Agriculture, trade
13. Georgia	1733	Refuge for debtors, agriculture

My dear cousin Anne,

New York
6 May 1765

How long it has been since I last put pen to paper. The work on the farm and unrest in the colony fill my days to the fullest. I shall try to do better. I hope this letter finds you, Walter, and the children in good health.

All is not well here in New York. Grumblings against the British government are heard daily in the streets of the town. People are unhappy with the events of the past two years. When the Seven Years' War ended, the colonists were relieved. The French were gone. The British colonies could now expand. Life would be better. This has not been the case.

When the war ended in 1763 the British government issued a Royal Proclamation. We colonists were forbidden to move west of the Appalachian Mountains. These lands were to be reserved for the Natives. What a shock that was. The British told us that it was necessary for the time being to avoid another costly war. Imagine! Why in heaven's name did we fight to drive the French out of the Ohio valley if the land was simply to be handed over to the Natives?

The British government has been getting more heavy-handed here in the past few years. New taxes seem to be the order of the day. The British are using the colonies to raise money. They claim these taxes are necessary. They tell us the Seven Years' War was very expensive. They say that we must help to pay the bill since the British armies were fighting here to protect us from the French. They also claim that the British army remains here today to protect us and that we must continue to share the burden of that cost. Colonists here don't like the idea of being taxed by a government as far away as Britain.

The Sugar Act of 1764 is an example of a very unpopular act here. It put a tax on molasses imported into the colonies from the West Indies. These taxes are not new. What is new is that the British mean business. They are cracking down on smugglers who have ignored taxes like this for years. Local customs officers now have the power to get tough and collect the taxes.

Most merchants are very disturbed by many of Britain's laws and old habits. They don't like the idea that we are allowed to trade freely only with Britain and her colonies. We should be free to trade where it is best for us. Why does Britain have the attitude that the colonies are there only to benefit her?

I greatly fear for the future unless there are changes. Colonists feel pressured by Britain. They want more freedom. They like making their own laws. They have their own elected governments to decide their future. Britain can't continue to control us and tell us what to do. I trust you already know of some of the things happening here. I pray that the problems will be solved before things get out of control.

Warmest regards from your cousin,

Russell Pitman

1. What is the mood of the people living in the colonies? Why?

2. Why is the British government introducing new taxes? How do the colonists feel about the taxes and the way they are enforced?

3. What trade restrictions has the British government put on the colonies? Why do the colonies object to these restrictions?

4. What does Russell Pitman fear will happen?

The problems grew worse over the next ten years. Britain imposed even more taxes to help reduce her huge debt from the Seven Years' War. The colonies began to band together. They were preparing for a fight. By 1775, the colonies were on the brink of revolution.

My dear cousin Anne,

New York
16 June 1775

I fear for the worst. It will surely be war with King George. The colonists here have been pushed to the limit. What will this mean for Diana and the children? There is much talk in the streets of complete separation from Britain. But I ask myself, can independence really be best for the colonies? If only things had worked out differently. There must be another way.

Many speak of British actions as being too harsh. Some colonists are determined to win independence at all costs. They are gaining more support daily. They remind us of the Stamp Act, the Townshend Acts, and the Tea Act. They claim that when we protested these measures, we were punished with even more strict measures. Such actions are unacceptable to them. People are outraged. The recent problems at Lexington and Concord are further signs of open hostility. The Continental Congress is moving closer to war with Britain.

I have talked secretly with two of my neighbours about leaving here. Revolution and independence are not for us. Yet, we dare not speak out. We shall try to make our way north to Quebec. Life in a British colony is what we want. We have talked of joining a British regiment.

All of this will be so difficult for the family, particularly the children. We have worked so hard to make a good life. We will have to give up so much.

I cannot say when next I shall be able to write.

Warmest regards from your cousin,

Russell Pitman

1. How does Russell Pitman feel about the growing problem?

2. What measures have made the problem worse?

3. The threat of war and separation from Great Britain is becoming more likely in the colonies. What is Russell Pitman planning to do? Why?

Skill Building: Recognizing Cause and Effect Relationships

One of the most important tasks for an historian is to examine cause and effect relationships. A **cause** is an event that makes something happen. An **effect** is the result. It is something that happens because the event took place. An event can produce many different effects.

Let's examine a simple cause and effect relationship that you might experience.

You are entered in a swim meet next week. You have been in the pool every day working hard. At the meet, you place third. This is a real improvement over your last meet. You are pleased with your placing and feel proud. Your coach and teammates praise your efforts. You receive the most improved swimmer's award for your level. You are determined to keep up your efforts.

The event (cause) is placing third in the swim meet. Can you list the results (effects)?

Cause (The event)	Effects (The results)
Placing third in the swim meet	1. Feeling pleased and proud of your improvement
	2. Receiving praise from coach and teammates
	3. Receiving the most improved swimmer's award
	4. Being determined to keep up the effort

Imagine your school team has just won a district championship. What effects might this event have? List them.

Historians also look for cause and effect relationships when they examine events in history. Study the effects of the Seven Years' War listed below.

Cause (The event)	Effects (The results)
The Seven Years' War (1756-1763)	1. The cost of the war created a huge debt in Britain.
	2. Britain decided to tax her colonies to help pay the costs of defence.
	3. The French territory in the north came under British control.
	4. Colonists in America began to resent the way they were governed by Britain.

In the next few pages, you will examine some real cause and effect relationships. They will help to explain the background to the American Revolution in 1776. This revolution was one of the most important events in the history of North America. It had an important effect on the character of Canada.

The Road to Revolution

Cause

Effects

1765: The Stamp Act

The British government passes a new tax law to raise revenue. Newspapers, legal documents, and other pamphlets must have special stamps purchased from British government officials. The money raised will be used to help pay for the defence of the colonies.

1. Colonists hold public demonstrations and distribute posters and pamphlets. One of the slogans on the posters is "No taxation without representation." Since they have no representation in the British parliament, they do not want to pay taxes approved by that body.
2. Stamp agents who try to enforce the law are tormented.
3. Colonists refuse to buy goods from Britain. This action is called a **boycott**.
4. An organization called the Sons of Liberty is formed to stop the collection of the tax.
5. Britain withdraws the tax in March 1766.

American colonists burning British stamps (like the one shown on the right) that they were required to purchase according to the Stamp Act.

1767: The Townshend Duties (Acts)

Another British tax measure is introduced. Colonists are required to pay a tax on all tea, glass, lead, paint, and paper bought in Britain.

1. Colonists refuse to buy goods from Britain.
2. Merchants who continue to trade with Britain have their shop windows smashed.
3. British soldiers are insulted in the streets and told to go home.
4. Britain withdraws the taxes in 1770 on all products except tea.

Cause	Effects
1768: The Quartering Act The British government requires colonists to supply food and housing for all British troops stationed in the American colonies. The British government argues that the troops are there to defend the colonies and the colonies should help to support them.	1. Colonists object to the costs of feeding and boarding the troops. They say it is an invasion of their privacy. They do not need British defence. 2. Street brawls take place between British troops and citizens in Boston.
1770: The Boston Massacre Colonists clash with a squad of British redcoats in Boston. The crowd begins to throw stones and become violent. The soldiers open fire on the crowd.	1. Five colonists are killed. For the first time there is bloodshed. 2. The British are accused of firing on defenceless citizens. British soldiers are arrested and put on trial, but only two are found guilty of manslaughter. 3. A Boston lawyer and writer, Samuel Adams, uses the event to stir public opinion against the British. He claims justice has to be done. 4. The colonies set up committees to share information and plans.

British troops firing on the colonists. The event came to be known as the Boston Massacre.

Cause	Effects

1773: The Tea Act
Britain grants the East India Company a monopoly to sell its tea in the American colonies. It is the only company allowed to bring tea into the colonies.

1. Colonists protest this interference in colonial affairs and boycott the imported tea. They turn the ships away at the ports.
2. In Boston, people disguised as Natives board ships in the harbour and dump the tea overboard. This event of 16 December 1773 is called the "Boston Tea Party."

The Boston Tea Party. What is the reaction of the people on the dock?

1774: The Intolerable Acts
Britain passes a series of harsh acts against any who dare to oppose the British government. The acts include terms that:
• Close the port of Boston
• Dismiss the government of Massachusetts
• Forbid public meetings
• Station more British soldiers in the Boston area
• State that British soldiers charged with committing crimes while on duty will be tried in Britain.

1. Colonists see these acts as the last straw. They are convinced that Britain intends to crush them.

Cause	Effects
1774: The Quebec Act The Quebec Act is passed to win the support of the French-Canadians. It gives the land in the Ohio valley to Quebec. The French may continue to go to the Roman Catholic church. The government of Quebec is to be appointed by Britain. French seigneurs may continue to hold their seigneuries. Roman Catholics will be allowed to hold public office in Quebec.	1. French-Canadians are pleased that their territory is enlarged, that they can practise their own religion, and that they can be appointed to the governing Council. 2. Colonists in the Thirteen Colonies are furious because they wanted to expand into the Ohio valley. 3. People in the Thirteen Colonies are proud of their elected governments. They feel Quebec should have an elected government rather than one appointed by Britain. 4. French-Canadian loyalty to Britain is almost certain if there is a war between Britain and the Thirteen Colonies.
1774: The First Continental Congress The Thirteen Colonies send representatives to a September meeting in Philadelphia. The representatives plan a course of action to deal with Britain.	1. Colonists express a desire for strong united action against Britain. 2. They decide not to buy any British goods. 3. Armed citizens called **minutemen** are organized to fight if needed. They would be ready in a minute to defend the colonies.
1775: Lexington and Concord The governor of Massachusetts knows colonists have been collecting arms and ammunition against the law. He knows they have them stored at Concord, 27 km from Boston. He orders British troops to seize the colonial supplies. Paul Revere, a Boston silversmith, rides from Boston to warn the people of Concord. As he gallops through the sleeping villages, he rouses minutemen with the cry, "The British are coming!"	1. British troops and minutemen clash outside Lexington on route to Concord. Eight colonists are killed. 2. In a second encounter at Concord about 73 British soldiers are killed and 200 wounded. 3. The British have to fight groups of minutemen at several places on their march back to Boston. 4. The idea of independence grows.

Cause	Effects
1776: The Declaration of Independence The Continental Congress declares the colonies independent of Britain on 4 July 1776.	1. The Thirteen Colonies of America separate from Great Britain. The American Revolution (1776-1783) begins.

The first announcement of the Declaration of Independence, 4 July 1776.

Settlers From America: The Loyalists

Not everyone living in the Thirteen Colonies wanted independence from Britain. About one-third of the American colonists were against it. But it was dangerous to oppose the Revolution. Your life and your property were in jeopardy. How much easier it would have been to follow the tide and join the rebels. The risk increased when the fighting broke out in 1775. Opposition was even more dangerous after American independence was won in 1783.

Who Were the Loyalists?

Colonists who were against the Revolution were called **Loyalists** or **United Empire Loyalists**. They did not want the colonies to break away from Britain and form a separate country. Being part of the British Empire had its advantages. Britain could be counted on for defence. It was an important industrial nation and bought the colonies' raw materials. King George III and the royal family deserved the loyalty of the people.

Some Loyalists opposed the very idea of revolution. They believed that rising up in armed rebellion to overthrow the government was wrong. To these colonists, the rebels were violent people. They could not be trusted. Some religious groups such as the Quakers and Mennonites became Loyalists because they opposed all war.

Not all Loyalists were British. They came from a variety of backgrounds. There were Germans, Dutch, Scandinavians, Natives, and Blacks. Some were rich and educated. Others were poor and uneducated. Some came from old colonial families, while others were more recent arrivals in America. They practised different religions and had different occupations. Most, however, were farmers, craftspeople, and labourers.

Treatment by the Patriots

The revolutionaries or rebels in the colonies called the Loyalists **Tories**. Tories were people who opposed change. The rebels did not think of the Tories as "loyal." It was just the opposite. By opposing the revolution, they were traitors to the colonies.

The colonial rebels called themselves **Patriots**. In most communities the Patriots set up Committees for Public Safety to hunt down the Loyalist traitors. When they were discovered, Loyalists were often treated brutally by mobs. Many were robbed of their possessions and driven from their homes. Some were tarred and feathered, though actual cases of this were not common. Just the threat was enough to frighten most Loyalists. Sometimes Loyalists were imprisoned in dark, musty prisons to wait out the war. Some were publicly executed to show the seriousness of their crime.

Loyalist Experiences

Read about the experiences of these Loyalists.

Benjamin Garrison: New York

Benjamin Garrison feared for the safety of his family. He decided to send them to Monmouth in New Jersey. He was certain they would be safer in a small out-of-the-way town. He was mistaken. Once the war began, these small towns were controlled by the rebels. Loyalists were easy to identify in such places. Benjamin Garrison was arrested on a visit to his family in Monmouth.

Suzanna MacDonald: New York

Alexander MacDonald joined the British army as the war began and was stationed in Halifax. Suzanna MacDonald remained in New York. One evening their home was ransacked by a gang of rebels. The rebels claimed to be looking for hidden weapons. They told Mrs. MacDonald that they would have her husband dead or alive.

Daniel Begal: New York

Daniel Begal joined Jessup's Rangers, a Loyalist regiment, in 1777. His wife and three small children were held in their home as hostages by the Patriots. The rebels hoped this would help them capture Daniel Begal. The family was released later in 1778 and sent to Canada.

Mary Hoyt: Connecticut

Mary Hoyt's husband had joined the British Royal Navy in 1776. Mary was frequently insulted and abused in her home community in Connecticut. Soldiers fired rounds into the house when marching by. On 17 February 1777, fifty armed men came to the house and broke open the doors. They rushed in, confined Mary, and destroyed all the furniture and clothing. Mary and her five children were left without clothing. One of the children died soon after.

James Nichols: Massachusetts

Reverend Nichols was accused of being a

Loyalist. Hot pine tar was poured over him. His skin blistered and shrivelled. While the tar was soft, he was showered with goose feathers.

Alexander Fairchild: Connecticut

Alexander Fairchild was convicted as a Loyalist and sentenced to two years in jail for his disloyalty to the cause of the Revolution. He was imprisoned in Newgate Prison in Connecticut. This was one of the worst prisons. Located 20 m underground in an old copper mine, the place was dark, cold, and filthy. Water trickled constantly from the top and earth shifted from the sides. This added to the misery and stench of wet bodies.

Moses Dunbar: Connecticut

Moses Dunbar refused to join the colonial militia and support the Revolution even after he was severely beaten. He was put in jail for fourteen days. After his release he fled and joined a Loyalist regiment. In 1777 he returned home to be married. He was betrayed by a friend who was a Patriot. A document from his regiment was found in his pocket when he was arrested. He was found guilty of treason and condemned to death. He was executed on 19 March 1777.

-Adapted from
The Loyalists: Revolution/Exile/Settlement
by Christopher Moore

Fleeing North

Loyalists fled to Canada in a steady stream during the American Revolution. Some gathered in camps to await the outcome of the war. In 1783 when the war ended, they realized they could never return to their homes.

Those still in the United States found themselves in a hopeless situation. Most were driven from their homes. They lost their lands and their businesses. Their only hope was to begin a new life in the British territory to the north.

Some wealthy Loyalists moved to Great Britain. But most could not afford the journey. They were forced to find safety in what was left of British North America. About 100 000 Loyalists left the Thirteen Colonies between 1775 and 1784.

A Loyalist family making the journey to British North America.

THE NATIVE ALLIES

The Mohawk, Oneida, Cayuga, Onondaga, Tuscarora, and Senaca made up the Six Nations of the Iroquois Confederacy. Their lands were located southeast of Lake Ontario. Most fought on the side of the British during the American Revolution.

The Iroquois were led by the Mohawk chief Joseph Brant (1743-1807), or Thayendanega as he was called by his people. Brant was a strong ally. He had fought with the British during the Seven Years' War. Though only fifteen at the time, he impressed the British. He became an excellent student of languages and an official translator for the British army.

When the American Revolution ended, all Loyalists wanted government help to recover their losses and resettle in British territory. The Natives of the Six Nations deserved this help as much as any other Loyalists. At the end of the war, the peace treaty between Britain and the United States did not include the Native allies in any of the terms. These Natives, who had fought for Britain, seemed to have been forgotten.

This mistake was later corrected. General Haldimand was instructed by the British government to repay the Natives for their suffering during the American Revolution. As a result, a section of land was purchased from the Mississauga in southwestern Ontario. It was more than 240 000 ha of forested, fertile land stretching along both sides of the Grand River. The area was similar to the Mohawk River country of New York State where the Iroquois had lived. Other Iroquois settled at Deseronto on the Bay of Quinte and at Cataraqui near Kingston, Ontario.

About 2000 Iroquois were brought to the Grand River area by Joseph Brant in 1784. Brant himself received land in Burlington, as well as a house and a military commission. He lived there until his death in 1807. Brant spent much of his time trying to improve the lives of his people.

A statue of Joseph Brant, from the memorial to him in Brantford, Ontario.

British North America Before the Loyalists

British North America in 1783 was made up of the colonies of Newfoundland, St. John's Island (later Prince Edward Island), Nova Scotia, and Quebec. Nova Scotia then included New Brunswick and Cape Breton Island. Quebec included the backwoods territory that was to become the colony of Upper Canada (later the province of Ontario).

Upper Canada Before the Loyalists

Present-day Ontario was not complete wilderness before the Loyalists arrived. The Native peoples and French had been there for centuries.

Native peoples had long-established communities in the region. In the 1650s, after the Huron-Iroquois Wars, the Iroquois had established villages along the north shore of Lake Ontario. *Teiagon* and *Ganatsekwyagon* were built around modern Toronto, at the mouths of the Humber and Rouge rivers. *Ganaraske* was located near Port Hope. *Ganneious* was near Napanee.

The French had been in Upper Canada for over 150 years before the Loyalists. The adventures of the coureurs de bois and voyageurs are still celebrated in song and legend. Missionaries also came to work among the Huron. When the Iroquois raids destroyed the missions, the French concentrated almost totally on the fur trade.

As the fur trade expanded, the French built forts in the backwoods territory. The first was Fort Frontenac, built in 1673 at the site of present-day Kingston. Other forts were established to protect the French territory, but the region was diffi-

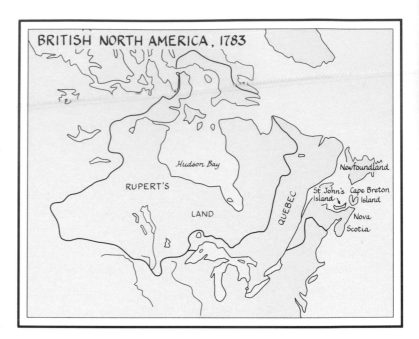

BRITISH NORTH AMERICA, 1783

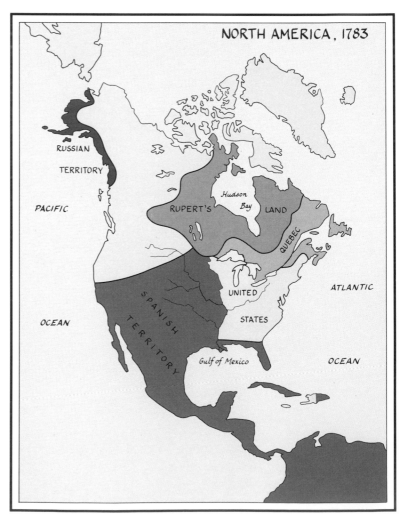

NORTH AMERICA, 1783

cult to defend. The forts were usually several days' travel apart.

English also established forts in the area that is today Ontario. The Hudson's Bay Company was formed in 1670 to promote the English fur trade. Forts were built on the shores of Hudson Bay and James Bay to protect English interests.

Besides fur-trading forts, there were dozens of small trading posts scattered throughout the wilderness of Quebec in the 1600s. They were built at the mouths of small rivers that ran into major waterways. Many were little more than fenced-in clearings with a few small buildings and a vegetable garden.

The French founded few settlements in the backwoods area west of Quebec and Montreal. Communities such as Detroit and Niagara were the exceptions. The backwoods of the west was seen mainly as a hunting ground for furs. The French feared that settlement would mean the end of the fur trade in the area.

Detroit

Detroit was an important pre-Loyalist settlement. Antoine de la Motha Cadillac founded a small fur-trading post on the Detroit River in 1701. It grew into an important military post called Fort Pont-chartrain, in honour of the French Minister of Marine. Soldiers there worked the land and grew their own food. The settlement spread on both sides of the Detroit River.

After 1734 the settlement on the Canadian side of the river began to expand. Land grants were given to ex-soldiers from the fort and to French settlers. The grants were laid out in long narrow strips running back from the riverfront. Houses built there were like those in Quebec. This settlement on the east bank of the Detroit River had several hundred inhabi-

tants when the British took over New France. Maps printed before 1793 show Detroit inside the boundaries of Upper Canada. It was an important settlement in the early history of the colony.

The Maritimes Before the Loyalists

Settlement in the Maritimes had also begun early in the 1600s. But growth and development were slow in the area. St. John's Island (Prince Edward Island) had a very small population before the Loyalists arrived. Most settlers were Highland Scots. There were also many Acadians who had survived the expulsion or made their way back to the island after 1755. Most of the land was in fact owned by landlords who didn't even live there. There were sixty-seven of these "absentee" landowners. Most lived in Britain rather than on the island!

Newfoundland also had a small population in 1783. Communities were thinly scattered across the island. Most Newfoundlanders depended on the cod fisheries of the Grand Banks. They traded mainly with Great Britain.

Nova Scotia in 1783 was a fishing and farming colony. The first settlement at Port Royal was established by the French in 1605. About 6000 French still lived in the colony in 1784. But almost half of the settlers traced their origins to New England. Many still had family and friends in the old Thirteen Colonies. Most of these former Americans lived along the southern and western shores of the colony. Other settlers of German, Scottish, and Irish background were scattered throughout the colony in small villages. The total population in 1784 was less than 30 000. Halifax was one of the most important communities.

Halifax

Halifax began as an English settlement. It was named in honour of the British Earl of Halifax, who organized its founding. The location was chosen because of its natural harbour. Halifax became an important trading port. About 2500 English settlers arrived in 1749. But most of these original settlers did not stay long. In fact, they left for New England before winter. They believed New England was the heart of the fishing industry and the centre of trade along the Atlantic coast.

After most of the original English settlers moved out, Americans moved in. The census in 1767 showed 3069 people. Over 1300 were Americans. Many different cultures were represented in the remaining population. Among them were 855 Irish; 302 English; 264 Germans and Swiss; 200 Acadians; 52 Scots; and 44 Blacks. The Germans and Swiss had come between 1750 and 1752 to help build the town. When the Loyalists arrived in Nova Scotia in the 1780s, Halifax was a growing community.

Loyalist Migration Routes and Settlements

What routes did the Loyalists follow to British North America? Where did they settle? What changes took place as a result of their arrival?

Nova Scotia

The arrival of the Loyalists had a great impact on Nova Scotia. The population of the peninsula doubled. Some 35 000 Loyalists chose to go to Nova Scotia. It was closer than Upper Canada and easier to reach. Shiploads of Loyalists set sail from ports such as Boston and New York and sailed up the Atlantic coast to the Maritimes.

Some Loyalists established new communities such as Shelburne. Between 14 000 and 15 000 settled across the Bay of Fundy in the valley of the Saint John River. In 1784 this settlement became the new colony of New Brunswick. Before 1780 the area had fewer than 2000 people of European descent. An additional thousand Loyalists settled on St. John's Island (Prince Edward Island) and Cape Breton Island.

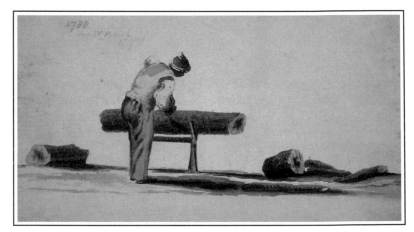

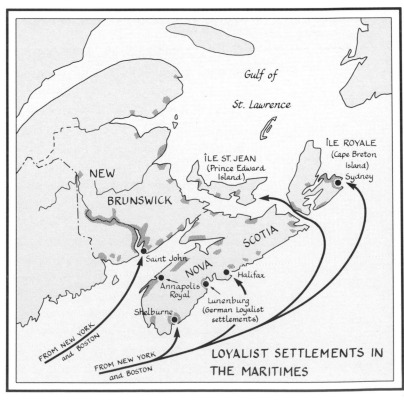

A Black woodcutter in Shelburne, Nova Scotia, 1788. About 3000 Blacks settled in Nova Scotia during and after the American Revolution.

LOYALIST SETTLEMENTS IN THE MARITIMES

Quebec

The largest number of Loyalists who came to Quebec were farmers from New York and Pennsylvania. Other groups came from Maryland, Georgia, New Jersey, and Rhode Island. They settled in the almost unoccupied territory at the head of Lake Erie, in the Niagara Peninsula, around the Bay of Quinte, and along the north shore of the St. Lawrence River. The southeastern part of present-day Ontario received the largest number of Loyalists.

The Loyalists began arriving in Quebec after 1774. Most came through the back country of New York following rivers, lakes, and portage routes. The main route was up the Hudson and Richelieu rivers to the St. Lawrence. They gathered in camps at places such as Sorel, Quebec.

But not all came through the back country. Some large groups travelled by sea up the Atlantic coast and the St. Lawrence River. In the fall of 1783, about 1300 Loyalists were led on such a sea voyage from New York City by Peter Van Alstine and Michael Grass.

The territory occupied by the Loyalists in 1784 was part of Quebec. Soon after their arrival, they asked the British government to make their territory a separate province. They wanted their own elected legislative assembly. They wanted their own laws based on the British system instead of the French. The British government agreed. The province of Quebec was divided in 1791. The western part became Upper Canada (present-day Ontario). The eastern part became Lower Canada (present-day Quebec).

The United Empire Loyalists played an important role in the history of British North America. Their arrival led to the creation of two new colonies: Upper Canada and New Brunswick. They brought with them new ideas and a new cultural richness. Remember that they came from a variety of ethnic backgrounds. They changed the face of British North America.

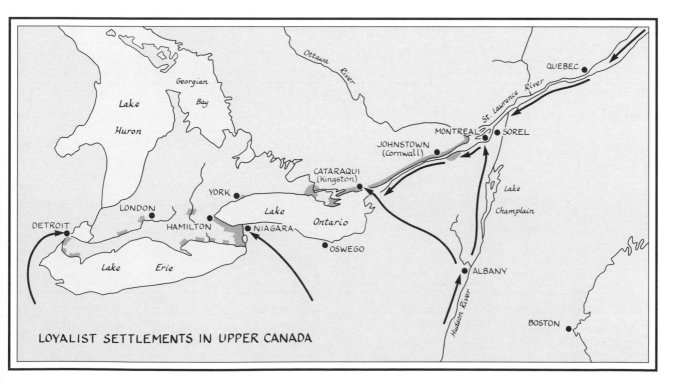

LOYALIST SETTLEMENTS IN UPPER CANADA

WHAT WAS UPPER CANADA?

What was this place "Upper Canada?" Today it is the province of Ontario. In 1784 it was part of the colony of Quebec. Between 1784 and today it had different names. From 1791 to 1840 it was called Upper Canada. From 1840 to 1867 it was called Canada West.

Examine the maps below. What was the area of present-day Ontario called in each map? How did the size of the territory change?

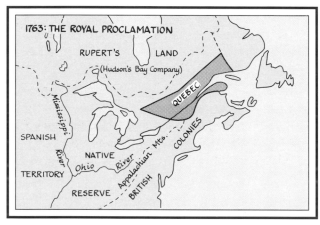

The British colonies in America were hemmed in. The area west of the Appalachian Mountains was reserved for the Natives. Upper Canada was Native territory.

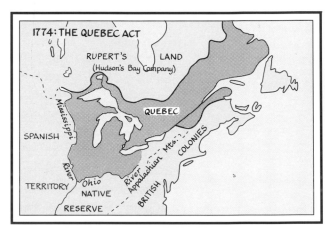

Britain gave the French-speaking colony of Quebec the area of the Ohio valley. Upper Canada was at the time still part of Quebec.

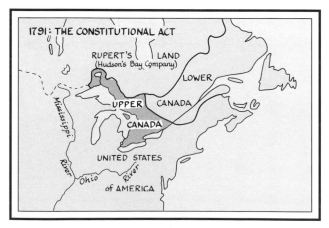

Quebec was split into two separate colonies. The French-speaking colony was called Lower Canada. The English colony on the "upper" St. Lawrence River was called Upper Canada.

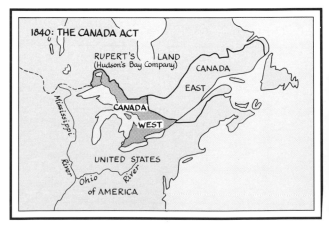

The two colonies of Upper and Lower Canada were re-united. Upper Canada became Canada West. Lower Canada became Canada East.

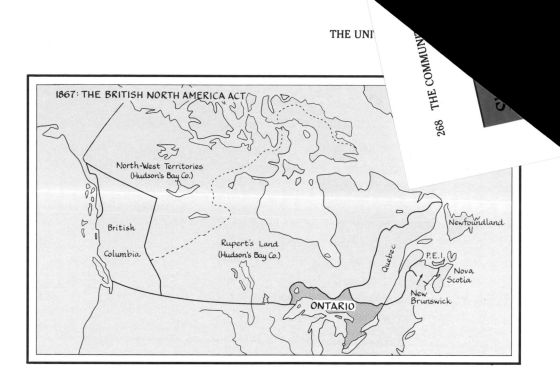

Canada West became Ontario, one of the four original provinces of Canada along with Nova Scotia, New Brunswick, and Canada East (which was again renamed Quebec). The other provinces joined Canada later.

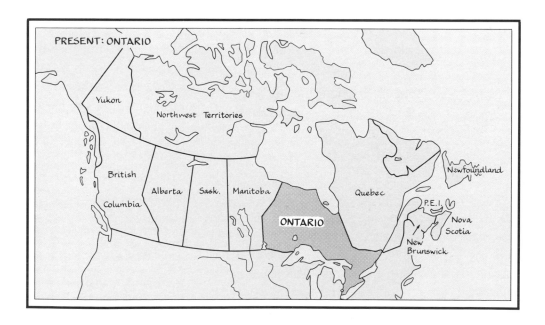

Today Ontario is the most populated province in Canada. Its present boundaries were defined in 1912.

Skill Building: The Decision-Making Organizer

Think about how many times you have to make decisions in a day. Some are small decisions such as "What should I wear today?" or "What should I have for lunch?" Other decisions are more important. If your family has to decide whether or not to move to a new town, they will want to know what you think. How would you feel about going to a new school, leaving your friends, and living in a smaller town. How will you decide? It isn't easy!

It helps to sit back and think through the problem carefully. What are the positive and negative sides? Let's look at a simple example first.

Your problem is: "Should I buy a new bicycle?" First write down the question. Then think of both the positive (Yes) and negative (No) sides and list them.

Problem	Yes	No
Should I buy a new bicycle?	-I need a new one	-it would take all my savings
	-my old bicycle is not safe	-my old bike can be repaired
	-there is a sale on	-I want a camera and tape deck
	-I have wanted one for a long time	-repairs cost much less than a new bike
	-it would have a good resale value	

Now how can you organize your thoughts even more carefully? Think about what kinds of things you were concerned about. For example, you considered your needs, the cost, the enjoyment, and the value of a new bike over your old one. These points were your criteria. You need to carefully evaluate each one. To help, you can make a decision-making organizer. Look at the example below. Notice how organizing the ideas has helped to clarify the points.

Problem Should I buy a new bicycle?

Criteria	Yes	No
Needs	-present bike is six years old -condition is a safety concern	-present bike can be repaired -expected use in future will be less
Cost	-there is a sale at two sporting stores -price will increase next year	-repairs to present bike would cost much less -a new bike would take my entire savings
Enjoyment	-I would have a new bike like Emile -it is something I have wanted for a long time	-I also really want a new camera and tape deck -I have just joined the camera club at school
Value	-the price rises each month I delay -it can always be resold in future with small loss	-there are always sales at various stores -I probably won't ride a bike as much in two years

Follow these steps to develop a decision-making organizer.

1. State the problem in the form of a question.

2. Identify the possible choices or **alternatives** across the top of the organizer–Yes or No.

3. Develop a list of the things you should consider before you make your decision. These considerations are the criteria.

4. List the criteria in the left column of your organizer.

5. Consider the positive and negative sides of all your criteria and enter your answers on the organizer. Use point form.

6. Review all of your points. Weigh the alternatives. Which column has the stronger points?

7. Make your decision.

8. Write a short paragraph explaining your decision. Which considerations were most important to you?

Now let's put your new skill to work. Imagine you are a Loyalist living in the Thirteen Colonies at the time of the American Revolution. You are trying to decide whether you should leave your home and move your family to Upper Canada. You have a good farm and the children are all happy there. Your savings are enough for the journey, but will not be enough for all of the supplies you will need when you arrive.

Use a decision-making organizer to help you decide. Consider the following criteria:

1. Money/Finances
2. The Family
3. The Situation in the Colony
4. The Situation in Upper Canada

Can you suggest other criteria or factors you should consider?

Arriving in Canada

Imagine trying to look after thousands of Loyalists, all arriving at one time!

How do you prepare for their arrival?

Where do you find land for them to settle?

How much land do you think they should receive?

Where do you find the necessary supplies to help them get started?

These questions had to be answered. The British government and the colonial governors had to decide how to take care of the Loyalists in British North America.

The Loyalists could be divided into three groups. First were the refugees who fled the Thirteen Colonies on their own during the war. **Refugees** are people who flee their homelands because of war or because they are mistreated. Second were those who left in groups under British military protection. These groups sailed from ports such as New York and Boston. Third were the soldiers who fought for the British and were released from duty at the end of the war.

Encampment of Loyalists at Johnstown, a new settlement on the banks of the St. Lawrence River.

Most of the Loyalists who fled to the Maritimes went under British military protection. The government directed most of them to the unsettled areas of the colonies. But in Quebec there were many more who came on their own. They caught the government by surprise. So many of them arrived during the war!

Finding places for the refugees to stay was not easy. Some went to live in French villages. Others settled in camps such as Sorel at the mouth of the Richelieu River. They felt safe there because British troops were nearby for protection.

By the end of the war there were thousands of Loyalists at Sorel. They were living in half-constructed buildings, tents, and hastily built barracks. They were given help by the British government while they waited for the outcome of the war.

Case Study: The Loyalists of the Upper St. Lawrence and the Bay of Quinte

Imagine that Russell Pitman was one of the Loyalists waiting at Sorel. Read about his family's experiences in this letter to his cousin. The family eventually settled in the Bay of Quinte region.

Cataraqui
26 October 1784

My dear cousin Anne,

We have arrived at the Cataraqui settlement. We came up the St. Lawrence River by bateau from Sorel in June. It was a journey none of us wish to repeat. Diana and I have received a grant of land in the Township of Ernestown on the north shore of the lake. Ernestown was surveyed last November and named in honour of Prince Ernest, the son of our beloved King George III.

The entire township is being settled by disbanded soldiers from my unit, Jessup's Rangers. A draw of location tickets was held. I drew lot 23 on the third concession. My days as a soldier with "The King's Loyal Americans" are over. The colonies of America and the Revolution are behind us. Now I begin a new life with Diana and the girls.

We have cleared part of our land and, with the help of neighbours, have constructed a cabin that will see us through the winter. It is a new beginning.

Warmest regards from your cousin,

Russell Pitman

In May 1784 the Loyalists from the camp at Sorel gathered just west of the Lachine rapids. The ice on the St. Lawrence had cleared. They were about to move up the river. The government had decided to resettle them permanently. They were on their way to new base camps. There they would be given grants of land along the shores of the upper St. Lawrence and the Bay of Quinte.

The journey up the St. Lawrence was dangerous. Nearly 200 km of rapids had to be navigated. The trip was made in flat-bottomed boats called bateaux. Each bateau could carry four or five Loyalist families. The boats travelled in flotillas of a dozen, each handled by an experienced crew of five. There were times when the crew had to use ropes from the shore to drag the boats against the current.

At night the travellers slept on the banks of the river. By day they were plagued by insects, hazardous waters, and often bad weather. The trip was slow. They travelled about 29 km each day. The entire journey to Kingston usually lasted ten days, but sometimes it stretched to a month.

Arrival at the base camp meant another disappointment. The farms were not ready. The surveying had not been completed. Life in tents and camps was not over for the Loyalists, but their hopes must have been high.

Loyalists landing at the Bay of Quinte. How would they have felt when they finally reached the shores?

Organizing the Land for Resettlement

In 1783 Governor Haldimand of Quebec had sent Samuel Holland to scout the lands around the upper St. Lawrence and Lake Ontario. He was to find the best locations for the new Loyalist settlements. Much of the land belonged to the Native peoples. Treaties had to be signed to obtain the land and avoid a war with the Natives.

In 1781 the Mississauga were persuaded to sell their lands in the Niagara region. In 1783 they surrendered lands along Lake Ontario and the St. Lawrence River.

Government surveying began in the fall of 1783. The land was organized into townships, concessions, and lots. Each lot was about 80 ha. The surveying was slow at first, but in March of 1784 it was speeded up. Thirty different surveying teams were used. The Loyalists were on their way!

The government created two sets of townships in the area. The first eight along the St. Lawrence River were called the Royal Townships. The second eight stretched west from Kingston and were called the Cataraqui Townships. Each township was a long, narrow strip stretching back from the waterfront, not unlike the seigneuries of Quebec. During the late spring and early summer of 1784, nearly 1500 men, 625 women, and 1500 children were resettled in these townships.

The layout of a typical township in Upper Canada.

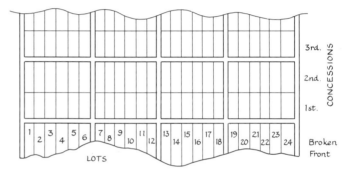

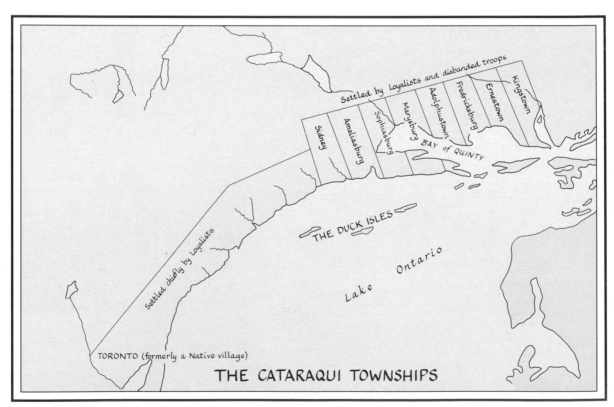

THE CATARAQUI TOWNSHIPS

Distributing the Land

The most important day arrived. That was the day the lots were assigned to the settlers. The government wanted to be fair to everyone. All Loyalists must be given an equal opportunity to get the choice locations along the waterfront. So the lots were assigned by drawing slips out of a hat!

The slip drawn was called a **location ticket**. It informed the Loyalists where to find their new homes by the concession and lot numbers.

Each head of a family—man or woman—was entitled to 40 ha and an additional 20 ha for each member of the family. The son of a Loyalist was entitled to 80 ha of land on reaching the age of eighteen. A daughter received 80 ha upon marriage.

The most generous land grants went to members of the military. Junior officers could receive up to 200 ha and senior officers up to 400 ha.

Some Loyalists did not even see their land. They sold it or gave it away, especially if it was back on the third or fourth concession. Loyalists with more than one grant sometimes sold the rear lot for clothing, seed grain, or livestock.

Providing Supplies for the New Arrivals

The government provided shelter and food to Loyalist refugees during the war. It also provided for them while they were at the base camps waiting for their land. They needed even the bare essentials of clothing.

To each man and boy over ten years:
> a coat, waistcoat, breeches, hat, shirt, blanket, shoes, leggings, and stockings.

To each woman and girl over ten years:
> two yards of woollen cloth, four yards of linen, stockings, a blanket, and shoes.

To each child under ten years:
> one yard of woollen cloth, two yards of linen, stockings, and shoes. Two children were to share a blanket.

The most important help came as the families took up their new land. There were no stores for hundreds of kilometres. Each Loyalist family was given a supply of flour, pork, some beef, and a little salt and butter. They also received seed for planting spring wheat, peas, corn, and potatoes. Finally, they got some basic farm tools—an axe, a spade, and a hoe.

Two families shared one plough and one cow. Every fourth family received a crosscut saw and every fifth family a set of tools that included chisels, augers, knives,

Drawing location tickets, 1784. Settlers would have been anxious to see whether they had drawn the choice lots on the waterfront.

pick-axes, and sickles. These were to be shared among neighbours. The government also left boats at convenient places along the river and bay for the settlers!

These supplies were provided for the first three years of settlement. After that time, the government hoped the family would be able to look after itself.

Getting a New Start

It was late in 1784 before the settlers reached their new land. What an experience that must have been–the first glimpse of the homestead! The families were greeted by forests, thick underbrush, fallen trees, and sometimes even swamp.

The first task was to prepare a clearing. The second was to build a rough cabin and some basic furniture before winter arrived. For many Loyalists, it was a lonely and difficult time. The nearest neighbour could be a great distance away. Many large land grants still remained empty. In the spring the soil would be prepared for the first crop of grain.

When the government supplies stopped, disaster struck. There was a bad crop in 1788. Summer drought and a severe winter, with nearly 2 m of snow on the ground until April, caused crops to fail. Then came "The Hungry Year" of 1788-89.

Many faced starvation. Reserve food supplies were gone by December. Extreme measures had to be taken to survive. The Loyalists turned to hunting animals and gathering plants to keep their families alive.

The stories of life in these years are filled with tragedy. Families survived by eating roots and wild plants and chewing bark stripped from trees. The capture of even the smallest animal for a pot of soup was considered a blessing. The survivors anxiously waited for the government relief expected in the spring. It had not been a good beginning in Upper Canada.

Activities

Looking Back

1. Define the following words and enter them in your dictionary.

cause	Tories
effect	Patriots
boycott	refugee
minutemen	location ticket
United Empire Loyalists	

2. Explain why each of the following British measures angered many citizens in the Thirteen Colonies.

    a) The Royal Proclamation
    b) The Sugar Act
    c) The Stamp Act
    d) The Townshend Duties
    e) The Quartering Act
    f) The Quebec Act

3. Why were the Loyalists against the American Revolution?

Using Your Knowledge

4. Make a map to show the different routes the Loyalists followed to British North America. Indicate what methods of transportation were used. Explain the advantages and disadvantages of each route.

5. What types of assistance did the Loyalists receive? Do you think the assistance was adequate or inadequate? Explain your answer.

6. Explain how land was distributed to the Loyalists. Do you think the system was fair? Why or why not?

7. The arrival of the United Empire Loyalists changed British North America. In what ways is this statement true?

Extending Your Thinking

8. **a)** You are a Loyalist living in the colony of New York in 1775. Your neighbour is a Patriot. Write a short conversation showing how you and your neighbour feel about the problems between Britain and the colonies. Be certain to present both sides of the argument clearly.
b) Choose a partner and act out your conversation for the class.

9. Imagine war is about to break out in Canada. You and your family do not agree with the war. You are forced to leave the country. Write a paragraph explaining how you feel.

10. You are a United Empire Loyalist who has just arrived at your new homestead on the Bay of Quinte. Write a letter to a friend in Pennsylvania explaining the problems you are having.

CHAPTER 18

Building the Community of Upper Canada, 1784-1850

At the time of the American Revolution, Russell Pitman had shared his experiences in letters to his cousin Anne in Liverpool, England. Their children continued the exchange of letters in the generation that followed.

In 1832 the Reid family decided to emigrate from Liverpool to Upper Canada. David Reid was eager to escape the crowded conditions of Liverpool and find suitable employment. His cousin Thomas Pitman, who lived in Thurlow Township on the Bay of Quinte, encouraged the family to come to Upper Canada.

The following letter was sent from Quebec City after the family had crossed the Atlantic. The letter is fictional, but the experiences are based on facts. What difficulties did the family experience on the voyage?

Dear Thomas,

Quebec City
14 September 1832

We have arrived in Quebec City. Much of our strength is gone, but I am thankful we are all still alive. Words cannot describe the horrors of our Atlantic venture. We had been warned that the voyage would be a difficult one. It was much worse than we could have ever imagined.

The crossing from Liverpool took us sixty-two days. Our ship was a cargo vessel out of Quebec City used to transport timber. Instead of returning empty, it has of late been outfitted to carry over ninety settlers to Canada. Crude bunks were built below deck in a space that could hardly accommodate thirty passengers, let alone over ninety. For the few meals we could cook, we had to use communal stoves.

It was like living in a dungeon. It was so dark and dank. We were stowed below the deck for most of the voyage. We were not allowed above in bad weather and that condition marked most of the journey. The hatch covers were not even watertight. In bad storms the straw of the bunk mattresses became soaked and began to rot.

I cannot describe the unbelievable heat of those quarters. The stench was at times almost unbearable. Seasickness was common and did not help such conditions. When the hatches were open the crew seemed amused at the steam rising from those sweltering holes. Seldom did crew members show any concern for our welfare.

I believe that the sickness on board was the most frightening part of the crossing. Passengers were struck by typhus and cholera. Seven of our company died and were buried at sea. My neighbour and friend Charles Maitland was among them. I shall forever remember his pain and agony at the end. His body had swelled so, and was covered in sores. Elizabeth and I have vowed to care for his widow, Ellen. Twenty-six others of our vessel have been held at the quarantine station on Grosse Island near Quebec City. They are suspected of carrying cholera. It seems to be so much worse this year than ever before. Your colony requires officials to hold any immigrants who might be carrying disease. A doctor must declare them clear of any infection before they can be released.

We shall be delayed here in Quebec another three weeks until strength has been regained by all. Our plan is to travel by bateau up the St. Lawrence to Kingston. There we will transfer to steamboat and venture on to Belleville. Then we will be close to you.

We all look forward to our arrival in Thurlow. We are eager to work on the farm with you and learn. Many of our fellow passengers are headed for farms as well. Others will look for work as domestic helpers or labourers on any canal or road project they can find.

Our journey thankfully nears its end. We shall be there soon.

Warmest regards,

David Reid

The Atlantic crossing. Describe the conditions below the decks of the ships.

The Population of British North America

Year	Upper Canada	Lower Canada	Nova Scotia	New Brunswick	Newfound-land	Prince Edward Island
1806	71 000	250 000	68 000	35 000	27 000	10 000
1814	95 000	335 000	n.a.	n.a.	n.a.	n.a.
1825	158 000	479 000	120 000	73 000	58 000	29 000
1831	237 000	553 000	277 000	94 000	76 000	33 000 (1833)
1840	432 000	717 000	203 000	156 000	n.a.	n.a.
1851	952 000	890 000	331 000	194 000	102 000	72 000 (1855)

n.a. = not available

Settlers from Europe

The arrival of the Loyalists increased the population of the British North American colonies. But in the early 1800s the total population was still small for such a large territory. So much good farmland was yet to be developed. The British government was anxious to open new areas to settlement.

A new wave of settlers arrived over the years 1815 to 1850. These were years of rapid growth for the colonies. Historians call the massive wave of incoming settlers **The Great Migration**. A steady stream of immigrants from Britain–English, Scots, Welsh, and Irish–crossed the high seas to British North America. In 1832 alone, 50 000 newcomers came to Upper Canada. In 1847, a famine year in Ireland, 100 000 immigrants arrived in the colony!

Reasons for the Great Migration

Unemployment

The year 1815 marked the end of a war in Europe that had lasted twenty-five years. During the war people easily found work. They were soldiers or they worked in the manufacture of weapons and war supplies. But the end of the war brought unemployment and hardship for many. Where could these people find new jobs and new opportunities?

The effects of the Industrial Revolution were also being felt in Britain. Machines powered by water wheels and steam engines were taking jobs away from many skilled workers and craftspeople. Hand weavers and spinners, for example, were no longer needed. These workers joined the unemployed.

Crowds of unemployed flocked to the growing industrial towns in search of jobs. The towns became crowded. People lived in dingy slum dwellings. Conditions grew steadily worse rather than better. Even those who found jobs were forced to work twelve to fourteen hours a day for very low wages and in wretched conditions. Children as young as six crawled into the coal mines carrying heavy loads. Other young children worked long hours in the factories.

People began to look for a way out. They considered **emigration** to another land such as British North America. To emigrate means to leave your country and move to another.

Over-Population in Europe

The population of Europe increased rapidly in the late 1700s. One reason for the growth was improved farming methods. Farmers had begun to take better care of their soil and crop yields increased. People had more food on their dinner tables. There were fewer famines. With a better diet, people also had more strength to fight disease.

Families of six or more children were common in Europe in the 1700s. But newborn children entered a dangerous world. One in five children died in their early years. In the poorer areas, it was more like one in three. By the late 1700s, conditions were improving. Fewer children died from lack of proper diet or from disease. Improved medical knowledge also contributed to the increase in population. Britain was becoming crowded. Land, good homes, and jobs were becoming scarce.

Enclosures and Clearances

Most European farmers did not own their land. They were tenants or **crofters** who rented from large landowners. Each year they gave the landowner part of their crop as rent. This system had been in place for generations. But the war that ended in 1815 brought changes. It created a great debt in Britain. The government began to tax landowners much more heavily.

The landowners found a solution to their financial problems in the growing factories. The looms in the woollen mills were producing more every year. They demanded a greater supply of wool. Raising sheep became very profitable.

Landlords removed their tenant farmers from the land in large numbers. They enclosed the land to raise sheep. That is, they fenced it in. The wool was sold to the factories. This movement in Scotland was called the **Highland Clearance**. In England it was called the **Enclosure Movement**. Thousands of tenant farmers and their families had to find new homes.

Irish emigrants leaving for America. What destinations are printed on the signs?

Famine

Ireland experienced a serious problem of its own. The most important food in the Irish diet was the potato. For several years in a row during the 1840s, the potato crop failed.

In 1845 a disease called **blight** infected the crop. The potatoes appeared normal when they were dug up, but within a few days they went black. They were unfit to eat. Famine struck. There was little food to replace the diseased crop.

The crop failed again in 1846. Starvation spread across the countryside. Terrible diseases such as typhus and cholera followed the famine. Terror filled Ireland. People by the thousands looked for opportunities to leave the country.

Encouraging New Settlements

Government Policies

Britain was eager to see more people settle in British North America. After 1815 government policies encouraged new settlers. Immigrants were offered free passage from Britain and thousands took advantage of the opportunity. They included disbanded soldiers from Britain, unemployed weavers and their families from Scotland, and struggling farmers from Ireland. They settled in the Atlantic colonies and in the Peterborough, Perth, and Rideau River areas of Upper Canada.

The government program to help immigrants was very successful. Over 6500 settlers were assisted between 1815 and 1825. There was just one problem. The program was very expensive for the government. New ways had to be found to bring immigrants to the colonies.

Private Land Companies

Private land companies were one solution. Land developers were granted large sections of government land known as Crown land. In return the developers promised to bring settlers to the colonies. They made a profit by selling lots to the settlers. Sometimes the developers also received additional grants when their original lands were sold.

In the Maritimes, the New Brunswick and Nova Scotia Land Company worked to attract settlers in the early 1830s. The company cleared land, and planned and built a community in Stanley, New Brunswick.

The Talbot Settlement

Thomas Talbot was a land developer in Upper Canada. In 1803 he gave up command of a British regiment to settle on the north shore of Lake Erie. Talbot was given 2000 ha of land near present-day St. Thomas in southwestern Upper Canada. He received a bonus of 80 ha for every new settler he brought to the land. His estate finally grew to 8000 ha and he became one of the largest landholders in Upper Canada.

Talbot spent the first years building roads and mills. The first settlers arrived in 1809. They came slowly at first, but by 1820 the original land grant was settled. Fifty thousand people settled on over 200 000 ha of new farmland.

Talbot spent fifty years supervising the growth of his colony. He personally interviewed everyone who wanted to live there. If he disapproved, the would-be settler was turned away.

He told his settlers how much of their 20 ha lot they had to clear. The settler received no record of the purchase until the clearing was done! The only record was a pencil scrawl over a lot on Talbot's map. If the settler didn't measure up, the name could easily be removed! The settlers also agreed to clear a road in front of their lots. The roads in this part of Upper Canada were among the best.

The Canada Company

One of the largest land companies was the Canada Company. It was founded by John Galt in 1826. Galt received a grant of over 400 000 ha in Upper Canada called the Huron Tract. It stretched from present-day Guelph to Lake Huron.

Towns were established at Guelph and Goderich on Lake Huron and a road was constructed between them. Galt and the Canada Company were responsible for settling thousands of people in what is today western Ontario. It was through the efforts of developers such as Talbot and Galt that much of southwestern Ontario was settled.

An ad for the Canada Company, printed in 1836.

Making a Home in the Forest

Catharine Parr Traill came to Upper Canada from England in 1832 and settled in the Peterborough area. In 1836 she wrote a book called *The Backwoods Of Canada*. This is how she described her new home in the backwoods:

I went to see the newly-raised building, but was sorely puzzled, as it presented very little appearance of a house. It was merely an oblong square of logs raised one above the other, with open spaces between every row of logs. The spaces for the doors and windows were not then sawn out, and the rafters were not up. In short, it looked a very queer sort of place, and I returned . . . a little disappointed, and wondering that my husband should be so well pleased with the progress that had been made. A day or two after this I again visited it. The timbers were laid to support the floors, and the places for the doors and windows cut out of the solid timbers, so that it had not quite so much the look of a birdcage as before.

After the roof was shingled, we were again at a standstill, as no boards could be procured [obtained] nearer than Peterborough, a long day's journey through horrible roads. At that time no sawmill was in progress. . . .

We have now got quite comfortably settled, and I shall give you a description of our little dwelling. The part finished is only a portion of the original plan; the rest must be added next spring, or fall, as circumstances may suit.

A nice small sitting-room with a store closet, a kitchen pantry, and bed-chamber form the ground floor. There is a good upper floor that will make three sleeping rooms.

When the house is completed we shall have a verandah in front and at the south side . . . in which we can dine, and have the advantage of cool air, protected from the glare of the sunbeams. The Canadians call these verandahs 'stoups'. Few houses, either log, or frame, are without them. . . . These stoups are really a considerable ornament, as they conceal in a great measure the rough logs, and break the barn-like form of the buildings.

Our parlour is warmed by a handsome Franklin stove with brass gallery and fender. Our furniture consists of a brass railed sofa, which serves upon occasion for a bed; Canadian painted chairs; a stained pine table; green and white muslin curtains; and a handsome Indian mat which covers the floor. One side of the room is filled up with our books. Some large maps and a few good prints nearly conceal the rough walls, and form the decoration of our little dwelling. Our bed-chamber is furnished with equal simplicity. We do not, however, lack comfort in our humble home; and though it is not exactly such as we would wish, it is as good as, under existing circumstances, we could expect to obtain.

–Adapted from
The Backwoods of Canada
by Catharine Parr Traill

1. How did Catharine Parr Traill feel when she first saw her new home? Why did she describe it as a "birdcage"?
2. What problems did she and her husband have as they were building their new home?

3. Do you agree that Catharine Parr Traill's house was a simple and humble one? Give reasons for your answer.

The home Catharine Parr Traill described was much more comfortable than most pioneer homes. Catharine Parr Traill was a gentlewoman. She was more fortunate than many other pioneers of the time. To others less fortunate, her home was a dream for the future.

Clearing the Land

When the pioneer families reached their wooded homesteads, they must have wondered how they could ever turn this wild forest into a productive farm. The task must have seemed impossible. There were two things to be done immediately. The land had to be cleared and a temporary shelter had to be built.

Everyone–men, women, and children–helped to clear the land. Trees were cut using simple hand axes. Neighbours helped one another. Brush and undergrowth were hacked away and dragged or rolled into huge piles. The piles were then set ablaze. The burning was always dangerous since the fire could easily spread into the nearby forest.

Settlers at work clearing the land.

When the trees were felled, the fields were still spotted with stumps. Most would take up to ten years to decay! Some could be burned and pulled up with the help of oxen, but this was hard work. Settlers used the pulled-up stumps for fences or boundary markers.

The First Home

The first temporary log cabin was called a **shanty**. Usually it was quite small. It wasn't much larger than a small room in an average home today. When the settlers later built better homes, the shanties became sheds for the farm animals.

The shanty roof was often made of bark and didn't always keep out the rain. Most shanties had only a dirt floor and no windows. The only opening was the doorway, covered with a blanket or rug. But even without windows, there was ventilation. Gaps between the logs provided welcome relief from the heat of summer. But the gaps created serious concerns in the winter!

Winter was not the only problem for shanty dwellers. They were often a great distance from their nearest neighbour. Pioneer life in the first clearings was quite lonely.

The Second Home

The second pioneer home was much larger than the shanty. It was more like the house described by Catharine Parr Traill. Usually it included more than a single room. There was a small upstairs room or at least a loft for sleeping.

Look at the picture of a typical second home. Can you imagine how it was built? First, logs were cut and squared with an axe or saw and notched at the ends so that they would fit neatly together. Not a single nail was used! Gaps between the

A settler's shanty. What evidence is there that this picture shows the settlers' first year on the homestead?

The second home. What new developments can you see on the farm in this picture compared with the one above?

logs were filled with moss or wooden wedges and clay to keep out the cold. Cutting, hauling, and placing the logs was back-breaking work.

The roof was made of split cedar logs or perhaps hand-made shingles. The floor was covered with rough planks. Unfortunately there was no basement. As a result, heavy frosts and rotting wood often caused the house to shift and made the floors uneven. The door and window openings were cut after the walls had been raised. Few people enjoyed the luxury of glass windows. Oiled cloth or paper was used to cover the openings.

The main feature of the house was the fireplace. It was made of stone and could be 2.5 m wide. It provided the only source of heat and also served as an oven for cooking.

Neighbours worked together to build their homes. There was often a party to celebrate when the work was done. Imagine how it must have felt to have a permanent, new home at last!

Farming the Land

What to Plant?

The first crops were planted as soon as a little land was cleared. The settlers needed to grow their own food to survive, especially when government supplies ran out. At first they concentrated on growing enough for the family. But as time passed they were able to produce a little extra. They took their extra crop to market in the towns. It was exchanged for manufactured goods such as iron tools and for cash.

The main crops were grains. Wheat, rye, oats, and barley were grown on the stump-studded fields. Wheat became the most profitable crop in Upper Canada.

Wheat flour made excellent bread and bread was an important part of the pioneer diet.

A few ambitious farmers planted orchards of apples and peaches. The Native peoples also taught the early settlers how to grow corn, squash, melons, pumpkins, and gourds. All pioneers planted vegetable gardens. They grew turnips, cabbages, peas, beans, carrots, and potatoes. The vegetables were easy to grow and could be stored for the long winter.

Preparing the Soil

Farming was much simpler in pioneer times, but it was back-breaking work. All a farmer needed was a wooden plough, a harrow, cradle scythes, flails, and perhaps a pair of oxen. The tools could probably all be kept in one small building.

Before planting, the ground had to be broken up with a hoe or mattock. The pioneers used hand tools because it was too difficult for animals to pull a plough through a stump-filled field.

If the stumps presented no serious problem, a wooden plough was used to cut through the hard ground and turn the soil. Most early ploughs were homemade and pulled by a yoke of oxen. The farmer walked behind the plough to guide it and keep it in the ground. Horses were seldom used because it was too easy for them to break a leg on the rough ground.

After ploughing, the land was **harrowed**. That is, it was levelled or made flat for planting. The harrow was like a large rake that broke up the clumps of soil.

Planting and Harvesting

Grain was sown by broadcasting. The farmer carried the seeds in a bag slung

Methods of building log homes.

Squared logs with bark left on the outside.

Squared logs stripped of bark.

Round logs with a roof made of basswood bark.

Farm tools from about 1830.

Sickle

Plough

Flail

Harrow

over the shoulder. The seeds were scattered about by hand as the farmer walked through the field. Rain washed them into the soil.

Corn planting followed the same practices that the Huron had used. The soil was shaped into mounds and a fish was placed into each one for fertilizer. The farmer dropped five or six kernels of corn into each seed mound and covered them.

The grain crop ripened by August and was harvested almost immediately. Rain or an early snow could damage the crop. A sickle or scythe was used to cut the grain. The scythe had a longer blade than the sickle and could cut more grain. When a cradle was attached to the scythe, the grain stalks could be gathered more easily into bundles. An expert cradler could cut about 1.5 ha of grain in a day.

After the grain was cut, it was gathered and bound. Then it was moved to the barn to be **threshed**. Threshing knocked the small grains out of their shells. It was often done with a flail. The flail was a flexible stick. Sometimes it was made of two pieces of wood joined by a leather strap.

The grain was spread on the floor of the barn and then hit with the flail. Sometimes horses or oxen were walked over the grain to break the shells.

Next came the **winnowing**. Winnowing separated the grain from the unwanted shells called chaff. The farmer placed both the grain and the chaff into a wooden tray and shook it lightly in the wind. The heavier grain remained in the tray while the lighter chaff was blown away.

The grain was now ready to be ground into flour at the local grist mill. The mill was often many kilometres from the farm.

Cutting grain with a cradle scythe.

Threshing with flails.

Winnowing.

Sometimes the farmer arrived only to find several other farmers already there. Everyone had to be patient. They might be away from home for several days.

Getting corn ground into meal wasn't as difficult as getting wheat ground into flour. The settlers borrowed an idea from the Native peoples. They used hominy blocks. These blocks were burned-out hardwood stumps. The corn was crushed in the hollow stump using a long-handled pestle.

Skill Building: Developing Listening and Discussion Skills

Have you ever been in a discussion and not had a chance to get a word in? Or have you noticed how sometimes people just talk around in circles and never make a clear point? These are frustrating experiences.

Good discussion skills are important life skills. Think about how many times you have been involved in a discussion. You probably often discuss with your friends what you would like to do on Friday after school. Or you might have a serious discussion with your family about whether to move to a new town. You also have discussions in class every day.

It is important to learn how to take part positively and listen carefully in a discussion. You can learn these skills by practising in small groups. In some discussions, a chairperson helps to keep everyone on topic and makes sures everyone has a chance to speak.

Here are some strategies to help you develop your skills.

Finding a Focus

1. Decide on the topic for your discussion. Develop a question about your topic. The question will give your discussion a focus. For example:

Topic: The Great Migration
Focus question: Why did so many people leave Europe in the early 1800s to go to British North America?

2. Be certain that all members of your group understand the focus question.

3. Each group member should:

a) form an opinion on the question

b) organize important ideas and information to support his or her opinion.

Setting the Ground Rules

1. Select a member of the group to act as chairperson. The chairperson leads the discussion. He or she makes sure everyone has a chance to speak and stays on topic. When one point has been fully discussed, the chairperson should bring up a new point to keep the discussion going.

2. Another member of the group might be selected to act as an observer. The observer should keep notes on how well group members do during the discussion. He or she should check that people present their positions clearly, listen carefully, give others a chance to speak, and participate in the discussion after they have given their initial opinions.

3. Decide the order in which group members will speak to start the discussion.

How to Start

1. The chairperson asks each member of the group, in turn, to state an opinion on the question. Each person briefly presents the most important points in his or her argument.

2. Listen carefully to each person's contribution. Think about ideas you could add or new arguments you could present. Be ready to participate in the discussion.

3. The chairperson then opens the discussion. Group members can expand on the points raised or add new ideas as they think of them. Remember to let everyone speak. Don't interrupt.

Helpful Hints

1. Try to make your ideas clear by using comparisons. For example, if your idea is a difficult one, relate it to something most people are familiar with.

"Isn't what we are talking about here just like ..."
"This is similar to what we do today when we ..."

2. Practise paraphrasing. That is, state another person's position in your own words. Then you can be sure you really understand what the other person has said.

"I see, you mean that ..."

3. Try to discuss one idea at a time. Don't jump into a new point until one idea has been completely discussed.

4. Always listen carefully.

Try It

Now it's time to practise your skills. Discuss the following question in small groups.

Topic: The best settlers for Upper Canada

Focus question: What qualities did early settlers in Upper Canada need to be successful?

The Timber Trade

Next to farming, the timber trade was the most important activity in Upper Canada. Britain needed timber for its wooden sailing ships. White pine for masts was in great demand. The strength of Britain's defence was her navy.

Britain's supply of timber from Europe was cut off by a war with the French leader Napoleon in the early 1800s. More and more Britain depended on the colonies of North America for timber. Wood was exported first from the ocean ports of Nova Scotia and New Brunswick. Later, in the 1820s and 1830s, timbering became important in the Ottawa valley and the northern parts of Upper Canada. By 1839 wood made up 80 percent of all exports from British North America.

The Lumbering Camps

Lumbering became a way of life for many in the pioneer communities. The season began in the fall. Canoes carried the lumberers and their supplies to the camps in the forests. Thousands went to live in the shanties of the lumber camps as the timber trade grew in importance.

Imagine the demand for food in these camps. So much food was needed it helped the growth of agriculture in Upper Canada! Huge breakfasts were devoured at dawn each morning before the gangs headed into the woods.

A shantyman from the Ottawa valley described his life this way:

I'm satisfied with my life. I'm not suffering any real hardships. I feel at home and I love the freedom. The food is good and there is lots of it. My one complaint is that there isn't much variety in the meals.

For breakfast we usually have baked beans, sometimes with a little molasses, bread and green tea. We take our lunch with us in little cotton bags out into the woods where we are working. It's usually boiled salt pork and bread and tea. Likely it's frozen because most of the time we have to bury our lunch in the snow to keep the ravens from getting it. How they love to tear open those cotton bags and eat our lunches in the morning while we are working! When lunch time comes we usually sit around an open fire to boil our tea and thaw our sticks of bread by holding them close to the fire.

Supper is the main meal of the day.

Usually there is a huge camp kettle of boiled beef and another one of boiled potatoes. There might also be more salt pork and there is always plenty of bread. For dessert we might have boiled rice with raisins, stewed dried apples with cinnamon, or brown apples that have been dried and quartered. . . .

–Adapted from
Notes on the History of Renfrew County

The axemen carefully selected the trees they would cut. The best white pine might tower 50 m high. Considerable skill was needed to bring these trees down safely. A good axeman could drop a tree on a precise spot. His skill and power were essential to the profit of the camp.

There were many reports of gambling and fighting in the camps. The lumberers worked hard and tensions ran high. Drinking sometimes led to problems. The stories of life in the lumbering camps upset many of the gentler folk of Upper Canada!

Once the logs were felled they were squared to fit more easily into the timber ships. Rounded edges wasted important space. Squaring was done with an adze and a heavy broad-axe which could weigh as much as 4 kg! Actually, squaring timber was very wasteful. About a quarter of the log was cut away and left on the ground. In winter the logs were hauled out of the woods to the rivers with teams of oxen.

Rafting the Logs Down River

Spring was the time of the "drive." The logs were rafted down river on the high waters of the spring snowmelt. The drives were the only way to take the logs on the long journey to the sawmills. The lumberers worked furiously to get the logs into the river at the right time.

The drive was the most hazardous part of the lumberer's job. Imagine the scene. The lumberers must work quickly to tie the logs into huge rafts. They use birch and hazel saplings as rope. The rafts must hold secure or rough water will break them up. Some rafts are 90 m long and 18 m wide! They are so large that a house can be built on them. Each has a crew of up to fifty men. They live in tents or cabins right on board the rafts.

With skill they guide the rafts downstream using oars. Sometimes favourable winds help out. There is always danger. The crew must be on the lookout for rocks and keep away from the shoreline. A good raftsman can ride through rough, icy water standing on a spinning log! Many lives could be lost during the spring drives.

Rafting methods were somewhat different on the Ottawa River. The timbers were put together in small rafts called **cribs**. These were not as strong as the St. Lawrence rafts, but they were suited to the Ottawa River and easily handled. In smooth water, several rafts could be linked together like the cars of a train.

Large log rafts on the river. What evidence can you see that the lumberers lived on the rafts?

Philemon Wright ran the first timber raft down the Ottawa River to Quebec in 1806. His son later invented the timber slides or special alleyways used to get the small rafts around waterfalls.

Sawmills also developed as part of the timber trade. By 1854, at the peak of the trade, there were 1618 sawmills in Upper Canada. They produced planks for the houses and barns in the communities. Plank buildings were replacing the old log homes. Boards from sawmills in Upper Canada were also exported to Europe.

The Decline of the Timber Trade

The timber trade in British North America began to decline in the 1850s. Britain's lumber supply from the Scandinavian countries was re-established after the Napoleonic Wars. Squared timber from Canada was less in demand. It was cheaper for Britain to import timber from Europe than from North America. Ship-building was also changing. As the century advanced, wooden ships were being replaced by ships with steel hulls.

Boiling wood ashes to make soap.

The Potash Industry

Another important export from Upper Canada was **potash**. Potash was made from the ashes of burned trees. It was in great demand in Europe. Potash was used to make glass, soap, and fertilizer.

As the pioneers cleared their land, they burned the brush and logs. Women and children collected ashes from the fires for potash. The pioneers added water to the ashes to produce lye, a solution rich in natural chemicals and used to make soap. The lye was boiled in heavy iron kettles to thicken it.

Pioneers earned cash by selling their potash. Many asheries developed in the early communities of Upper Canada. An ashery refined the potash before it was exported to Europe. Huge oak barrels of potash were shipped each year.

The problem with the industry was that it did not last long. Once the land was cleared and the brush burned, there were fewer ashes. The potash industry shows, though, how resourceful the early pioneers were. Even the ashes from trees were turned to a profitable use.

Transportation in Upper Canada

Going Down the Road

Road-building in Upper Canada began with the arrival of the first settlers. But road-building did not mean what it does today. In the early years it meant clearing a path through the woods! Later roads were built by laying logs side by side through swampy areas. These were called **corduroy roads**.

Most main roads were built by the government. Some though were built by companies such as the Canada Company. Other companies developed just to construct roads. They were allowed to collect tolls–that is, people who used the roads had to pay every time they travelled on them. Traffic wasn't heavy on these early roads. The average family in Upper Canada didn't even own a horse.

The Stagecoach

Have you ever thought that a stagecoach might once have gone down your street? Stagecoaches were being used in British North America by 1800. They first appeared in important centres such as Niagara. They carried passengers and mail. In the 1820s a regular stagecoach line opened between York and Kingston. The coaches were run by private citizens or companies. Service was not very reliable in the early years. By the 1830s coach lines began to connect the towns, villages, and farming communities north of York. Daily service became available year-round.

A stagecoach was drawn by two pairs of horses. The coach itself was small and reminded many of a box. Leather curtains hung at the sides and the back and

covered the luggage holder at the rear. All coaches were equipped with shovels and axes. Passengers could be called upon to help the driver free the coach from the mud or remove a fallen tree from the road!

A traveller could count on being cooped up in one of these small boxes for several hours with two or three companions, even for a short journey. A long journey from Kingston to York was another matter. A one-way trip could take from one to four days. It depended on the

A corduroy road. Why would travel on these roads have been uncomfortable? What advantages would they have had over dirt roads?

Struggling through the mud in an early stagecoach.

weather and the condition of the roads.

Travelling along these rough roads in a stagecoach was not a comfortable experience. The coaches had no springs. They were supported on their frame by heavy leather straps. The coach swayed and jolted with every bump along the way. A traveller was lucky to emerge with nothing worse than a few bruises.

The Conestoga Wagon

The Conestoga wagon was brought to Upper Canada as early as 1799 by settlers from Pennsylvania. They used it as their home on the journey to the colony. The rounded top was made of canvas. The box of the wagon was narrow and deep and was made by boatbuilders. It was curved like a boat and was waterproof. When the wheels and gear were removed, the wagon could be used as a boat to cross rivers.

Settlers travelling with the Conestoga wagon.

Going Down the River

The first real highways in Upper Canada, as in New France, were the waterways. The first settlements were located on the shores of lakes and rivers. Anyone who travelled in the colony by road appreciated the advantages of travelling by water!

By the end of the 1700s timber rafts were going down the St. Lawrence River. They were steered by oars and helped along when possible by sails. They carried the products of the colony down to Quebec where they were transported across the ocean. Upper Canada had no seaport. Flour, grain, pork, and potash were carried on the timber rafts. But going down the river was dangerous business. It meant travelling through rapids. Losses were heavy.

The Durham Boat

Durham boats transported passengers and goods along the shores of Lake Ontario and the St. Lawrence River. Usually the boats travelled in groups of five or six. If an accident happened, there was always someone to come to the rescue.

The Durham boat was a flat-bottomed craft like the bateau. What made it different was its rounded bow and square stern. Its bottom was sometimes covered with iron to prevent damage from rocks. It had sails, and the crew used long poles to get through rapids or strong currents.

Changes in Transportation

The Steamboat

The important changes in transportation came with the introduction of steamboats and canals. The first steamboat on the

Great Lakes was the Frontenac, built in 1816 at Bath near Kingston. By the 1820s steamboats were carrying passengers and cargo back and forth between the great falls at Niagara and Kingston. Thousands of settlers were transported to their new homes by steamboat. By the 1830s steamboats were being used even on the smaller lakes and rivers. They improved the speed and comfort of travel considerably.

The lake steamer "Great Britain." This was the largest steamer to travel on Lake Ontario in 1839.

Canal-Building in Upper Canada

"Canal fever" swept Upper Canada from 1825 to 1850. Canals made it possible to navigate a ship all the way from Quebec to Lake Michigan. Naval vessels could enter the heart of the continent and defend the province against an American invasion if needed. And the St. Lawrence River became the trade outlet for the entire Great Lakes region.

Americans knew the importance of canal development. In 1825 New York State built the Erie Canal. It linked Lake Erie at Buffalo with the Hudson River and the ice-free port of New York. The canal meant trouble for merchants in Upper Canada. It was taking away their business.

The first major canal-building project in Upper Canada was the Welland Canal, built between 1825 and 1829. It linked Lake Erie to Lake Ontario, bypassing Niagara Falls

The Welland Canal helped to make the St. Lawrence-Great Lakes waterway a rival to the Erie Canal. The first Welland Canal was very different from the present one, which can accommodate long lake freighters. The modern canal is one of the largest in the world.

The Welland Canal project was begun by a merchant from St. Catharines named William Hamilton Merritt. He was a second generation Loyalist. Merritt set up a company that received a land grant and a loan from the government of Upper Canada. The British government also helped with the costs in return for a promise. Government ships should have the right to pass through the canal toll free.

The Rideau Canal was another major building project in Upper Canada. This canal linked the Ottawa River with Lake Ontario at Kingston. The governments of Upper Canada and Britain financed the project. It was planned as a defence

The opening of the Welland Canal, November 1829. Why was this an important event for Upper Canada?

measure. It would be another way of linking Montreal and the ports along Lake Ontario in the event of war.

The Rideau Canal took six years to complete. Over 4000 workers were involved. They worked sixteen hours a day and six days a week under terrible conditions. Mosquitoes and blackflies plagued them during spring and summer. They developed swamp fever and malaria labouring in the swamps and marshes. After the stagnant water was drained from the marshy areas, a foul-smelling mist rose from the decaying plant life. Trees had to be cut back to provide better air circulation for the workers. Over 500 lost their lives in the work camps.

The Rideau Canal was completed in 1832. It cost about one million pounds! This was the most expensive military work ever constructed by the British government in North America. It stretched more than 210 km and contained forty-seven locks. The canal became important for moving immigrants and products between the St. Lawrence and the Ottawa area.

In 1841 plans were made for canals around the rapids on the St. Lawrence below Lake Ontario and for the enlargement of the Lachine and Welland canals. The minimum depth of the canals was increased to about 3 m. This depth allowed vessels sailing the Great Lakes at the time to pass through the canals. The project was completed in 1848. It was then possible to navigate the entire distance from the Atlantic Ocean to the Great Lakes by way of the St. Lawrence.

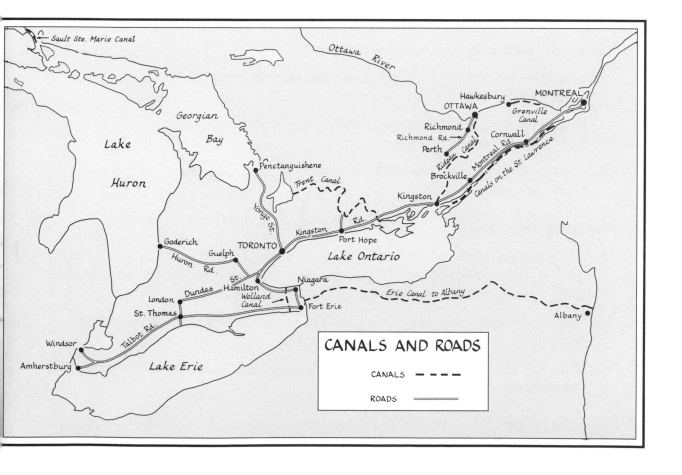

CANALS AND ROADS

CANALS — — — —

ROADS ═══════

Activities

Looking Back

1. Define the following words and enter them in your dictionary.

The Great Migration
emigration
crofter
enclosure movement
blight
shanty

harrowing
threshing
winnowing
timber cribs
potash

2. Why did so many immigrants come to British North America from 1815 to 1850?

3. Describe a typical pioneer farm in the early days of Upper Canada. Include details on how the land was cleared, the first home, and what crops were planted.

4. Explain how each of the following tools was used by the pioneers. Include a sketch.
   a) adze
   b) cradle scythe
   c) harrow
   d) flail

5. Why did the timber trade decline in the 1850s?

Using Your Knowledge

6. Describe what crossing the Atlantic was like for most immigrants. What was the worst part of the voyage? Explain your choice.

7. What do you think were the most serious problems a pioneer family faced in their first years? Explain your answer.

8. Imagine you are a lumberer in Upper Canada. Write a paragraph describing why you enjoy your work.

Extending Your Thinking

9. You are a land developer in Upper Canada in 1822. You have been granted a large tract of land in the backwoods. Draw up a list of rules and regulations for a group of settlers you will bring from Britain.

10. Reread Catharine Parr Traill's description of her home. Draw a floor plan of the home and label each room. Include notes on how each room was used.

11. In groups develop panels for a mural showing the steps pioneers took to produce their first crop.

CHAPTER 19

Organizing the Community of Upper Canada

After the Loyalists Russell and Diana Pitman had settled in the township of Ernestown, Russell continued to write to his cousin in Liverpool, England. Anne was anxious to hear news of how they were getting on and how the colony was developing.

My dear cousin Anne,

Ernestown
26 November 1791

As I mentioned in my last letter, our homestead continues to grow. Our crop yield this past harvest is the best since our arrival in Ernestown. Diana and the children are all well. At last, things seem to be working out for the better.

The big news here this year is our new Constitutional Act. It has made the territory west of the Ottawa River a colony separate from Quebec. Now we are called Upper Canada. The French-speaking area east of the Ottawa River is called Lower Canada.

This is an important change for the Loyalists who came here from America. We came because we wanted to remain British. Yet the colony of Quebec where we settled was mostly French and governed by military governors. Our French neighbours had a different language and religion. Their laws and seigneurial system were not what we were used to.

It became a problem. The French wanted to keep their ways. More and more the English demanded English laws and an elected government like they had in the old colonies. After all, there was an elected representative government in Nova Scotia and New Brunswick. Why shouldn't there be a representative government here? The British solution to the problem was to divide Quebec into two separate colonies. They realized they were faced with two different groups of people.

The result is that now we have English laws and an English system of owning land. Most important of all, we have the British system of government in our new colony of Upper Canada.

Warmest regards from your cousin,

Russell Pitman

In the last two chapters you saw how the colony of Upper Canada was settled and how it developed. In the section called "What Was Upper Canada?," you saw how a colony separate from Quebec was created in 1791. What about how it was governed?

As you can see from Russell Pitman's letter, the Loyalists wanted their own colony. As early as 1785 they began to ask Britain to make their townships self-governing. The letter tells us some of the reasons why they wanted to be separate.

In 1791 they got their wish. The British government passed the **Constitutional Act**. The colony of Quebec was split. The lower province, called Lower Canada, was home to French-speaking Canadians. The upper province, or Upper Canada, was home to the Loyalists who then numbered about 12 000.

Government in Upper Canada: 1791

The government of Upper Canada was to be headed by a Lieutenant-Governor appointed by Britain. The Lieutenant-Governor appointed two different councils to help run the colony. The first was the Executive Council which included close advisors. It had five members appointed for life. The second was the Legislative Council which had the power to make laws for the colony. It had seven members who were also appointed for life.

The most important part of the government to the people was the Legislative Assembly. The Assembly was elected for a four-year term. Its members represented the citizens in the government. It gave the people of Upper Canada a say in the affairs of the colony. But the governor

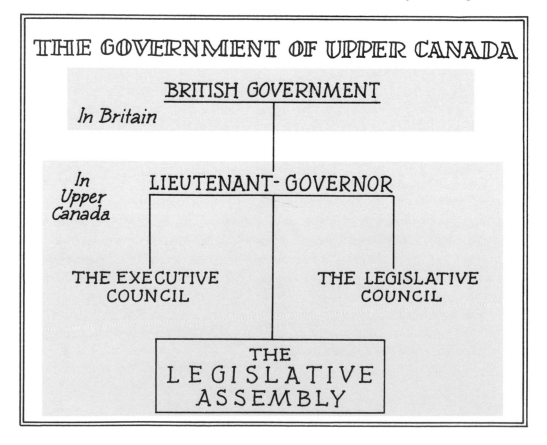

THE GOVERNMENT OF UPPER CANADA

In Britain — BRITISH GOVERNMENT

In Upper Canada — LIEUTENANT-GOVERNOR

THE EXECUTIVE COUNCIL   THE LEGISLATIVE COUNCIL

THE LEGISLATIVE ASSEMBLY

or the appointed councils could refuse to accept any laws passed by the Assembly. The elected representatives of the people had the least power. The appointed members of the government still had the most power.

Elections in Upper Canada

Elections were different in early Upper Canada from what they are today. Women did not have the right to vote. They were not granted the right to vote in Ontario until 1917! Voting in the countryside sometimes went on for a whole week rather than just a day as it does today. Rural people then had to travel great distances to the voting stations. Voting would go on for at least three days in centres like Toronto.

Voting was "open." The secret ballot was not introduced until 1874. Men came to the voting place and announced their choice for everyone to hear. People thought this system would keep the voting honest since everyone could keep count and nothing was secret. But can you think of what disadvantages this system might have? Voters didn't always vote for their true choice. Often they voted for the same candidate as their boss. It was safer to do this than take the chance of losing your job!

SKETCHES OF UPPER CANADA

Elizabeth Simcoe came to Upper Canada in 1792 with her husband John Graves Simcoe, the first Lieutenant-Governor of Upper Canada. She was a remarkable and energetic woman. She kept a diary while she lived in Canada and sketched many of the locations she visited. Her diaries are important sources of information about events and places in Upper Canada from 1792 to 1796.

Read her description of her arrival at Kingston, then the largest town in Upper Canada. Look at her sketch of the mill at Gananoque.

Sunday, 1 July 1792 Kingston

We rose very early this morning in order to take a view of the mill at Gananoque before we proceeded on our way to Kingston. The scenery about the mill was so pretty that I was well repaid for the trouble of going. Then we returned to our large boat and proceeded. After passing Grande Island and Isle Cauchois, we drew near to Kingston, which we were aware of before we saw the houses, as we discerned the white waves of Lake Ontario beyond, looking like a sea, for the wind blew extremely fresh.

Kingston is six leagues from Gananoque, and is a small town of about fifty wooden houses and merchants' storehouses. Only one house is built of stone. It belongs to a merchant. There is a small garrison here and a harbour of ships.

They fired a salute on our arrival, and we went to the house appointed for the commanding officer, at some distance from the barracks. It is small but very airy, and so much cooler than the great house in Montreal that I was very well satisfied with the change. The Queen's Rangers are encamped [half a kilometre] beyond our house, and the bell tents have a pretty appearance. The situation of this place is entirely flat, and incapable of being rendered defensible. Therefore, were its situation more central, it would still be unfit for the seat of government.

–From the diaries of Elizabeth Simcoe

Elizabeth Simcoe's sketch of the mill at Gananoque.

John Graves Simcoe

John Graves Simcoe was the first Lieutenant-Governor of Upper Canada. He was no stranger to the Loyalists. During the American Revolution he had served as a British officer with the Queen's Rangers in Virginia.

Simcoe brought tremendous energy to his job. His goal was to develop the colony beyond the areas settled by the Loyalists. He arrived in Upper Canada with Elizabeth Simcoe and their children in the early summer of 1792. They journeyed up the St. Lawrence and stopped first at Kingston. Kingston, with about fifty houses, was the largest town in Upper Canada! There Governor Simcoe issued a proclamation calling for the election of the first Legislative Assembly.

The Simcoes then moved on to Newark (Niagara-on-the-Lake), the capital of the colony at the time. They were surprised to find that it was little more than an outpost in the forest!

The first elected assembly opened on 17 September 1792. Its early decisions were important ones. Some settlers in Upper Canada had brought slaves with them. The assembly decided that no more slaves would be allowed into the colony. Children of slaves presently in Upper Canada were to be freed at the age of twenty-five. Their children were to be free at birth.

As part of his plan to develop new sections of the colony, Governor Simcoe chose a site in the western area of the province for the capital. He called the site London and the river on which it was situated, the Thames River. Simcoe believed that this location would be easier to defend against any possible attack by the Americans.

While London was being prepared, Simcoe moved the capital temporarily to

The opening of the first assembly in Upper Canada, 1792.

York (Toronto) in 1793. Later the British government decided to establish the capital permanently at York. When Simcoe left Upper Canada in 1796, York was still a village of fewer than twelve blocks!

Organizing Land and Settlers

Governor Simcoe introduced the land survey system called the **Chequered Plan**. Townships were to be a standard size of 14 by 19 km. Each was to have 14 rows with 24 lots of 80 ha. One-seventh of the land in each township was for support of the church. These lands were called the **clergy reserves**. Another seventh was set aside to raise money for the Crown.

Simcoe's plan was to spread these reserves throughout the township in a checkerboard pattern, rather than keeping them all together. This idea proved to be a mistake. Many reserve lots remained unsold wilderness and slowed road development. Settlers might agree to clear a road past their farms, but not past vacant land!

Governor Simcoe realized that roads were essential for the development of the colony. Two important roads built during his term were Dundas Street from Burlington on Lake Ontario to the Thames valley, and Yonge Street from York to Lake Simcoe. He also knew that wheat production would be important. Upper Canada could become a great supplier to Britain. But first the colony needed more farmers. Governor Simcoe offered free grants of land to all Loyalists still remaining in the United States. These new arrivals were called the **late Loyalists**.

The settlers had to swear allegiance to the Crown. They also had to promise to clear 2 ha of their land, build a home, and open a road along the front of their property. Large numbers of Americans took advantage of the offer. Many came out of loyalty to the King, but others came for the free land. Not long after Simcoe departed, the Americans in Upper Canada outnumbered the Loyalists.

John Graves Simcoe spent only four years as Lieutenant-Governor of Upper Canada, but his leadership was very important in the history of the colony.

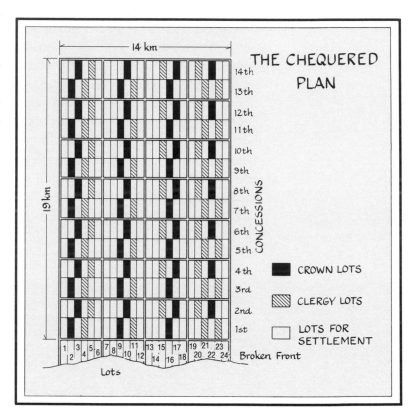

Laws and Courts

Laws in Upper Canada were based on the laws in Great Britain. Courts were established to keep order in the colony. They made sure people obeyed the laws. The courts appointed **sheriffs** to arrest lawbreakers and bring them before the courts.

The courthouse in the early years was little more than a log cabin in the woods. A **magistrate** or **justice** was appointed by the government to hear cases in the court. The magistrate was much like a judge today.

As townships were formed in Upper Canada, they appointed their own police officers. The earliest officers were not paid. They served a term of only one year. Regular police forces developed after 1829. Toronto appointed a police chief and five officers in 1835.

Anyone accused of a crime was brought to the courthouse. The charge was read in front of the magistrate and a trial followed. According to law in Upper Canada, the accused was entitled to trial by jury. A jury is a group of citizens selected by the court to hear the facts of the case. The jury would decide whether the accused was guilty or innocent. If the verdict was guilty, the sentence would be handed down by the court.

A trial in Simcoe County. Why might the accused have reason to fear the punishment?

People could be arrested for stealing, forgery, and not paying their bills! The most common crime, though, was assault. It seems that whiskey was too cheap and easy to obtain. Drunkenness usually led to quarrelling and fighting.

People looked at crime differently in pioneer times. Stealing, even something of little value, was a more serious crime than injuring someone. The law was more concerned about protecting property than people! No one paid much attention to why people committed crimes. It was more important that criminals be punished.

Punishment could be very harsh. Horse-stealing and forgery both received the death penalty. Hangings were public events that attracted citizens from great distances. People who didn't pay their bills were put in jail. Criminals could be whipped with the lash. They might also be "burned in the hand" or "branded on the tongue" with a hot iron. Some were forced to wear a ball and chain. This practice continued in York (Toronto) until about 1875.

Someone found guilty of a crime could be sentenced to the **pillory**. This was a platform on which the criminal stood. The criminal's arms were locked between two timbers supported on a pole. The whipping post and the pillory were usually located right in the town market. Mud was often thrown at criminals in the pillory by people passing by.

In 1804 a woman in Toronto was sentenced to six months imprisonment for being a nuisance. She also had to stand in the pillory on two market days for two hours at a time. A man was given the same penalty for speaking out against the government.

Sometimes prisoners were banished. That is, they were told to leave Upper Canada within eight days. Usually these people fled to the United States. The death penalty was handed down to anyone who disobeyed or returned.

THE YORK JAIL: 1810

One of the earliest jails in the colony was the York (Toronto) Jail. It was built in 1800. It was a squat, unpainted clapboard building. A cedar-log stockade hid it from the street. The stockade was made of logs over 4 m high, each sharpened with an axe to a point at the top. The large double doors were seldom opened. A block of wood was suspended on a chain over these doors and when it was pulled, a bell rang inside.

The cells were unheated and there were no beds. The prisoners were forced to lie upon straw on the wooden floor. It was not until 1813 that makeshift straw beds, raised above the floor, were supplied to sick prisoners.

All the prisoners got to eat was dry bread and water. Even this was not distributed regularly. Sometimes a famished prisoner ate three days supply of bread in one. If the prisoner had relatives in York, they were sometimes allowed to bring food. There was no prison clothing. The prisoners wore the clothing they brought with them.

–Adapted from *Toronto in 1810*
by Eric Hounsom

Pioneer Churches

Making a new start meant isolation and loneliness for many new settlers. Life was hard and often drab. Church helped the people to deal with their everyday problems. The services brought people together. They were encouraged to sing and forget the roughness of their daily lives for a time.

At first religious services were held in the homes of church members. But once the settlers had put up their log homes, they often came together to build a church. The church was one of the first public buildings in a community. The members of the church donated their time, labour, and some supplies to complete the building. The first Protestant church in Upper Canada was the Zion Church in Williamsburgh, Dundas County. It was built by the Lutherans in 1789.

Pioneers brought with them the Christian religious beliefs they had practised in their home countries. There were many different religious groups. Among them were members of the Church of England, Methodists, Roman Catholics, Lutherans, Baptists, Presbyterians, Quakers, and Mennonites. All shared one common goal. They wanted to keep their beliefs and to worship as they always had.

The Church of England

From the earliest days in Upper Canada, the Church of England was the "established" church. That is, it was the church that received government support. It held a privileged position in the community. It was the only church allowed to use money from the sale of the clergy reserves. Before 1798, it was also the only church allowed to conduct marriages in Upper Canada.

John Langhorn was a clergyman of the Church of England. In 1790 he settled in Ernestown Township and constructed a church at Bath. The members of his congregation were scattered throughout eastern Upper Canada. He tried to make regular visits to them, but he would only perform marriages at his church. And it had to be before eleven o'clock in the morning! If the couple did not arrive in time, no matter how long or how far they had travelled, they had to wait until the next morning. Reverend Langhorn always asked the groom to pay three coppers to the clerk, but he never took any money for himself.

The Methodists

The Methodists were one of the most active religious groups in Upper Canada. They sent the first **circuit riders** into the scattered settlements of the colony. The circuit was the area that the preachers covered in their travels.

How imposing they must have looked as they rode into the settlements all dressed in black with a broad grey hat, booted and spurred! The circuit riders were often called "saddlebag" preachers because they carried their hymn books and Bibles in saddlebags flung across their horses. They were constantly on the move preaching the gospel.

One Methodist missionary who came to the colony in 1810 described his experience:

We crossed the St. Lawrence in romantic style. We hired four [Natives] to paddle us over. They lashed their canoes together and put our horses in them, their fore-feet in one canoe, their hind-feet in another. It was a singular load and a dangerous one too, for some part was rough, especially the rapids.

A Methodist circuit rider. Why would these preachers have been welcomed in the backwoods settlements?

Circuit riders organized camp meetings when they arrived in the settlements. These large religious gatherings could last several days. People from all sections of the circuit would gather to worship if they could. It might be a long time before the preacher could return to the area!

BARBARA HECK (1734-1804)

Barbara Heck settled in Augusta Township on the St. Lawrence in 1785. In the 1760s Barbara and her husband Philip Embury had founded the Methodist Church in North America. When she arrived in Upper Canada, Barbara Heck began holding the first Methodist services in the colony.

One hundred years after her death, a monument was erected in her honour at her gravesite near Prescott, Ontario. It reads:

Barbara Heck put her brave soul against the rugged possibilities of the future and under God, brought into existence American and Canadian Methodism, and between these her memory will ever form a most hallowed link. In memory of one who laid foundations others have built upon.

The Plain Folk

Among the pioneers of Upper Canada were members of religious groups called Quakers and Mennonites. The Quakers were mainly English in origin. The Mennonites were German. These two groups were the "plain folk."

They were called the "plain folk" because they believed in plain religion and plain dress. They were against war and taking oaths of allegiance to any government. Their only allegiance was to God.

The plain folk had been persecuted in Pennsylvania and New York because of their beliefs. Americans did not like their refusal to swear an oath of allegiance. The plain folk wanted a new home where their beliefs would be accepted. Upper Canada was attractive. There was good, cheap land. Governor Simcoe welcomed them. He promised that they would not have to bear arms.

Philip Dorland of Adolphustown was a Quaker. He was elected to the first Legislative Assembly of Upper Canada from the Middle District. To take his seat in the Assembly, Dorland had to make the long trip to Newark. He rode the distance on his horse following old Native trails.

When Philip Dorland arrived in Newark, he was asked to take the oath of office. He refused. He is reported to have said, "My yea is a yea and my nay is a nay and there is no reason to take an oath." Philip Dorland was not allowed to take his seat in the first Legislative Assembly. He saddled his horse and rode the long way back home.

Many plain folk from the United States were excellent farmers. Large numbers settled in Upper Canada in the early 1800s. They trekked north in the heavy, broad-wheeled Conestoga wagons. The greatest number settled in the Niagara Peninsula. Others settled in the Bay of Quinte area, and in Markham and Vaughan townships.

THE

THIRD READING-BOOK,

FOR

THE USE OF SCHOOLS;

CONTAINING

SIMPLE PIECES IN PROSE AND VERSE,

WITH

NUMEROUS EXERCISES.

ARMOUR & RAMSAY, MONTREAL.
RAMSAY, ARMOUR & CO., KINGSTON.
A. H. ARMOUR & CO., HAMILTON.

1843.

ADAMS'S NEW ARITHMETIC.

ARITHMETIC,

IN WHICH THE PRINCIPLES OF OPERAT-
ING BY NUMBERS

ARE

ANALYTICALLY EXPLAINED,

AND

SYNTHETICALLY APPLIED;

THUS COMBINING THE ADVANTAGES TO BE DERIVED BOTH FROM

THE INDUCTIVE AND SYNTHETIC MODE
OF INSTRUCTING.

THE WHOLE
MADE FAMILIAR BY A GREAT VARIETY OF USEFUL AND INTERESTING
EXAMPLES, CALCULATED AT ONCE TO ENGAGE THE PUPIL IN THE
STUDY, AND TO GIVE HIM A FULL KNOWLEDGE OF FIGURES IN THEIR
APPLICATION TO ALL THE PRACTICAL PURPOSES OF LIFE.

DESIGNED FOR THE USE OF

SCHOOLS AND ACADEMIES

IN THE UNITED STATES.

BY DANIEL ADAMS, M. D.
AUTHOR OF THE SCHOLAR'S ARITHMETIC, SCHOOL GEOGRAPHY, ETC.

KEENE, N. H.
PUBLISHED BY JOHN PRENTISS.
SOLD BY THE BOOKSELLERS IN NEW-YORK, PHILADELPHIA, BALTI-
MORE, AND CINCINNATI, OHIO.

1836.

The covers of two textbooks used in the schools of Upper Canada in the 1830s and 1840s.

Pioneer Schools

How different school was in the early days of Upper Canada! The first classes were held in the teacher's home. As the community grew, a public school was built. Usually it was a small, simple log cabin. The families in the community contributed money to pay for the school and the teacher's salary.

In 1807 the Public Schools Act was passed. This Act set up eight grammar schools in Upper Canada. Grammar schools were like our high schools today. Each grammar school was given a hundred pounds per year to hire a teacher. But the pay was very low and good teachers were hard to find. Sometimes the teachers knew little more than the basics of the subjects they taught!

Children were not required to go to school as they are today. Many children were needed to help on the farms, so they did not go to school regularly. Also, all of the grammar schools were located in towns. Students in the country often had to walk several kilometres to get there. And for some families school fees were an expense they could not afford. Few children attended school much beyond the age of twelve in the early days of Upper Canada.

What might a pioneer classroom be like? How would it be different from classes today? Imagine looking in on a class in 1816. The classroom in the small log school house has a low ceiling. It is poorly lighted and has little ventilation. The floor and desks are made of rough pine. You notice there are no backs on the seats.

The students are seated facing each other. Girls are on one side of the room and boys are on the other. A stove for heating stands in the centre.

There don't seem to be many school supplies. You discover that paper is in short supply and expensive. The students write on small slates and share books. You see copies of *Murray's Grammar, Murray's English Reader, Walker's Dictionary, Goldsmith and Moore's Geography, Mavor's Spelling Book,* and *Walingame's and Adams's Arithmetic.* Most are printed in the United States.

The schoolmaster is standing at the front of the class. In his hand is a birch stick. This reminds all of the students to pay attention. A "severe caning" awaits any student who misbehaves. Anyone who gives a wrong answer or even misspells a simple word is in trouble!

The lessons are in reading, writing, and arithmetic. The students in the classroom are of different ages and grades. The schoolmaster teaches a lesson to each group separately. Some students are busy trying to memorize assigned lessons. Others are reciting the lessons they have just learned. It must be difficult to study with the noise of students reciting lessons!

The Pioneer Village

How did villages in Upper Canada develop and why? Some such as Kingston and Newark (Niagara-on-the-Lake) began as military forts. York developed as a centre for the colonial government. Other villages grew up at ideal locations such as around a natural harbour, on a river, or at a crossroads. Many became trading centres. Sometimes though, villages developed quite by accident. A resourceful pioneer chose a location to build a mill or tannery and a village grew up around it. Brantford is an example.

A pioneer village looked very different from small communities today. In the early years you could expect to find stumps in the middle of the streets. You might see cows wandering about. Dogs running in packs were a nuisance. The streets were mud traps, particularly in the spring and fall. People who took a walk through the village might need a complete change of clothes when they returned!

What a difference there was between life in the villages and life in the backwoods! In the villages there were neighbours nearby to talk to. And there was so much more to do. You could go for a stroll through those muddy streets to the trade shops. You could stop along the way to chat with neighbours. You always knew that in times of crisis or emergency you were not alone.

Look at the map and illustrations on page 307. They are based on Upper Canada Village, a living historic village near Morrisburg, Ontario. This village is an important tourist and heritage site. Let's look around.

The village is located on the St. Lawrence River. Notice the names of the streets. Most of the important industries and trade shops are found at the end of "Mill Street" near the river. The sawmill at the very bottom of the street is the most important industry in the community.

As you walk up Mill Street you come to the blacksmith's shop. Inside, the blacksmith is hard at work by the hot fire. The blacksmith does more than just shoe horses. He builds carriages and buggies, repairs equipment, and makes small items such as hoes, rakes, shovels, and axes. Some of these tools are hanging on the walls, ready to be picked up by their new owners.

Further up the street you come to the cabinet maker's shop. The cabinet maker fashions beautiful pine cupboards, tables,

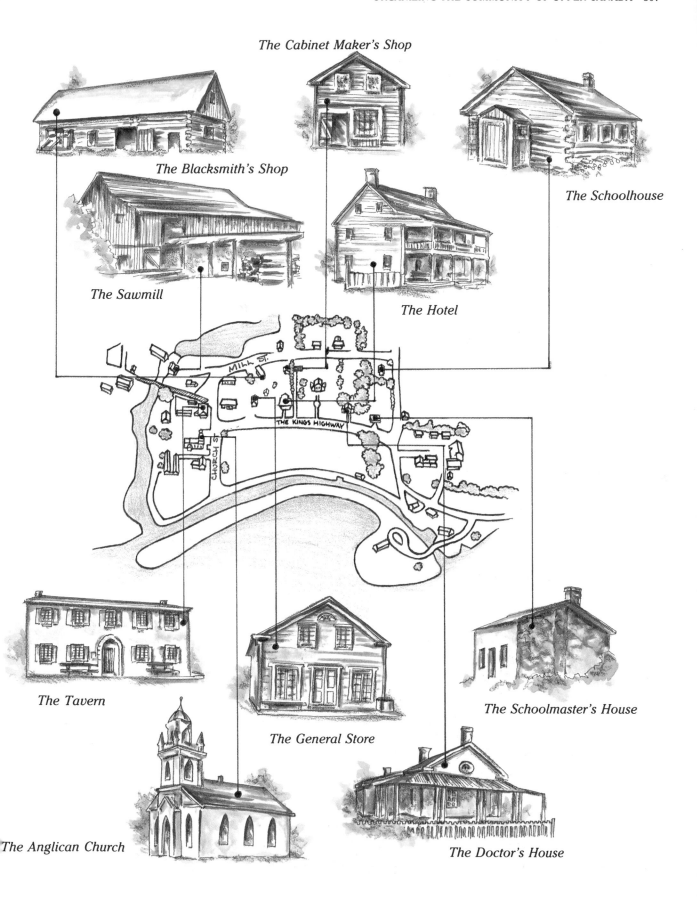

The Cabinet Maker's Shop

The Blacksmith's Shop

The Schoolhouse

The Sawmill

The Hotel

The Tavern

The General Store

The Schoolmaster's House

The Anglican Church

The Doctor's House

benches, and chests of drawers for kitchens and bedrooms. From great chunks of curly maple, cherry, butternut, and walnut he also makes fine furniture for dining rooms, as well as clock cases and canopy beds.

Next you stroll back down Mill Street to the top of Church Street. It's not hard to imagine how the street got its name. The church is the first thing you notice from the top of the street. This Anglican Church was an important church in the village.

Beside the church, near the junction of the two roads, is the tavern. The tavern, you discover, is the community centre for the village. There is a beautiful ballroom on the second floor. It serves as a hall for political meetings and as the court of law for the village.

A stagecoach stops at the tavern for fresh horses on its way through the village. The tavern is conveniently located for travellers and is close to the river where the bateaux pass. The kitchen is a scene of bustling activity. You hear the visitors chatting in front of the open fire where food is being boiled, roasted, and baked for dinner.

From Church Street you turn the corner onto the King's Highway. You are still in the heart of the village. Just up the highway is the general store. Villagers and visiting farmers can buy almost anything they need there. You see pairs of shoes, sacks of flour, door hinges, and some of the tastiest sweets ever made. The shelves are crowded and not too well organized. But look at the prices! You can buy 0.5 kg of sugar for 10¢, 0.5 kg of cheese for 12¢, and a dozen eggs for 8¢.

The storekeeper tells you that most people buy things on credit until harvest time. Not many villagers have a great deal of cash. The local farmers might pay in bushels of wheat or oats. Then the storekeeper sells the grain to the local miller.

The hotel on the King's Highway has a second story balcony at the front. Travellers stay in the hotel as well as at the tavern, but the hotel depends mostly on local people for business. The village lawyer's office and the barbershop are on the ground floor of the hotel.

Further along the King's Highway you come to the doctor's house. The doctor has an examining room right inside the house. You see a chair for pulling teeth and all the surgical instruments. They all look very scary! You learn that doctors made their own medicines and pills. They spent much of their time attending to accident cases when people were injured working in the woods, on their farms, or on the river. There was no anaesthetic then to dull the pain. The doctor was often paid in produce from the farms or craft shops as well.

Finally you visit the schoolmaster's house and the new log schoolhouse. The schoolmaster keeps a vegetable garden and small pasture at the back of the house. People in the community pay him in kind. His furniture was made by the local cabinet maker, his buckets by the village cooper, and the family's shoes by the village shoemaker. All of this is in exchange for educating the artisans' children.

Shoeing oxen at the blacksmith's shop in Upper Canada village.

YORK IN 1810

The population of York in 1810 was 630. Today it is over 2 000 000. The main buildings in the town included the Parliament Buildings, two fortified blockhouses for defence, buildings for troops, a jail, a customs house, a post office, and one church. Businesses and industries included six hotels, a tannery, wagon factory, shipbuilding yard, general store, open-air market, potashery, distillery, brewery, slaughter house, bakery oven, newspaper office, printing shop, market garden, watchmaker's store, and about six other stores including a bookstore. There were also more than 100 houses.

Town lots were about half a hectare in size. Most residents had a stable and many owned a horse, cows, pigs, or chickens. There were always a few squared logs, fence rails, or rough-sawn boards on the property, drying out for use the following year. Many families made their own furniture. Many homes also had flower gardens and most had vegetable gardens.

All houses had a cistern of some sort to hold washing water. The cistern was a keg or barrel placed under a roof gutter. Most people got their drinking water from the Don River. They carried it home in wood or leather buckets or in tin pails. The streets were not lighted and those travelling at night usually carried lanterns. The footpaths were beaten earth. Sometimes they were covered by gravel or flagstones. In the spring thick planks might be laid over the pools of water.

People had different opinions about York in 1810. A visiting American called it "a pleasant town containing a great many frame houses, but the land is rather low and unhealthy." A young York resident visiting England said, "I am so prejudiced in favour of York, that I think it is the neatest and prettiest place I have ever seen." But his brother at home in York called it "a miserable hole." Joseph Bouchette in his book on travel noted, "It promises to become a very handsome town."

–Adapted from *Toronto in 1810*
by Eric Hounsom

The Town of York

Growth was slow in York in the early years. As the capital of the province, the town was an American target during the War of 1812. York was occupied for a time in April 1813 by the Americans. Many buildings were burned, including the pioneer Parliament Buildings. When the war ended in 1815, the population was still only 720.

York developed steadily in the 1820s, but the 1830s was the decade of the greatest progress. The prosperous farms surrounding the town helped its growth. In 1834 the town took back its Native name of Toronto. It elected its first mayor, William Lyon Mackenzie. The town then had over 9000 residents.

By the late 1830s Toronto was about the same size as Kingston. Kingston was the largest town in the province. The large immigration from Great Britain during the decade helped the population of Toronto grow.

King Street in Toronto, 1836. The 1830s were years of growth for the town.

Largest Communities in Upper Canada: 1830

Kingston	3 587
York (Toronto)	2 800
London	2 415
Hamilton	2 013
Brockville	1 130

Largest Communities in Upper Canada: 1850

Toronto	30 775
Hamilton	14 122
Kingston	11 697
Bytown (Ottawa)	7 760
London	7 035

Skill Building: Co-operative Group Work

Have you ever played hockey, baseball, or some other organized team sport? If you have, you understand the importance of teamwork. Each team member has a specific position to play or a specific job to do, but everyone works together. Team members co-operate to reach their goal. They understand that they "sink or swim together."

Being able to work co-operatively is an important skill. It is important for more than just team sports. It will help you in school and later in your jobs.

You can practise developing co-operative group skills in your classroom. Here are some steps to follow:

1. Organize the class into groups of three or four. These groups will be called the **home groups**.

2. In your home group, examine the topic and sub-topics for research.

Topic: Government in Upper Canada
Sub-topics: 1. How the government was organized
2. Elections in pioneer times
3. The work of Lieutenant-Governor Simcoe

3. Have the members of the home group number themselves 1, 2, 3, etc. Each member of the home group will be responsible for a different sub-topic.

4. Members of the home group will now form **expert groups** with other members of the class. That is: home group members with the number 1 form expert groups of three with students who are researching the same sub-topic. Home group members with the number 2 form expert groups of three with students who are researching the same sub-topic, and so on.

5. In your expert groups:
a) reread the information in the text on your sub-topic
b) discuss what you have learned and decide on the most important points
c) design an organizer each group member can use to summarize the most important points
d) together decide on an interesting way to present the information on your sub-topic to the home groups.

6. Return to your home group.

7. Take turns presenting the sub-topics to the group. Try to make it interesting and make sure that everyone understands.

8. After each presentation, take time to ask questions, make comments, and give praise.

Activities

Looking Back

1. Define the following words and enter them in your dictionary.

Constitutional Act	magistrate
Chequered Plan	jury
clergy reserves	pillory
late Loyalists	"established" church
sheriff	circuit rider

2. How did the Constitutional Act of 1791 change Upper Canada?

3. Why were the Quakers and the Mennonites called the "plain folk"?

4. School attendance was not very good in the early 1700s. Why?

5. List the reasons why villages developed in pioneer Upper Canada.

Using Your Knowledge

6. Use a comparison organizer to show the similarities and differences between one of the following:
   a) elections in 1830 and elections today
   b) education in pioneer schools and education today
   c) a pioneer village and a small village today.

7. Develop a timeline to describe events in the history of York from 1810 to 1850.

Extending Your Thinking

8. The year is 1796. Governor Simcoe is about to leave office. Write an article for your community newspaper outlining the contributions he made to the development of Upper Canada.

9. Organize your class into groups to create a bulletin board display on "The Pioneer Village in Upper Canada." Decide on the number of panels in the display and what each one will show. For example, you could include panels on the general store, the pioneer school, the doctor, and the blacksmith. Have each group research and prepare one panel for display.

CHAPTER 20

Everyday Life in Upper Canada

MAKING A LITTLE FUN OUT OF WORK

As soon as the ground was cool enough, I made a logging bee, at which I had five yokes of oxen and twenty men, four men to each team. The teamster selects a good place to commence a heap [start a pile], generally against some large log which the cattle would be unable to move. They draw all the logs within a reasonable distance in front of the large log. The men with the hand-spikes roll the logs one on top of the other, until the heap is about [2 m] high, and [3-4 m] broad. All the chips, sticks, and rubbish are then picked up and thrown on the top of the heap. A team of four good men should log and pick [0.5 ha] a day when the burn has been good.

My hive worked well, for we had [2 ha] logged and set fire to the same evening. On a dark night, a hundred or two of these large heaps all on fire at once have a very fine effect, and shed a broad glare of light for a considerable distance. In the month of July in the new settlements, the whole country at night appears lit up by these fires.

A logging bee. Working together often made the back-breaking job of clearing the land more enjoyable.

We managed to enjoy ourselves very much. After tea, dancing commenced, to the music of two fiddles, when the country-dances, reels, and French fours were all performed with much spirit. The music was very good, the dancing indifferent.

During the pauses between dances, some lady or gentleman would favour the company with a song. Then plays were introduced such as hunt the slipper, cross questions and crooked answers, and several others in which forfeits had to be redeemed by the parties making mistakes in the game–a procedure of course productive of much noise, kissing, and laughter. Refreshments were handed around in great production, and the entertainment would end up with a dance.

From *Twenty-Seven Years in Canada*
by Samuel Strickland

1. What is a "bee"?
2. What was the purpose of the bee described in this passage?
3. Describe the events after the bee.

Bees

A quilting bee at Upper Canada Village. Aspects of early life are relived at the village.

One of the nicest things about pioneer life in Upper Canada was the co-operation among the settlers. They came together to help one another with difficult tasks such as logging, clearing the land, and bringing in the harvest. If a barn needed to be built, neighbours and friends came from all over the district to lend a hand. People also worked together for tasks such as corn-husking, apple-coring, and quilting. These community ventures were called **bees**.

Quilting bees were very popular among pioneer women. The women assembled at one home with their materials. They grouped around the large quilt frame in front of the fire and shared news. At the same time, they worked together to produce something of beauty from tiny pieces of cloth sewn into fancy patterns. The finished quilt might be a gift for a future bride or for the coming sale at the church bazaar.

The end of a working bee was marked by a plentiful meal. It might include roast pig, boiled leg of mutton, fish pie, cold ham, cold roast mutton, salt pork, mashed potatoes, beans and carrots, a large rice pudding, freshly baked bread–and fresh blackberries or currant and gooseberry tarts for dessert!

A dance was held in the barn after the meal. It would last well into the night. When it finally came to an end, families

gathered their tools and headed home. They would talk for days about the good times they had shared.

Recreation and Leisure

Life in Upper Canada wasn't all work and no play! The pioneers turned many of their working activities into competition and sport. In the backwoods, ploughing matches, chopping contests, and hay-mowing competitions offered excitement and attracted local crowds.

Indoor games and activities included popular favourites such as checkers. Billiards, quoits, backgammon, chess, and various card games such as whist were also popular.

Sewing was a favourite indoor pastime among women. Many women produced works of embroidery called samplers. Sometimes they depicted rural scenes or included short verses. Often the work was framed and hung on the parlour or bedroom wall.

People also enjoyed outdoor activities such as fishing, hunting, horseback riding, canoeing, sailing, and picnicking. Lacrosse and cricket were popular sports.

The real time for recreation was the winter. Much of the settlers' work could not be done when the ground was frozen. Curling, sleigh-riding, and skating were great favourites. Sleighs were lined with bright-coloured cloth or bearskin. Buffalo robes might cover the driver. A farmer's sleigh was often filled with young people out for a ride on one of the backwoods roads. Skates were made of wood with iron runners and were fastened to boots by leather straps.

Auction sales were also a favourite pastime. They were often held when a person died or moved away. People came from all around. Auctions were a great opportunity to buy needed furniture or a luxury item that someone had wanted for a long time.

Growing up in Upper Canada

Imagine that Mary Elizabeth Pitman is the grand-daughter of the Loyalist settler, Russell Pitman. As a young girl of twelve, she too begins to write letters to her relatives in England. In the following letter she tells what it was like to grow up in Upper Canada in the early 1800s.

A family sleigh ride. How would the passengers in the sleigh have kept warm?

My dear cousin Charlotte,   *24 September 1818*

. . . and you asked me about what my brothers and sisters do. So I am adding a part to my letter.

There are five children in our family. Five or six is the usual number around here. Thomas, my older brother, is sixteen and my older sister Sarah is fourteen. Russell is ten and Diana has just turned nine. I am glad there are five of us. It makes work on the farm easier.

We all have our daily chores to do. They start when you are very young. When I was five I helped bring in firewood and gather berries. As I got a little older, I helped feed the livestock and look after Russell and Diana. Russell and Diana help out in the kitchen and in the garden out back. Sarah and Thomas help to bring buckets of water to the house and split logs for the fire. Most chores are done before school. All of us but Diana help in the fields. She will help next year.

It is not all work. We have fun too. You asked about toys. We had toys when we were little. Most of them were made by father or uncle Albert. Aunt Anne made corn-husk and rag dolls for us. She is very good at needlework too. She taught us how to knit and sew after mother died. She also taught us how to make tallow candles, churn butter, and milk a cow.

Mostly though we make our own fun. The smaller ones like tag and hide-and-seek. Two years ago a travelling circus came to Belleville. Diana loved the clowns. Russell decided he would like to be a magician!

The circus arrives in town.

We all love to play ball. You might laugh at the ball though. It is really a stuffed stomach from a pig! We also play horseshoes. Sometimes older children even play with the adults. Thomas is very good at throwing ringers.

You asked what we wanted to do when we grow up. Thomas wants to stay on the farm for certain. Sarah would like to work as a dressmaker in Belleville. Sometimes I think I would like to be a school teacher. So would Russell. Father says Russell would get paid twice as much as me for teaching in the school. I have lots of time to decide.

Please write to me as soon as you can.

With affection,

Mary Elizabeth Pitman

1. Why would Russell be paid twice as much as Elizabeth if he became a school teacher?
2. What bias does this show?
3. How do you feel about it?

Getting Married

There weren't that many opportunities in pioneer times for young people to meet someone to marry. Chances were probably better in the villages than in the backwoods! Many young couples met at church events or community bees. Sometimes though, marriages were arranged by parents.

When the young couple "went together," they were said to be **courting**. The couple was usually chaperoned. This means an older friend or relative was usually with them when they were together. Seldom were they left alone. Sunday night was for courting. Even the strictest parents in Upper Canada understood this!

When a young couple decided to marry, they had to have the **banns** read. Reading the banns meant that the upcoming marriage had to be announced from the pulpit of the church on three Sundays in a row. A marriage notice was also posted on the wall or door of the church. Reading the banns had been law in Britain since 1753. It was also law in Upper Canada. It was intended to stop hasty marriages!

Young men were expected to have land before they married. The couple needed to provide for themselves and a family. In all likelihood, if a young man was ready to get married he had 20 ha of land and at least some of it was cleared. He might also have a cow, and possibly a yoke of oxen and a few sheep. A few basic items of furniture such as a bed, a table, and some chairs would also be needed. The bride often brought linen and bedding that had been woven at a bee held in her honour.

Marriages were performed in the church or at the bride's home. The ceremony always took place in the morning. By a law passed in 1793, only ministers of the Church of England could perform the ceremony. If there was no church within 28 km, the couple could be married by a justice of the peace. Justices of the peace were appointed law officers. They were required to use the Church of England service for the marriage.

Couples wanting to be married by a minister who was not of the Church of England had to make the long journey to the United States. In 1798, Church of Scotland, Calvinist, and Lutheran ministers were allowed to perform the marriage ceremony in Upper Canada as well. Methodist and Baptist ministers could not legally perform the service until 1830. After that young couples in the backwoods could wait until the saddlebag preacher came to their area.

A wedding was a cause for celebration in the pioneer community. Family and friends gathered to mark the occasion. The reception was a grand opportunity to taste all of the delights from the pioneer kitchen. Preparations began well in advance.

Newlyweds did not go on a honeymoon as they do today. They stayed at the home of the bride's family. They could expect a visit from the young people of the community. The noisy celebration by the visitors to honour the new couple was called a **chivaree**.

Usually young people assembled at the couple's house after dark and serenaded them with noisemakers. They used horns, drums, kettles, whistles, cowbells, tin pans, or anything that would make a noise. The young couple would listen for a while. They pretended not to hear! Then they invited the noisemakers into the house. Refreshments were served and the evening often ended with a sing-song.

A country dance in 1800.

Looking After the Basics

Running the pioneer farm was a partnership. It was the responsibility of both men and women. Women worked in the fields and tended the vegetable gardens. They milked the cows and completed the million and one tasks that had to be done to manage the pioneer household. There were no electrical machines or appliances to make things easier! Men worked in the fields and tended to the livestock. They made furniture and kept the buildings in good repair.

The early settlers didn't bring many household goods with them when they came to Upper Canada. The Loyalists brought only the few prized possessions they could carry. Later immigrants from Britain sold what little they had before taking passage to Canada. For the new arrivals, it was really a new beginning. Nearly everything needed in the new home had to be made.

But not everything could be made on the farm. Rifles, glass, candle moulds, and metal items had to be bought. Sometimes they were purchased from travelling peddlars called tinkers who visited the backwoods. Sometimes the farmer had to make the long trip to the local village shops.

Making Candles and Soap

Very little was thrown out in the pioneer home. The fat from farm animals was saved to make candles. The fat was cut up into little pieces and boiled in a pot with a little water. When it was boiling hot, it was put through a flannel strainer into a dish. The boiled fat was called tallow.

As in New France, candles were sometimes made by the dipping method. Another method was to use a mould. Lengths of wick were placed into the candle moulds. Then tallow was poured into the moulds and allowed to cool. More tallow was added later to each mould since the tallow shrunk when it cooled. Sometimes wild ginger or herbs were added to give the candles a fragrance. When the tallow cooled, the candles could be removed from the moulds.

Candles were carefully stored away in a cool, dry place until needed. They had to be covered so the mice wouldn't get at them.

To make soap, tallow was mixed with

lye. In the early years lye was made by combining ashes from hardwood trees with rain water. The tallow and lye were stirred together until thick. Then the mixture was poured into a lined wooden box. When it cooled and hardened it was cut into bars. Glycerine and wild ginger leaves could be added to make the soap fancy!

Clothing

Many pioneer women were skilled at spinning wool into yarn to make the clothing for the family. The wool was first combed or **carded** to clean it and free it of tangles. Then it was spun into yarn on a spinning wheel. The yarn was used to knit socks and mittens or was woven into cloth on a loom.

Home-spun cloth was a dull grey colour–the colour of raw wool. But the cloth didn't have to be a dull grey. Wool could be dyed.

Pioneer women knew how to make dyes from natural materials. Goldenrod from the fields was boiled to make a yellow dye. The bark of the butternut tree was used for a brown dye. A pale-fawn shade could be made by boiling the outer skins of onions! Bloodroot produced a deep red and blackberries a purple. Dyes were not used for everyday clothing. They were reserved for the family's best clothes.

Furniture

Most home furnishings were made during the winter when there was some free time. The first furniture in the shanty was very simple. Cut logs served as stools or chairs. Crude planks were fashioned into the first family table and benches.

Beds were often built right into the cabin walls. They had neither springs nor mattresses. Instead, cord lacing was tied across the bed frame. The cords stretched and sagged with use and had to be tightened regularly.

Trundle beds were also common. A large drawer was built at the floor in the frame of the main bed. This drawer was pulled out at night to form a bed for

A mould for making candles.

Weaver on a loom making a rag rug at Black Creek Pioneer Village just outside Toronto, Ontario, where aspects of pioneer life are recreated.

young children. It was stored away during the day to make more room in the cabin. Other furniture included a pine cupboard and a few shelves. These would be enough to hold the possessions of the family.

Nearly all kitchen tools were made of wood and were called **treen** or **treenware**. There weren't many china or glass dishes in the early days. These came later as transportation improved and they could be imported from Europe. Treen included plates, spoons, and scoops but seldom forks. Forks seem to have been limited to wealthy settlers.

Kitchen utensils from a pioneer home. Identify how each utensil was used.

Many of the early wooden bowls were made from maple burls. A **burl** is a growth found on the side of a maple tree. The Native peoples taught the settlers how to hollow out the burls and polish them. They made hard, sturdy bowls that seldom cracked. Water buckets and barrels were made by hollowing out various lengths of logs.

Food

What kinds of foods did the early pioneers have? Game such as deer and rabbit and game birds such as pheasants, grouse, partridges, and ducks could be hunted. Fresh fish including salmon, trout, and bass could be caught in the rivers and lakes. But farmers did not always have a great deal of time to hunt and fish. The diet of the backwoods pioneer was limited.

Salt pork or salt beef was the most common meat diet most of the year. Salting kept the meat from going bad. The meat was cut into pieces and put in a solution of salt and water. It was left until the solution worked its way through the meat.

Vegetables were plentiful however. The Native peoples taught the pioneers how to grow corn and pumpkins. Cabbage, turnips, potatoes, carrots, onions, beans, and peas were also grown in pioneer gardens. Wild plants such as fiddlehead ferns, wild rice, raspberries, strawberries, gooseberries, and cranberries were gathered for the table as well.

Fresh bread was baked in the pioneer ovens. It was made from corn or wheat flour. Tea, coffee, and sometimes cocoa were available in most villages and towns. Backwoods settlers though had to rely on substitutes. The most popular was hemlock tea. Another kind of tea was made from corn.

Making Butter and Cheese

Most families kept a cow or two for fresh milk. From the milk they could also make butter and cheese. Butter was made in a hand-operated butter churn. Cream was shaken and mixed in the churn until the fat in it became solid. The fat was then removed from the churn, washed in cold water, and placed in a large wooden bowl. It was "worked" with a wooden paddle to force out any remaining liquid. Salt was added for flavour. Sometimes, to be fancy, pioneers shaped the butter in wooden moulds.

To make cheese, rennet was added to the milk to make it curdle. Rennet was made from salting and drying the stomach of a new-born calf or lamb. When the milk curdled, it separated into curds and whey. **Curds** are solid lumps. **Whey** is a liquid. The curds were then removed and cut up. Again salt was added for flavour. The curds were then put into a cheese press. Pressure was gradually increased until the cheese became a solid block.

The Doctor and the Dentist

There weren't many doctors in Upper Canada. Most pioneers went to the doctor only in extreme emergencies. Besides, poor roads often prevented doctors from visiting patients in isolated areas. Hospitals were also scarce. One of the first opened at York in 1829. The Kingston General Hospital opened in 1832.

There was always someone in the pioneer community who could treat common disorders. Often it was a woman who would be nurse, doctor, and druggist in one!

Most home remedies came from the forest. They were made from plants, roots, berries, and seeds. Bloodroot, catnip, cherry bark, black adder, smartwood, and wormwood were all used. These herbs were mixed with things like lard, vinegar, resin, or beeswax. Many of the mixtures brought relief to the patient. Some had no worthwhile effect at all!

Pioneer Medicines and Cures

Stomach-ache	*- Catnip tea*
Indigestion	*- Dried burdock tea*
Blood disorders	*- Cherry bark tea*
Burns	*- Black elder, lard resin, and beeswax mixed into a salve*
Heart stimulant	*- Motherwort*
Liver problems	*- Dandelion tea*
Bleeding	*- Juice from the burnet rose*
Swelling	*- Smartwood steeped in vinegar*
Baldness	*- Mashed garlic rubbed on the scalp*
General cures	*- Wormwood tea*

A doctor's office at Upper Canada Village. Notice the bottles of remedies on the shelves.

In pioneer times people didn't have their teeth filled as we do today. A problem tooth was left until it had to be removed. The patient knew when the pain reached an unbearable level that the time had come!

Almost anyone who wanted to be a dentist could set up a practice. There were few regulations in the early days. One of the main requirements was the physical strength to pull a tooth as quickly and painlessly as possible.

An instrument with a hook on the end was used to pull the tooth. The instrument was called a turnkey. The dentist loosened the gum with a pocket-knife and then inserted the hook of the turnkey. Patients must have grasped the rungs of the chair tightly and shut their eyes while the tooth was pulled.

Communicating with the Outside World

The Newspaper

With travel conditions as poor as they were, the backwoods settlers longed for news from other communities. They wanted to know what was happening in

the world. A newspaper was a welcome treat. Newspapers were often read aloud to other members of the community. Anyone fortunate enough to borrow an American newspaper had an eager audience.

The first newspaper in Upper Canada was the *Upper Canada Gazette*, published at Newark on 18 April 1793. In 1798 the paper moved to York and it became the *York Gazette* in 1813. Kingston began to publish its own newspaper, the *Kingston Gazette*, in 1810. Other towns followed. But the population in the colony wasn't large enough to support many newspapers.

The *Upper Canada Gazette* was printed weekly. The colony did not have a daily paper until 1853. By modern standards the *Gazette* was a very small newspaper. It was simply one large sheet folded to make four pages of print. It could not be bought on the street or in the stores. The only way to get it was by subscription order or by picking it up at the printing office. When people finished reading the paper, they passed it along to friends and neighbours.

The news in the *Gazette* really wasn't all that new. World news was usually copied from newspapers printed in the United States or Britain. If the news came from Europe, it might be five months old! Even news from the United States might be a month old.

To the modern reader, the newspaper would have appeared very dull. About all it contained was a small bit of local and foreign news. The local news told about social events in the community and surrounding area, decisions of the local government, and of course births, marriages, and deaths. There were no pictures and there was no sports section, though there were drawings.

A notice in Brown's Toronto General Directory, 1856. Why might people be willing to try this remedy before going to a dentist?

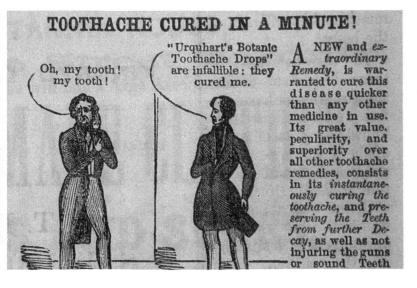

TOOTHACHE CURED IN A MINUTE!

Oh, my tooth! my tooth!

"Urquhart's Botanic Toothache Drops" are infallible: they cured me.

A NEW and *extraordinary Remedy*, is warranted to cure this disease quicker than any other medicine in use. Its great value, peculiarity, and superiority over all other toothache remedies, consists in its *instantaneously curing the toothache*, and *preserving the Teeth from further Decay*, as well as not injuring the gums or sound Teeth

The Mail

The pioneers also dearly looked forward to receiving mail. Many had close family and friends in Europe, the United States, or other parts of Upper Canada or the Maritimes. A letter often brought welcome news and could be a comfort from loneliness.

Upper Canada set up a regular mail service in 1810. Every two weeks in the winter, a mail courier left Montreal for Kingston and Toronto. The trip took sixteen to eighteen days. The postage from Montreal to Kingston was ninepence. Service in the summer was less regular because it depended on the sailing schedule of government schooners.

By 1815 there was a weekly service from Montreal to Toronto. Mail was going as far west as Amherstburg and Sandwich (Windsor). Upper Canada had nine post offices. Stores along the letter carriers' routes served as pick-up and drop-off locations.

A letter in these times was usually one sheet of paper folded and sealed with wax. Charges for postage were based on the number of sheets. It cost about a dollar in 1810 to send a one sheet letter to England. The person receiving the letter paid the postage. In some cases the poorest pioneers could not even afford to pick up their mail.

The postal service had serious problems. It was very slow to say the least. A letter mailed from England in November wouldn't arrive in Upper Canada until the following spring. There also weren't enough post offices. People had to travel great distances to reach the nearest office or count on travellers to bring them their mail. Settlers constantly voiced their anger about the quality of the mail service.

Skill Building: Communicating History through Role Playing

What was it like to be a pioneer farmer or a village doctor? How did the new settlers feel when they finally had a new home? What were pioneer bees really like? To answer these questions, you can try to put yourself in the place of the early pioneers. Imagine what they thought and felt and what they would do. You can play a role like an actress or actor in a movie or play.

Role playing is one of the most exciting ways to make history come alive. By acting out a scene, you can feel that you were actually there. Role playing helps you to understand what the problems and events of the past were really like.

Try the following activity.

1. Work in groups. Each group should choose one of the following topics:

a) visiting the doctor　　　　**d)** holding a chivaree

b) visiting the dentist　　　　**e)** trying a criminal in court.

c) celebrating after a bee

2. Assign character roles to each member of the group. Think about who would be at the scene and what they would be doing.

3. Discuss a storyline for your presentation. What will happen?

4. Write a short script. What will people do and say? Think about the sort of language and accent that would be authentic. Make your presentation about 10 or 15 minutes long.

5. Decide on costumes and props (if any). You may need to do some research. Pictures or illustrations can tell you what people wore, for example.

6. Rehearse until you are satisfied that you have a quality presentation.

7. Present your role play to a group. You could make a tape or video recording to share with others later as well.

8. Ask your audience what they thought of your presentation. Were your characters realistic? What did they learn from the scene? How did they feel? Could they imagine they were there too?

Activities

Looking Back

1. Define the following words and enter them in your dictionary.

    bees   burl
    courting   treenware
    banns   curds
    chivaree   whey
    carding

2. Why were bees held in Upper Canada?

3. What chores were pioneer children in Upper Canada expected to do?

4. What complaints did pioneers have about the mail?

Using Your Knowledge

5. Develop an organizer to compare leisure activities for children and adults in Upper Canada. Organize your information into separate categories for indoor and outdoor activities.

6. Develop a timeline to describe a typical day for a pioneer woman, man, or child.

7. How were medicine and dentistry in Upper Canada different from what they are today?

8. Write a paragraph describing a pioneer wedding and reception in Upper Canada.

Extending Your Thinking

9. In groups, design a single edition of the *Upper Canada Gazette* for 1812. Remember that the paper was one large sheet folded into four pages. Include local and world news, announcements, and advertisements.

10. Create a typical daily menu for a pioneer family in the backwoods.

11. Design and organize a collage of illustrations on one of the following:
    a) pioneer leisure activities
    b) pioneer furniture
    c) pioneer arts and crafts.

CHAPTER 21

Conflict and Change–
The War of 1812

THE BATTLE OF QUEENSTON HEIGHTS

British and American troops battle at Queenston Heights, 13 October 1812.

It was 1812. Some 6300 American soldiers were ranged along the Niagara River between Lake Ontario and Lake Erie. Upper Canada was about to be invaded. The commander of the British forces, Major-General Isaac Brock, waited along the same front for the attack. With him were 1500 soldiers and some 250 Natives.

Brock thought the Americans would attack his headquarters at Fort George. Queenston was 11 km to the south. It had been left with only 350 defenders and three cannon.

Late that stormy evening Brock conferred with his officers. Then he wrote dispatches until midnight. He lay down to rest, but at 3 a.m. he was awakened by the boom of guns at Queenston.

The distant gunfire continued. At 4 a.m. a messenger galloped in with news that twenty-four guns in Lewiston were hammering Queenston and American troops were crossing the river. Brock, already in the saddle, ordered his second-in-command, Sir Roger Sheaffe, to stand ready. Then he set spurs to his horse Alfred and sped along the river road for Queenston Heights. His ride that wet, blustery night was a race to save Canada.

A second messenger met him. The attack on Queenston was mounting, the soldier shouted. Brock sent him on to Sheaffe. Every available soldier was to be sent to Queenston.

Brock galloped into Queenston before dawn. His old regiment, the 49th, with stinging musket fire and one feeble 6-pound cannon, had held the first wave of American invaders to the beaches. The sight of Brock, massive in his crimson tunic, an arrow-pattern sash from the Shawnee Chief Tecumseh fluttering at his waist, lifted their hearts. They cheered.

Halfway up the heights gunners with a single 18-pounder hammered at the American shoreline. A few kilometres to the north, the Canadians' third gun, a 24-pounder, methodically thumped the enemy. Across the river some 2000 American troops waited for boats. If only the Canadians could hold until Sheaffe arrived.

Wild cries and musket fire broke out suddenly behind Brock. Into sight burst 350 American infantry. They had scaled the sheer, slippery, unguarded face of Queenston Heights.

"Follow me!" shouted Brock. He rallied 200 men, led them on the run to the foot of the Heights, and took cover behind a low stone wall.

"Take your breath, you'll need it presently!"

They cheered him again. Brock dismounted, sent his panting horse away with an apologetic pat for the punishing ride, and drew his sword. His men fixed bayonets. They poured over the wall and up the hill, directly at the enemy's centre.

Brock, always in the lead, was a spectacular target. A bullet struck his wrist. He went on. The enemy fell back. Then a rifleman stepped from the trees, took aim, and shot Brock through the chest. He died almost immediately.

The death of General Brock on the battlefield.

His friend and aide-de-camp, Colonel John Macdonell, took over. Riding Brock's horse, he rallied the troops. Then, he too, fell mortally wounded. The Canadians retreated carrying dead and wounded comrades. Alfred, Brock's charger, lay dead on the battlefield.

A lull fell over the Heights. Across the river, hundreds of Americans did not budge.

Near noon Sheaffe closed in on Queenston with a remarkable cross-section of Upper Canada: Natives, 300 regulars, a battery of field guns drawn by farmers' horses, and 250 militia including a company of Blacks who had fled slavery in the United States. Sheaffe took a Native trail and gained the Heights behind the enemy line.

By 3 p.m. the invaders were in trouble. The defenders of Queenston village turned a hail of musket fire on the Heights. Sheaffe's redcoats charged with fixed bayonets. Natives closed in from the flanks. The Americans fired one nervous fusillade, then many turned and ran. The rest threw down their weapons.

Some 300 Americans had been killed or wounded and nearly 1000 were taken prisoner. Sheaffe had more prisoners than soldiers of his own! British and Canadian casualties totalled 112.

Brock and the Battle of Queenston Heights had united the colonists as never before.

–Adapted from *Heritage of Canada*

The Battle of Queenston Heights was the most important battle in the War of 1812 between the United States and Britain.

1. Who were the main characters in the battle?

2. From the description, which side looked like it had the best chance to win as the battle began? Why?

3. What was the result of the battle?

4. Describe the battle in your own words.

Causes of the War of 1812

On 18 June 1812, President James Madison of the United States signed a declaration of war against Great Britain. This action marked the official beginning of what became known as the War of 1812. The Americans and the British were at war for the second time in less than thirty years. What had caused another war?

Skill Building: Investigating the Causes

An accident has just happened. The police officer investigating the accident asks three main questions:

1. What happened?
2. What were the effects? For example, was anyone hurt?
3. Why did it happen?

These three questions ask about the event, its effects, and its causes. In Chapter 17, you looked at an event and saw how it could have many different effects. You read about some of the causes and effects that led up to the American Revolution.

Historians ask the question "Why?" For example, they ask "Why did the American Revolution take place?" They investigate not only the effects of an event, but also the causes. An event can have many different causes.

How can you investigate the causes of an event? Here are some steps to help you:

1. Suppose the event is the Great Migration. Develop a question to help you identify the causes of the event. For example: "Why did so many people leave Europe in the early 1800s and go to British North America?"

2. Use an organizer like the one shown to record your information. List the event and your focus question at the top of the organizer.

3. Examine a variety of sources on the event. Go through your textbook and check the library.

4. Identify all the possible causes of the event. List them down the left side of the organizer.

5. Identify the people or groups involved with each cause. Ask: "Who was concerned about this?" "Who was affected?"

6. Identify the effects of each cause you have listed. Ask: "What happened because of this?" Enter the effects on your organizer.

7. When your organizer is complete, review each cause. Which cause do you think was the most important? Explain your choice.

Event: The Great Migration
Focus question: Why did so many people leave Europe in the early 1800s and go to British North America?

Causes	People Involved	Effects
1. Unemployment in Europe	people who had worked in war industries; skilled workers and craftspeople	-overcrowding in towns -poverty
2. Over-population in Europe	everyone	-overcrowding -land, homes, and jobs were scarce
3. Enclosure Movement	tenant farmers and landowners	-tenants were thrown off their land
4. Famine in Ireland	people in Ireland	-people starved and died of diseases -people wanted to leave the country

Now it's your turn. In this chapter you will read about the War of 1812. Use a cause and effect organizer to investigate the causes of the war. Decide which cause you think was the most important. Explain your choice.

Trade Barriers

Britain and France were at war in Europe. They had been at war since 1793. In 1806 the French leader, Napoleon, decided to try to defeat Britain by destroying her trade. He made a declaration: No British ships or goods were to be allowed into Europe. No country was to trade with Britain. If any country did trade with Britain, its ships and cargo would be seized by France.

Britain likewise declared that no country would be allowed to trade with France. The penalty would be seizure of ships and cargo. These moves created great problems for the United States.

The United States wanted to remain **neutral** in the war. That is, they did not want to support either side openly. The government believed that American merchant ships should be able to trade freely with any country they chose. But when the trade barriers went up, the Americans were caught in the middle of the fight.

Britain had the best chance of enforcing its threats. The large British navy was considered the best in the world. In the first year after the barriers were declared, the British stopped and searched twice as many vessels as the French. Americans resented this interference with their trade. They were not at war. Why should they be punished for trading with anyone?

Trouble on the High Seas

There were other problems on the high seas. The British navy needed many trained sailors. They were not easy to find in Britain. Life as a sailor in the Royal Navy was not good. The pay was poor. The food was bad. Few wanted to join.

Conditions were so bad that Britain had to force sailors into the navy. Men were sometimes beaten up, drugged, and kidnapped into service. Thousands of British sailors deserted or "jumped ship" because of the terrible conditions.

Sailors who deserted could not return to England. They would be arrested. Their only hope was escape to a neutral English-speaking country such as the United States. Many of the deserters got jobs in the American navy where the pay was better. Others found jobs on American merchant ships.

The British developed a plan to prevent the loss of more sailors. They needed their sailors to defeat Napoleon. The navy was told to stop merchant ships of any country and search for runaway British sailors. Trouble began when British captains began stopping and searching American vessels and removing crew members.

Americans felt these searches were an insult. The British claimed they took only British deserters. The Americans disagreed. They strongly resented the searches.

A crisis occurred in June 1807. The US warship Chesapeake was ordered to stop for a search by the British frigate Leopard. The Chesapeake was close to the coast of the United States and refused to stop. The Leopard attacked her. The Chesapeake was crippled and boarded by the British. Four sailors were identified as British deserters and removed. In fact, only one of the sailors was a deserter. The Americans were outraged.

Western Expansion

In the years after the American Revolution, the population of the original Thirteen Colonies had grown rapidly. Americans began moving out of the crowded east into the west. The Native peoples were concerned about the advance of settlers into their territory.

burned. Tension between Britain and the US increased.

American Nationalism

As Canadians, we feel a sense of pride in our country. That feeling of devotion to our country is called **nationalism**. It is good to be proud of your country. But sometimes, nationalist feelings can lead to problems with neighbouring countries. This happened in the United States in the years before the War of 1812.

Some Americans in the west wanted to see the day when the United States would control all of North America. These people were called **War Hawks**. They believed there was good reason for war with Britain. An attack on Canada was the easiest and closest way to get at Britain. The capture of Canada would be a prize–a welcome addition to the United States.

The War Hawks were anxious for war. But not all Americans felt this way. Many did not want another war with Britain. When the US government voted to declare war, the decision was close. Many of the eastern states, which traded heavily with Britain, opposed the war.

War Breaks Out

All of the colonies of British North America were involved in the War of 1812. Militia were drawn from Upper and Lower Canada and the Maritime colonies. But the main target of the American invasion was the colony of Upper Canada.

The Invasion of Upper Canada

Some Americans, like the War Hawks, thought Upper Canada was theirs for the taking. First, Britain was busy in Europe in a war with France. She would not be able to help a colony thousands of kilometres

The Shawnee chief, Tecumseh. Tecumseh was to play an important role in the war.

The Shawnee chief, Tecumseh, and his brother, the Prophet, led the Native peoples in defending their lands against the coming settlers. Native attacks on American frontier settlements increased. Americans believed the Natives were getting guns from British fur traders. They believed that the British Indian Department was encouraging the attacks. In November 1811, US troops attacked Tecumseh's headquarters at Tippecanoe Creek. Tecumseh was forced to abandon camp. The village and crops were away. Second, about sixty percent of the people living in Upper Canada were recent American immigrants. Many Americans thought these people would be sympathetic to their cause in the war. Third, the population of the United States was ten times that of British North America. The US had an army of over 7000 troops plus militia.

The outcome of the war seemed certain. The capture of Upper Canada would not be difficult, or would it? What advantages do you think the Canadians had? First, they could count on help. They had the support of the British and several Native groups. Second, they were fighting in familiar territory. They knew the routes to move troops and supplies quickly and efficiently. Third, they were fighting for their very survival. The American invasion had to be stopped if they were to remain a colony separate from the United States.

The Events of 1812

The British military commander in Upper Canada when the war broke out was General Isaac Brock. He had been in the British army since he was fifteen years old. Before arriving in Canada in 1802, he had fought in Europe.

Brock was concerned that the large number of Americans living in Upper Canada would not support him in a war against the United States. Something bold had to be done to win their loyalty, and it had to be done quickly.

Brock needed early victories to bring the Upper Canadians to his support. He achieved his goal. Quick victories were won in the first months of the war. Fort Michilimackinac was seized by the British and in August, Brock took Fort Detroit.

Brock was assisted in his attack on Detroit by the Shawnee Chief, Tecumseh.

Tecumseh had joined the British when the war began. He had gathered a Native army in western Upper Canada and had taken part in many skirmishes on the Detroit frontier.

A large number of American troops were stationed near Detroit under the command of the American general, William Hull. Natives had been attacking Hull's supply lines. He sought protection inside Fort Detroit. Brock crossed the river with 1300 soldiers and Natives and launched an all-out attack on the fort. The Americans were terrified by the Native attack and surrendered on 12 August without a fight. The victory lifted the spirits of the Canadians.

The American attempt to invade Upper Canada at Queenston Heights in the Niagara region came on 13 October 1812. The Canadians were victorious, though the battle was a difficult one and General Brock was killed. You read about this battle at the beginning of the chapter.

Yet another American attempt to invade Upper Canada took place in December. An army of 5000 Americans tried again to cross the Niagara River. Their efforts ended in confusion and defeat.

The brass compass said to have been given to Tecumseh by General Brock in 1812.

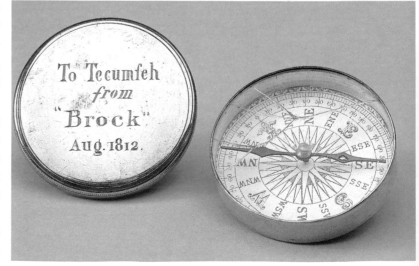

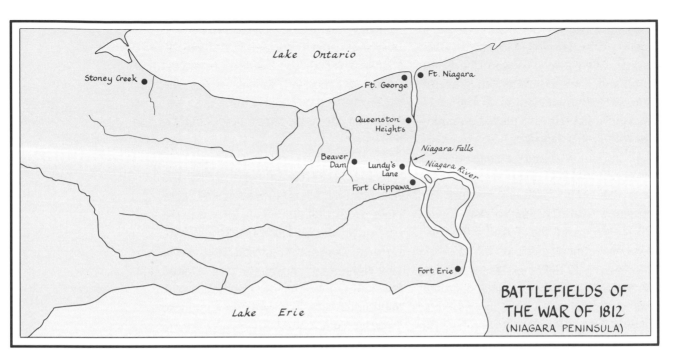

BATTLEFIELDS OF
THE WAR OF 1812
(NIAGARA PENINSULA)

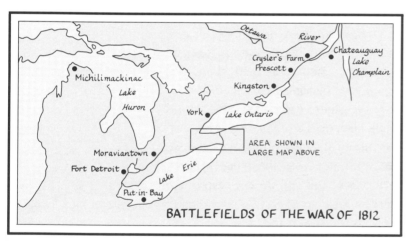

BATTLEFIELDS OF THE WAR OF 1812

The Events of 1813

The United States was once more on the attack in the spring of 1813. Their targets were York, Kingston, and the forts along the Niagara River.

American forces arrived at the harbour of York, the capital of Upper Canada, on 27 April 1813. General Sheaffe, commander of the British forces, tried to defend the town, but they were no match for the larger American force. The defenders were driven from Fort York and the Americans took possession of the town. During their four-day stay, they burned the Parliament buildings and other parts of the town.

At the end of May 1813, the Americans launched another attack on Niagara. A force of 2000 Americans took Fort George. Fort Erie and Fort Chippawa were abandoned by the British as they pulled back their troops.

By June, the Americans had over 5000 troops in the Niagara area. Numbers though do not always decide battles. The Americans were defeated at Stoney Creek near present-day Hamilton. The British commander Major-General Vincent attacked the Americans in the dead of night on 6 June. The battle was short-lived. The Americans were taken by surprise and suffered heavy losses. A daring and bold venture had once again proved worthwhile.

On 24 June another large American force was defeated, this time at Beaver Dam. The Americans were trying to capture a supply depot. It was at Beaver Dam that Laura Secord became a Canadian legend. She is said to have slipped through enemy lines to warn the British commander of the American advance. That warning made British victory possible. Native fighters also played an important role in this victory.

All important military engagements in 1813 were not on land. The Great Lakes were the scene of many battles. The Americans were anxious to gain control of Lake Erie. Like the British, they had a fleet of six armed vessels on the lake. The difference was that the American ships were larger and better equipped with guns. An important naval encounter took place at Put-in-Bay on 10 September. The Americans were victorious. The battle on Lake Erie gave them control of the western peninsula of Upper Canada. British troops, including Tecumseh and his followers, were forced to retreat eastward.

The Americans followed the retreating British to Moraviantown in the Thames valley. There the British commander decided to make a stand. On the left he had the Thames River for protection. On the right he had a thick woods and swamp. The American attack came in the centre of the line.

The Americans quickly took control at Moraviantown. Only the Natives seemed to fight with any determination. When the Shawnee leader Tecumseh was killed, the Natives also fled. Over 600 British soldiers were captured at Moraviantown. The American victory came late in the year. As winter set in, the Americans withdrew to Detroit.

The British had greater success at the eastern end of Lake Ontario in 1813. The Americans struck north from Lake Champlain. A second American force moved east down the St. Lawrence River. Both were heading for Montreal. This was a very important move for the United States. If the Americans seized Montreal, they could cut off supplies to Upper Canada. They would be able to starve Upper Canada into surrendering. Neither American force reached its destination.

The first American army was halted on 26 October at Chateauguay, just south of Montreal. Colonel Charles Michel de Salaberry led a French-Canadian force of about 800, called the Voltigeurs. They were greatly outnumbered by the Americans. De Salaberry told his troops to make as much noise as possible when the battle began. He wanted to give the Americans the impression that the French-Canadian force was larger than it really was. The battle was short and decisive. The American commander

The battle at Put-In-Bay on Lake Erie, 1813. The better-equipped American fleet defeated the British and gained control of the lake.

De Salaberry rallying the troops at the battle of Chateauguay in 1813. The small French force halted the American advance on Montreal.

abandoned the fight and fled to the United States. The Voltigeurs had defended Lower Canada against the American invaders.

The other American army was defeated at the Battle of Crysler's Farm. These diary entries of Corporal David Radcliffe of the British infantry tell of the events at the Battle of Crysler's Farm. The entries are fictional, but the events are fact.

November 10

The night is damp. A cold sleet is blowing in off the St. Lawrence. We have set up headquarters on the farm of John Crysler. He is a farmer and lumber trader as well as a member of the Legislative Assembly. He tells us he was a drummer boy in the Revolutionary War and came here as a Loyalist in 1784.

We have housed our troops as best we can in makeshift shelters. Lieutenant Colonel Morrison is in charge and is working on our defence plan.

Word has just come of an American force of several thousand camped near the farm. They came down the river under cover of night from Sacket's Harbour. Canadian militia report firing on them from the riverbank. The Americans avoided a force that followed them from Kingston and they got past the guns at Prescott. Their progress was stopped by river rapids. They must intend to march down the King's Highway to Montreal!

November 11

Today we drove the Americans from the field. Our force of about 600 was greatly outnumbered. Some say the Americans had a force seven times that of ours. But the battle site gave us some advantages. The open meadows provided us a clear view and we were protected on the right by the St. Lawrence River and on the left by thick woods. Our fire power was too much for the Americans.

November 12

The Crysler family stayed in the farmhouse basement for safety during the fighting. Now we are using the farmhouse and the outbuildings as a temporary hospital to treat the wounded. Morrison says our casualties number 179, but the American losses were likely twice that. We have taken 150 American prisoners.

The year 1813 drew to a close. Victory was no nearer for the United States than it had been a year and a half before. Upper Canada was still free of American troops and reinforcements were on their way from Britain. The war in Europe was reaching an end.

LAURA SECORD (1775-1868)

It is said that Laura Ingersoll Secord overheard American officers planning the attack on Beaver Dam. The Americans were using her house as a temporary headquarters at the time. While the Americans were dining, Laura Secord got past the American sentries. She took a cow so that the Americans would think she was on her way to the pasture. Her 30 km journey to the British lines is said to have taken hours. There are monuments to Laura Secord in Lundy's Lane, Niagara Falls and on Queenston Heights. She is one of the heroines of the War of 1812.

Laura Secord warning Fitzgibbon of the impending American attack on Beaver Dam in 1813.

To perpetuate the name and fame of Laura Secord who walked alone nearly [30 kilometres] by a circuitous, difficult, and perilous route through woods and swamps and over miry roads to warn a British outpost at DeCew's Falls of an intended attack and thereby enabled Lieut. Fitzgibbons on the 24th June 1813, with less than 50 men of H.M. 49th Regt., about 15 militiamen and a small force of Six Nations and other Indians under Captains William Johnson Kerr and Dominique Ducharme to surprise and attack the enemy at Beechwoods (or Beaverdams), and after a short engagement, to capture Col. Boerstler of the US Army and his entire force of 542 men with two field pieces.

–From the text of the Laura Secord
monument at Lundy's Lane, Niagara Falls, Ontario.

The Events of 1814

In 1814 the war between Britain and France in Europe ended. Now Britain was free to concentrate on defeating the Americans. The British planned three major attacks in 1814. The first would be on the capital at Washington. The second would be a strike south from Lake Champlain into New York. The third would be an assault on New Orleans.

But the most dangerous event of the year was an attack launched by the Americans in July. The location was Lundy's Lane on the Niagara Peninsula. This battle was the longest and bloodiest of the war.

On 25 July an army of 2650 Americans met a British force of about 3500. The Americans suffered 853 casualties. The British and Canadians had 878 killed, wounded, captured, or missing. It was not a clear victory for either side. The British and Canadians won because the Americans withdrew. The Americans had learned that fresh British troops were marching to meet them.

The British advance on Washington took place on 24 August 1814. All but two of the public buildings in the American capital were destroyed. Even the official residence of the President of the United States was burned. Later it was

The British attack on Washington, 24 August 1814. The President's house was burned in the attack. Can you find it in the engraving?

painted white to cover the burn marks. Ever since the residence has been called the "White House." The British finally had their revenge for the attack on York.

The strike south from Lake Champlain into New York did not meet the same success. The British used a large force of experienced veterans from Europe. They faced a weaker American army. Yet when the British learned that their naval support had been defeated, they turned back.

The attack on New Orleans really did not take place in 1814. It happened in early January of 1815. This was three weeks after the war had officially ended! Communication was so poor that word did not get through in time to stop the battle. The British military intended to close off the Mississippi River and destroy American trade. The American force defending the port was small.

The British attack turned out to be a disaster. The troops marched against the Americans openly in shoulder-to-shoulder formation. They were easy targets. The Americans had 71 killed or wounded, but the British suffered over 2000 casualties.

The battle of New Orleans was a decisive victory for the United States. The American general, Andrew Jackson, became a national hero. The battle though had no effect on the outcome of the war since it was already over. Lives had been wasted needlessly.

Results of the War

Britain and the United States were tired of fighting by the end of 1814. There had been no clear winner in nearly three years of fighting. It did not appear that there ever would be a clear winner. Only one thing was certain. Neither side would win without paying a terrible cost.

The British were ready to negotiate for peace. They had not completely lost the desire to fight, but they felt that their goal had been accomplished. Canada was safe from takeover by the United States.

The Americans were also ready to negotiate. People in New England wanted peace so that trade could be restored. Besides, the end of the war in Europe between Britain and France had removed many of the problems that had started the war. For example, search and seizure on the high seas was no longer the issue it had once been.

Britain and the United States signed a treaty ending the War of 1812 on Christmas Eve, 1814. It was called the **Treaty of Ghent**. The treaty basically put things back the way they were before the war. All territory seized during the war was returned to the original owner. No mention was made of the problems that had caused the war.

Some important decisions, however, were made. Arguments over the boundary between Canada and the United States were resolved. The forty-ninth parallel of latitude became the Canada-US boundary from the Lake of the Woods to the Rocky Mountains. The border east of Lake of the Woods along the Great Lakes to the Atlantic colonies remained much as it had been before the war.

The boundary line west of the Rockies, however, remained in dispute. This area was valuable fur country. Both countries would occupy the area for ten years until they could decide how to divide it.

The Rush-Bagot Agreement of 1817 came about as a result of the peace settlement as well. This agreement was designed to remove problems that might lead to future wars. It limited the number and type of warships Britain and the United States could have on the Great Lakes.

What did the war really mean to Canadians? Many colonists had lost their lives in the fighting. A great deal of private property was destroyed. But British North America had defended itself. The invasion by the United States was stopped. Colonists were proud of their victory. They were proud to be Canadians. A new feeling of "community" was created.

But the events of the past were not forgotten. The Loyalists had suffered during the American Revolution at the hands of Patriots. Now, a generation later, the Americans had tried to invade Canada. Many disloyal American settlers had been driven out of the British colonies during the war.

Anti-American feelings grew stronger after the War of 1812. Large-scale American immigration into Upper Canada ended. Americans no longer received land grants after 1815.

Instead, the government of Upper Canada favoured Britain as a source of immigrants. British settlers were offered free passage to Canada, free land, and rations for eight months. Thousands came from Britain in the decades after the War of 1812.

The early communities of Canada were the Native communities, New France, Upper Canada, and the Maritimes. Each struggled to establish its own identity. Together they had stood against the Americans in a fight for their common survival. In the years ahead they would be united as one country. Their history would become part of the foundation on which the Canadian nation would be built. Their cultures would be woven into the fabric that we call Canada's multicultural heritage.

The signing of the Treaty of Ghent 1814. The War of 1812 was over.

Activities

Looking Back

1. Define the following words and enter them in your dictionary.

   neutral   War Hawks
   nationalism   Treaty of Ghent

2. Why did Britain have a problem getting sailors for the navy? What measures did they use to secure sailors?

3. Montreal was an important target for American forces in 1813.
   a) Why did the Americans want to attack Montreal?
   b) Why did the Americans fail in their attempt?

4. Why were the Americans and the British both ready to negotiate a peace treaty in 1814?

Using Your Knowledge

5. Which side had the best chance to win at the beginning of the war? List the advantages and disadvantages of both sides.

6. Reread the account of the Battle of Queenston Heights. Write a paragraph explaining why the Americans were defeated.

7. Create a timeline showing the important events in the War of 1812.

8. On a map, show the routes the American forces took in 1813 to advance on Montreal. Indicate the battle sites and which side won the battles.

Extending Your Thinking

9. Imagine you are an editor of a newspaper in Upper Canada. Write an editorial explaining how the War of 1812 has affected your colony and its people.

10. Research one of the following key personalities in the War of 1812. Develop a personality profile for your choice.

    a) Laura Secord   **c)** Isaac Brock
    b) Tecumseh   **d)** Charles Michel de Salaberry

11. You are a resident of York in April 1813. Write a journal account of your experiences during the four days of the American occupation.

ACKNOWLEDGEMENTS FOR QUOTED MATERIAL

32 Reprinted with permission–The Toronto Star Syndicate; **34** Reprinted with the permission of *The Toronto Sun*; **44-47** Adapted with the permission of Campbell House and the Sir William Campbell Foundation; **64-65** From *Glooscap and His Magic: Legends of the Wabanaki* by Kay Hill. Used by permission of the Canadian Publishers, McClelland and Stewart, Toronto; **66, 122** Quoted with the permission of The Champlain Society, Toronto; **88** From *Indian Legends of Canada* by Ella Elizabeth Clark. Used by permission of the Canadian Publishers, McClelland and Stewart, Toronto; **102-103** Adapted from "Lamkisn" in *Stories from the Six Worlds: Micmac Legends* by Ruth Holmes Whitehead, Nimbus, 1988; **136** Illustration courtesy of Hilary Stewart; **153** The Canadian Press; **155** The Globe and Mail; **156** Reprinted with permission–The Toronto Star Syndicate; **161** The Globe and Mail; **162** The Canadian Press; **163-164** Reprinted with permission of *Canada and the World Magazine*, Oakville, Ontario; **171** From *The Vikings* by Jon Nicol. Reprinted with permission; **222** Quoted with permission of NC Press Limited; **259-260** Adapted from THE LOYALISTS by Christopher Moore © 1984. Reprinted by permission of Macmillan of Canada, a Division of Canada Publishing Corporation; **324-326** From HERITAGE OF CANADA, Revised Edition © 1978, 1984 The Reader's Digest Association (Canada) Ltd., Montreal. Reproduced with permission.

PHOTO CREDITS

AO = Archives of Ontario
Canapress = Canapress Photo Service
Glenbow = Glenbow Archives, Calgary, Alberta, Canada
Granger = The Granger Collection, New York
MTL = Metropolitan Toronto Library
NAC = National Archives of Canada
NFB = National Film Board of Canada
NMC = National Museums of Canada, Canadian Museum of Civilization
NS Museum = Nova Scotia Museum
ROM = Royal Ontario Museum, Toronto, Canada

1 Box stove NMC 77-142; Native Woman and Child AO ACC.16462-63; Blacksmiths AO ACC.9355 S14678; Tombstone MTL/J. Ross Robertson Collection T17058; Pioneer home British Columbia Archives and Records Service HP60002 D-598; Pioneer man and woman British Columbia Archives and Records Service HP80408 E-2392; **4** John Holland; **6** John Holland; **7** Photos from Gertler/Denison Family Album; **13** John Holland; **14** (top) R. Poissant/Publiphoto, (bottom) John Holland; **15** John Holland; **18** General Motors of Canada Limited; **19** John Holland; **25** Courtesy of the Japanese Canadian Cultural Centre; **26** Folk Arts Council of Winnipeg Inc.; **27** Canada Wide Feature Service Limited; **33** (top) NAC PA74583, (bottom) Hockey Hall of Fame/Galloway Collection; **35** P. Carpentier/Publiphoto; **38** John McLean; **42** Knickles Studio and Gallery/Wilfred L. Eisnor; **43** Courtesy of the ROM; **44** Courtesy of Campbell House; **45** Courtesy of Campbell House; **46** Courtesy of Campbell House; **48** Prince Edward Island Tourism; **49** Canapress; **51** (top) MTL 974-6-2, (bottom) MTL T13569; **53** City of Toronto Archives, William James Collection #78; **55** NAC C59560; **57** "Conflict between Good and Evil" by Carl Ray, 1975, The McMichael Canadian Art Collection; **61** Courtesy of the Canadian Museum of Civilization through the service of the Museum of Indian Archaeology (London), An Affiliate of The University of Western Ontario; **62** (bottom left) Artist Ivan Kocsis, all photos courtesy of the Canadian Museum of Civilization through the service of the Museum of Indian Archaeology (London), An Affiliate of The University of Western Ontario; **63** (bottom left) Canadian Museum of Civilization S88-133, (bottom right) Peterborough Kawartha Tourism & Convention Bureau; **64** Isotrace Laboratory, University of Toronto; **73** Henry Georgi/Miller Comstock Inc.; **74** Dawn Goss/First Light; **75** Robert Hall/Miller Comstock Inc.; **76** George Hunter/Miller Comstock Inc.; **77** Miller Comstock Inc.; **78** Thomas Kitchin/First Light; **79** G.W. Caulfeild-Browne; **83** Neg./Trans. no. 2431(2) Courtesy Department of Library Services American Museum of Natural History; **88** Courtesy Arnold Jacobs/Photography Tim Johnson; **90** Canadian Museum of Civilization S71-2176; **91** (top) Courtesy of the ROM, (bottom) Canadian Museum of Civilization S71-2178; **92** "Nicholas Vincent Isawanhonhi" by E. Chatfield, NAC C-38948; **94** Courtesy of the ROM; **96** Courtesy: NFB; **97** (top) Courtesy of the ROM, (bottom) "Huron Deer Hunt"/After a drawing by Samuel de Champlain, NAC C-113066; **100** (top left) Ponomareff/Ponopresse Inc., (bottom left) NMC S75-477, (top right) NMC S75-468, (bottom right) NMC S75-441; **105** (top) NS Museum, (bottom) NS Museum; **106** (top right) MTL/John Ross Robertson Collection T15835, (bottom) Courtesy of the ROM; **107** NS Museum; **110** Notman Photographic Archives, McCord Museum of Canadian History; **112** MTL/John Ross Robertson Collection T15823; **114** NS

Museum; **115** (top left) NMC S77-1845, (top right) Courtesy of the ROM, (bottom) NS Museum; **116** Micmac News; **120** Reeves/Glenbow File No. ND-24-44; **121** (top right) J. Anderton/Glenbow File No. NA-408-1, (bottom left) E. Harper/Glenbow File No. NA-2794-10; **122** Reeves/Glenbow File No. ND-24-49; **124** NMC 81456; **126** Calgary Herald/Glenbow File No. 1; **127** Alberta Culture and Multiculturalism; **128** W. Kilroe/Glenbow File No. NA-768-4; **130** (bottom left) Glenbow File No. NA-1666-5, (top right) Glenbow File No. NA-313-3, (centre photos) Courtesy of the ROM; **131** Glenbow File No. P-74-3; **134** British Columbia Archives and Records Service PDP 2145; **136** British Columbia Archives and Records Service HP33784 B-3660; **137** Collection: Vancouver Art Gallery, Emily Carr Trust; **138** Bill McLennan/University of British Columbia Museum of Anthropology; **140** Launching of Bill Reid's canoe at Skidegate, Haida Gwaii, BC (Queen Charlotte Islands), Courtesy of the UBC Museum of Anthropology/Photo Jacquie Gijssen; **141** British Columbia Archives and Records Service HP57607 C-9278; **143** J. Gijssen/University of British Columbia Museum of Anthropology; **144** "In Potlach Regalia with Talking Stick" by Joanna Simpson, NAC C74700; **146** © Ulli Steltzer 1984 from "A Haida Potlach" by Ulli Steltzer, published by Douglas & McIntyre. Reprinted by permission; **147** (top left) NAC PA23081, (bottom left) Courtesy of the UBC Museum of Anthropology, "Woman mask", alder carved by Haida artist Bill Reid, 1970, photo: Bill McLennan, 22 cm x 17 cm x 11 cm; (top right) Haida Raven Rattle, 19th century wood, paint, 11.0 x 31.7 x 10.3 cm McMichael Canadian Art Collection Purchase 1974, 1974.6, (bottom right) Courtesy of the ROM; **148** Collection: Vancouver Art Gallery; **151** "The First Prescription in Canada" By C.W. Jefferys, NAC C6680; **152** Courtesy of Yvonne Garbutt and the Whetung Art Gallery; **153** P. Andrews/Publiphoto; **154** David Lavell; **156** Canapress; **157** (top) Canapress/Winnipeg Free Press, (bottom) Mark Zuehlke; **158** J.P. Danvoye/Publiphoto; **159** Canapress; **161** Canapress; **165** Copyright: Greg Staats/Courtesy: Jane Corkin Gallery, Toronto; **167** Bill McLennan/University of British Columbia Museum of Anthropology; **169** "The Habitant Farm," by Cornelius Krieghoff, 1856/The National Gallery of Canada, Ottawa. Gift of Gordon C. Edwards, Ottawa, 1923. In memory of Senator and Mrs. W.C. Edwards; **170** Granger; **172** NMC 77-401; **173** (top) Publiphoto, (bottom) "Cartier Taking Possession of New France, Gaspe 1534" by Charles Walter Simpson, NAC C13938; **175** Publiphoto; **177** MTL D-24-8; **180** Nova Scotia Tourism and Culture; **181** NAC C655; **182** "Habitation at Quebec", engraved after the original published by Samuel de Champlain in Paris, 1613, NAC C09711; **184** NAC C5750; **187** "Fur Traders at Montreal" by George Agnew Reid, NAC C11014; **189** First Light TK 3595B; **192** "Étienne Brûlé at the Mouth of the Humber", 1956 , by F.S. Challener, Government of Ontario Art Collection, Toronto, Photo Credit: Tom Moore Photography, Toronto; **193** "Shooting the Rapids" by Frances Ann Hopkins, NAC C2774;

195 Sainte-Marie Among the Hurons, Midland, Ontario; **198** (top) "Arrival of the Ursulines at Quebec, 1639" by H.R. Perrigard, NAC C-11232, (bottom) Publiphoto; **199** Archives des Soeurs de la Congregation de Notre-Dame, Montreal; **200** "Louis Joseph, Marquis de Montcalm", 1956, by June McCormack, Government of Ontario Art Collection, Toronto, Photo Credit: Tom Moore Photography, Toronto; **203** Granger; **207** "Representation of the French Girls Arriving at Quebec" by C.W. Jefferys NAC C10688; **208** The Confederation Life Gallery of Canadian History; **209** Eugen Kedl; **211** Bibliothèque nationale du Québec; **214** "Portrait de MGR François de Laval", Copie d'après la gravure de Claude Duflos, 1708, Ecole canadienne Pc 84.1, Societe du Musee de Seminaire de Québec; **216** "Seigneurial System" by C.W. Jefferys, NAC C73398; **218** "A View of the Chateau-Richer, Cape Torment, and Lower End of the Isle of Orleans near Quebec" by T. Davies, National Gallery of Canada, Ottawa; **220** NMC J-4909; **221** Courtesy: NFB; **224** (top) J.C. Hurni/Publiphoto, (bottom) Courtesy: NFB; **225** (top) Courtesy: NFB, (bottom) MTL T14887; **226** Black Creek Pioneer Village; **228** (top) "Planting May Tree" by C.W. Jefferys, NAC C73399, (bottom) "La Danse Ronde; Circular Dance of the Canadians" by George Heriot, NAC C251; **230** "Histoire de l'Amerique septentrionale", In Bacqueville de la Potherie, C.C. LeRoy, NAC C4696; **231** (top) B. Martin/Publiphoto, (centre) Courtesy of the ROM, (bottom) NAC C09673; **232** NAC; **233** NAC; **235** Courtesy of the ROM; **236** (top) "La mort de Montcalm", 1902, by Marc-Aurele de Foy Suzor-Cote, oil on canvas, Collection: Musee du Quebec, Acc. No. 43.176, photo by Patrick Altman; (bottom) Archives des Ursulines de Québec; **239** State Historical Society of Wisonsin/Painting by E.W. Deming; **240** Artist: Claude Picard, Saint-Basil, N.B., Courtesy: Canadian Parks Service, Atlantic Region; **241** Courtesy of the ROM; **242** Nova Scotia Tourism and Culture; **244** Archives nationales du Québec à Québec; **249** "Harvest Festival", c. 1850, by William Berczy, National Gallery of Canada, Ottawa, No. 16648; **254** (both) Granger; **255** The Metropolitan Museum of Art, Gift of Mrs. Russell Sage, 1909 (10.125.103); **256** Granger; **258** Granger; **260** "The Homeseekers", 1910, by G.A. Reid, Government of Ontario Art Collection, Toronto, Photo Credit: Tom Moore Photography, Toronto; **261** Courtesy of Tourism and Convention Services — The City of Brantford; **264** "A Black Wood Cutter At Shelburne, Nova Scotia, 1788" by W. Booth, NAC C040162; **269** "Encampment of the Loyalists at Johnstown, a New Settlement on the Banks of the River St. Lawrence in Canada, taken June 6th, 1784" by James Peachey, NAC C2001; **271** "Landing of the Loyalists", by Rev. Bowen Squires, Collection: Hastings County Museum, Photo by Richard Lumbers; **273** "Loyalists Drawing Lots for the Land", c. 1921, by C.W. Jefferys, Government of Ontario Art Collection, Toronto, Photo Credit: Tom Moore Photography, Toronto; **277** "On Board an Emigrant Ship in the Thirties" by C.W. Jefferys, NAC C073435'; **279** NAC C3904; **281** AO, P1812; **282** "Clearing The Land"

INDEX

911